From Bellslea to Brora
THESE ARE MY HEROES
(FIFTY YEARS OF FRASERBURGH FC)

by

Mike Barbour

Grosvenor House
Publishing Limited

All rights reserved
Copyright © Mike Barbour, 2010

Mike Barbour is hereby identified as author of this
work in accordance with Section 77 of the Copyright, Designs
and Patents Act 1988

The book cover picture is copyright to Mike Barbour

This book is published by
Grosvenor House Publishing Ltd
28-30 High Street, Guildford, Surrey, GU1 3HY.
www.grosvenorhousepublishing.co.uk

This book is sold subject to the conditions that it shall not, by way of
trade or otherwise, be lent, resold, hired out or otherwise circulated
without the author's or publisher's prior consent in any form of binding or
cover other than that in which it is published and
without a similar condition including this condition being imposed
on the subsequent purchaser.

A CIP record for this book
is available from the British Library

ISBN 978-1-907652-20-2

Contents

Foreword		v
Chapter 1	The Fabulous Fifties	01
Chapter 2	The Not so Swinging Sixties	19
Chapter 3	The Seventies, So Near and Yet so Far	70
Chapter 4	The Eighties, The Broch go Local Again	130
Chapter 5	The Nineties, Cups, Shields and a League Title to Come	163
Chapter 6	The Noughties, a Dream Fulfilled	210

Acknowledgements

It is often the case, when a book is completed, that a declaration is made confirming that the text is entirely the author's own work. With this book, the words are mine, but without the support of a succession of people and organisations, this work might never have been completed at all. Special thanks must therefore go to the following: Duncan Brown, Express Newspaper Group, Aberdeen Journals, The Sunday Post, and to the Family of the late Jan Borowski, for their various permissions regarding photographs included in the book. I am grateful to Bill Watson, for his help in providing and preparing initial pictures and further thanks must go to Davie Henderson, for his permission also and for his valuable help in preparing the photographs I have included. My thanks must also go to Finlay Noble and Fraserburgh Football Club for their kind help with photographs and for continuing support in putting everything together. Prudence Smith, Audrey McDonald, Mike McLean, Martin Hicks and Bill Jackson all know what it took to put my story into print and I am grateful for all of their time, effort and support in helping it all become a reality.

I cannot finish without mentioning my partner Eileen. Thank you for your patience and support and for putting up with my love affair with Fraserburgh Football Club for so long.

Any errors and omissions in these pages are entirely my own.

Michael Barbour
June 2010

Foreword

This is my story of the heartaches and jubilations of Fraserburgh FC, otherwise known as, 'the Broch,' or, 'the Burghy,' and of the players whom I watched, over the years, in the famous black and white stripes. I was born and brought up at 41 Cross Street; a badly hit Bellslea free kick over the Pole's Garage roof would have landed at my front door. Most of my childhood, Saturday afternoons were spent at the matinee, watching the likes of, 'Zorro,' and, 'Robin Hood,' as my father used to work every Saturday afternoon and so was unable to take me to football matches. That, however, was about to change.

One Saturday afternoon my friend Davie Noble and I were at the, 'Granda,' swings and were attracted by the roar of the crowd coming from the adjacent Bellslea Park. Clambering up the chute, we peered over the dyke at the excited onlookers. The year was about 1957 or 1958 so it must have been a big match as all we could see were 'heids' so, just like every other 'loon' at the time (somewhat financially challenged), we skipped over the dyke and crawled through the long grass at the, 'clinic,' end. Arriving home after the match, I found my mother somewhat displeased to say the least, and she jarred me, saying that I'd only get trampled amongst, 'a' that mannies,' but that day was the beginning of my love affair with the Broch.

Chapter One

The Fabulous Fifties

The late fifties were a golden age for the Broch, of championships, cup finals and Scottish Cup classics, with local household names taking to the pitch every Saturday: Stephen, Strachan, Bradford, Emery and McCall, to name but a few.

In season 1957-58 the Broch were drawn away to Peterhead in the first round of the Qualifying Cup and a Johnny Strachan goal earned the visitors a replay at Bellslea Park on October 12th, the following week. Goals from Meldrum and a flashing header from Stephen gave the Broch a 2-1 victory and set up a second round clash with Clachnacuddin at Grant Street. It was to be an epic encounter with Clach fielding: McDonald, Lytham, Wheeler, Patience, McLean, Chisholm, Grant, Beaton, Sinclair Urquhart and Donnachie against the Broch's: Thomson, Mowatt, McKenna, Clelland, McCall, Auld, Robb, Stephen, Bett, Smith and Meldrum.

The Broch went 1-0 ahead through Stephen but were pegged back by a Clach equaliser. Smith nudged the visitors ahead only for Clach to pull level for a second time and force the replay at Bellslea. The following Saturday, October 26th, the two teams had another thrilling encounter. Whilst the first half produced only one goal from Smith, giving the Broch the lead, the second half burst into life after three minutes when Sinclair struck the equaliser. Events seemed to replay themselves as Best edged Fraserburgh in front after 55 minutes, only for Sinclair to drag the visitors level yet again. The Broch refused to give in, and came back with a Stephen goal to take the lead yet again. With the clock ticking down Clach were awarded a free kick, and Chisolm, almost inevitably, hit a screamer into the top corner to make it 3-3. A few minutes later the referee blew for time. No extra time or penalties were played in those days, so the tie was to be repeated, yet again.

On 2nd November the Broch met Clach at Boroughbriggs for a match that turned into a true classic. Clach took the initiative, attacking from the kick off, and Donachie rewarded their aggression with a goal after six minutes. The Broch were struggling to get into the game and it was no surprise when Sinclair made it 2-0. Nine minutes later, crucially, Bett pulled one back, providing a lifeline for the second half.

What a transformation in the second half! Rumours spread about the contents of the half time tea as Auld made it 2-2 with the Broch's first attack, and on 62 minutes the Broch took the lead for the first time through Meldrum. When Stephen made it 4-2 after 78 minutes there was no way back for Clach, and Meldrum's goal, his second and the Broch's fifth, had the ground ringing with cries of 'come awa the Burghy'!

For the semi finals, played on 9th November 1957, the Broch were drawn at home to Buckie. They fielded: Thomson, Mowatt, McKenna Clelland, McCall, Auld, Robb, Stephen, Bett, Smith and Medrum, with: Low, Stewart, Reid, Thain, Dutch, Jeffrey, Craigie, Cowie, Andrews, Smith and Christie lining up for the visitors. Stephen caused a sensation when he put the Broch 1-0 up in the first minute, but Buckie hit back three minutes later with a Cowie strike. Meldrum's penalty regained the home side's advantage, and with half time approaching Stephen made it 3-1 with a crashing drive. Just after half time Meldrum scored again to make it 4-1, and on 75 minutes grabbed his hat trick to put the Broch on easy street. Christie reduced the deficit after 85 minutes, but it was too little, too late, and the Broch recorded a 5-2 victory. From goal keeper to outside left the whole team were heroes that day, particularly Bunny McCall, who never missed a single ball all day.

FROM BELLSLEA TO BRORA THESE ARE MY HEROES

So it was up to Telford Street to meet Inverness Caledonian in the 1st leg, Caley fielding: Mowatt, McDonald, McGilvray, Christie, Bolt, McIntosh, McBeath, McKenzie, Clyne, Chisolm, Munro, whilst the Broch team remained unchanged from the semi final-winning side. A dull first half had few incidents of note, with the highlights being Stephen's shot off the post and a Clyne header that flashed over the bar. However, within one minute of the second half Stephen had put the Broch 1-0 up thanks to a cross from Smith, much to the delight of the large travelling support. The Broch were in the driving seat and when Stephen went on a mazy run he left the Caley defenders in his wake. His deep cross was deflected into the Caley net to double the Broch's lead. It was then Smith's turn to take the Caley defence for a run, and when he was floored by a clumsy tackle inside the box referee W Syme had no hesitation in pointing to the spot. Meldrum coolly slotted home to make it 3-0 to the visitors. As the final whistle went it was a great thought to think that we could win the Qualifying Cup for the first time at the Bellslea.

The second leg of the tie against Caley has long been in the memories of those that witnessed the 23 November game, a tie that drew a 2,300 strong crowd. With their 3-0 first leg advantage the Broch started where they had left off at Telford Street. Auld sent a flashing header over the bar in the first minute as the goal keeper stood rooted to his spot. The Bellslea erupted after 20 minutes when Meldrum gave the Broch the lead and when he added a second three minutes later it looked all over for Caley. Their fate was sealed when Emery crashed a 20 yarder into the top corner to give the Broch an unassailable advantage. On the stroke of half time Caley's McBeath thought he had pulled one back, but his strike was disallowed for an infringement. Caley finally got their name on the score sheet on 75 minutes when an own goal from Auld gave them the faintest glimmer of hope. However, it was too little too late, and when the final whistle sounded the Bellslea crowd went wild with delight. It was a fantastic day for the Broch and for their supporters, aptly crowned by Bobby Auld lifting the cup. Disappointing news for Broch supporters was the signing of Cliff Meldrum after the game, by Cardiff City, but we wished him well. It was also reported that pubs all over the town were doing a brisk trade. For the non – drinkers you could watch John Wayne in, 'Fort Apache,' or dance to Pat Paterson and his music, admission was 3 shillings (that's 15p in modern money.)

I seem to remember the team going round the Broch after the game sitting on the top of a bus, with the cup. The cup was displayed in the window of Barbour's Garage on Cross Street during the day, as my uncle, Jimmy Duthie, was Secretary of the Broch at that time. Otherwise, for safety reasons, it was kept in the house. As a boy, I didn't realise at the time how many great players had held that famous old trophy.

After all the celebrations had died down, it was back to league business and of course the dream of Scottish Cup glory. The Broch were on their way to Hampden to meet Queens Park. On the 15th of February, the Broch ran onto the hallowed turf – a great experience for the players. Teams:

Broch: Thomson, Mowatt, McKenna, Clelland, McCall, Auld, Strachan, Stephen, McRae, Smith, Robb.

Queens Park: Crampsey, Marmett, Kerr, Cromar, McKinnet, Holt, Church, Coates, McEwen, Omand, Perry.

The Broch kicked off and were holding their own until Perry put the home side 1 – 0 up. The Broch hit back, with McRae making it 1 – 1, before Cromar made it 2 – 1 with a penalty kick. Disaster struck the Broch when Clelland put through his own goal to make it 3 – 1 and soon after Coates made it 4 – 1 before Robb pulled one back to make it 4 – 2. The Broch had a goal disallowed just before half – time, so the score remained the same. The second half was even right up until ten minutes to go, when Queens hit three goals in a five minute spell. McEwen, Coates and Perry all scored, to make it 7 – 2, but it was a lot closer then the result suggested. There were over 150 supporters from the Broch, between cars and private coaches – a fair support for the time. Bertie Doig told me the men used to gather outside the old Post Office to get the scores, as not many people had phones at that time. The season ended with the Broch halfway up the league:

Played	Won	Drawn	Lost	For	Against	Points
28	13	3	12	68	67	29

Seven weeks of the school holidays were spent down at the Black Sands catching crabs with a 3d line and hook or up at the castle swimming in the, "Bather," as there were no swimming pools in those days. For any Brocher the Bather was, and still is, a rock pool just under the old fog horn. The summers seemed to be a lot warmer then, they would have to have been, as the tide went in and out of the Bather every day and the first dip took your breath away.

Holidays over and it was back to school, with season 1958 – 59 not far away. If it was half as exciting as the last one, there would be no complaints. The League cup was the usual four team section, comprising the Broch, Peterhead, Huntly and Deveronvale. This was a competition the Broch had never won. The first winners were Forres Mechanics in 1946 – 47 and Buckie had won it three seasons on the trot from 1955 – 1958, a great achievement, but it was time for a change.

On Wednesday 13th August, the Broch met their old rivals Peterhead at the Bellslea. Russell put the visitors 1 – 0 up, before Strachan equalised with a 25 yard drive. Aitken made it 2 – 1 from the penalty spot and then Meldrum made it 3 – 1. Strachan put the game out of Peterhead's reach with a fourth, making it a good start to the season. A 4 – 4 draw with Huntly, and the results with Vale and Peterhead going the right way, meant we just needed a point at Recreation Park to get into the semi – finals. The Broch ground out a 0 – 0 draw to achieve that target.

On Saturday 30th September, the Broch played Elgin City in the semi – final of the League Cup. Team:

Broch – Thomson, McKenna, Aitken, Birnie, McCall, Auld, Strachan, Smith, Meldrum, Bradford, Brander.

Over the years, if the Broch was going to win something, you could guarantee they would do it the hard way and this match was no exception. The game kicked off in sensational style, when the Broch goalkeeper, Thomson, had to go off injured. With no substitutes allowed, an outfield player had to don the jersey and you played the rest of the game with ten men. Billy Bradford stepped up and Elgin took advantage, with Clyne putting them 1 – 0 up. Birnie equalised, then Meldrum put the Broch 2 – 1 in front. Smith made it 3 – 1 from the penalty spot, before Elgin hit back to make it 3 – 2. The Broch were beginning to tire, and the extra man was taking effect. With Elgin camped in the Broch's half and the minutes ticking away, the Broch broke upfield in the 89th minute, winning a penalty. With usual penalty taker Smith struggling, Aitken was left to put the tie out of Elgin's reach, keeper Jenkins however made a tremendous save, but to no avail as the whistle blew shortly thereafter and the Broch were through, the hard way!

The final was played at Borough Briggs on September 13th, against Inverness Thistle. Teams:

Thistle: Urquhart, Glennie, McDonald, Godsman, Sanderson, Hendry, McLennan, Grant, Mitchell, Paxton, Moynihan.

Broch: Mowatt, McKenna, Aitken, Birnie, McCall, Auld, Bradford, Meldrum, Strachan, Smith, Brander.

The game was billed as a young and up and coming Thistle team against an ageing and experienced Broch side. In the first minute Thistle hit the bar, with the Broch defence looking on, but then the Broch hit Thistle with a quick one – two. Strachan scored in the 8th minute and Bradford a minute later. McLennan reduced the leeway in the 38 th minute and it stayed that way until half – time. Strachan scored again in the 60th minute and went on to complete his hat – trick in the 73rd minute. Paxton scored a consolation goal for Thistle to make it 4 – 2, and as the final whistle went a bit of history was made as Bobby Auld became the first Broch player to lift the League Cup.

To this day no other Broch skipper has lifted it, but it was happy days, with two trophies in the sideboard. Could we make it three by retaining the Qualifying Cup? It was a tall order.

Around that time not a lot of people had a T.V. There was always a group around the window of an electrical shop if the TV was on and you could buy a 17" screen T.V. from Murray Mackies for 69gns. That's £72.45 if my arithmetic serves me right. A Hotpoint washing machine would set you back £69.6s or a portable radio £23:2/- batteries extra. If you used to go to the Palace in Peterhead it would cost you 3.6d to get in to hear The Ambassadors, but back to the football.

There was no time to rest on laurels, as the Broch were drawn at home to Peterhead in the first round of the Qualifying Cup. Meldrum gave the Broch the lead in 6 minutes and there was no more scoring in a very uninspired derby match. The second round draw saw the Broch away to Keith at Kynoch Park, never an easy place to go. I wonder if my good friend Sandy Stables (Mr Keith) was there in his short trousers (only joking Sandy.) On October 4th the Broch were in a confident mood and went 1-0 up in 10 minutes through Meldrum. There was plenty of goalmouth action at both ends and Keith drew level on 33minutes. As half time was approaching, Brander made it 2-1 for the Broch, a perfect time to score. The second half was a real ding-dong affair. Keith were awarded a penalty in the 80th minute. Byiers hit it low and hard, but Mowatt got down well to save it. For the final 10 minutes it was safety first, "if in doubt, boot it out." What a relief as the referee blew the final whistle, with the final score Keith 1 Broch 2. As the old saying goes it's the result that counts, as we lived to fight another day.

The semi final draw was made, with The Broch travelling away to Ross County at Dingwall on October 25th. Ross Co dominated the first half and a slip by McCall let Ogilvie in to put County 1-0 up after 20 minutes. It stayed like that till half time, but five minutes after the break Stephen made it 1-1 with a flashing header from a Robb cross and the Broch were taking command of the game. Brander made it 2-1 on 55 minutes and Meldrum put the issue beyond doubt when he made it 3-1 in the 85th minute. The final score was Ross County 1, Broch 3. Broch fans were fairly getting spoiled with another cup final and the draw for the Scottish Cup to look forward to.

It was getting to that time of the year again, Guy Fawkes night. With my chums, I used to help collect for the Hanover Street Bonfire. If you don't know where that is, it's where the Bus Station now stands. At that time it was a large bit of waste land where the bonfire was sited every year. It was there, you could guarantee, that the Fire Brigade was called to put the bonfire out. There was always a carry on before it was put out. At that time bonfires were built quicker than the council workers took them away. Everybody would fill their wash houses or sheds with rubbish for the bonie. The Landings used to have a big one and Jubilee Crescent had another. Before November 5th they were usually burnt down two or three times. If you've never heard of the Landings it was a large bit of land across from McConachie's, but, as time went on, all of these places were built on. Guy Fawkes night doesn't seem to be the same and nowadays, with all the rules and regulations, you need permission to build a bonfire. It's a funny old world!.

Ah well, let's get back to the football. The Broch would play in the Cup final for the second year in a row. Buckie Thistle would be our opponents in the Qualifying Cup final on Saturday November 15th at Victoria Park. The teams were:

Buckie: Low, Cowie, Reid, Thain, Mutch, Jaffray, Sutherland, Yorkston, Stewart, Smith, Christie.

Broch: Mowatt, McKenna, Aitken, Brinie, McCall, Auld, Robb, Bradford, Strachan, Meldrum, Bradford.
Ref – T. Wharton, Glasgow.

The Broch took an early lead, with Strachan scoring in 4 minutes. Smith made it 1-1 on 20 minutes. Then Buckie were awarded a penalty and Danny Mowatt was the Broch hero as he saved Christies spot kick, just like he had at Keith in the second round. At half time, the score was 1-1. Five minutes after the break Strachan put the Broch 2-1 up but Buckie equalised in 68 minutess. The game ended 2-2 and all to play for at Bellslea next week.

November 22nd saw the 2nd leg of the Qualifying Cup. A bumper crowd turned up to see if the Broch could retain the trophy but it was not to be. There was disaster early on, when a Sutherland shot, which was going nowhere, hit McCall and deflected into his own net to put Buckie 1-0 up and 3-2 in the lead on aggregate. Soon after, the Broch hit back through Bradford to make it 1-1, but Sutherland put Buckie 2-1 up on 26 minutes (4-3 on aggregate) and it stayed like that till half time. The game then deteriorated, as nerves were getting to the players, with bad play and poor passing. The result could have gone either way as the ref' blew for time. What a difference a year makes as Buckie went up to collect the Cup, with the final score 4-3 to them on aggregate. Never mind, there was still the Scottish Cup to look forward to, and we were still in with a shout for the league.

An amazing game took place at Bellslea on Sat 27th December. The Broch were at home to Peterhead. We were 4-2 down at one stage, but hit back to win 5-4. Smith had put Broch 1-0 up, then Rose made it 1-1. Campbell made it 1-2 in 20 minutes. A Russell double in 20 and 27 minutes made it 1-4 (I've nae time for ex Brochers scoring for Peterhead against the Burgh.) Brander made it 2-4 in the 44th minute, and at half time it remained 2-4. Smith got his second goal in the 50th minute to make it 3-4, before Meldrum made it 4-4 on 60 minutes. It was one way traffic now and it came as no surprise when Strachan made it 5-4, "nice one Johnnie," and that was how it finished. In goals that day for the Broch was a certain J. Muirhead, better known in the Toolies as, "Beak" the Toolies Painter, "SORRY JIM!"

The Broch was really buzzing with the news we had drawn Dundee in the Scottish Cup at the Bellslea. This was what dreams were made of. Imagine household names such as Brown, Gabriel, Cox and Cousins playing at the Bellslea. As the game drew nearer, tickets were like gold dust, but I didn't have to worry about that. My mother wasn't too keen on letting me go to the match but my uncle, Jimmy Duthie, was Club Secretary. His wife Betty worked in the Tea Hut, so she persuaded my mother she would look after me.

On to the game on Saturday January 31st. The teams who took the field that day were:

Broch: Mowatt, McKenna, Aitken, Meldrum, McCall, Auld, Strachan, Bradford, Andrews, Smith, Brander.

Dundee: Brown, Hamilton, Cox, Henderson, Gabriel, Cowie, Curlett, Bonthrone, Cousin, Sneddon, Robertson.
Ref – H. Phillips, Wishaw.

The Broch lost the toss and kicked off shooting towards the clinic end. There was a nervous start by both teams but the Broch had two corners in the first few minutes, though these were easily cleared by the Dundee defence. McCall came to the Broch's rescue when Auld mis-kicked as Bonthrone headed over. On 43 minutes Dundee's Curlett headed against the upright - what a let off - but just a minute later the Broch forced another corner. Brander took the kick and Johnny Strachan met it at the back post to score. The Bellslea went wild as the ref blew for half time. Could we hold out, was all that was talked about? I wondered what was said in the dressing rooms?

The second half kicked off with Broch shooting into their favourite side, the "Pole's Garage" end and they nearly made it 2-0 when a repeat move of the first goal saw

Strachan heading past. Dundee were getting desperate and had two shots from 18 yards sailing over the bar and out of the ground. The Broch were defending well as a unit. Doug Cowie tried to rally his weary team, but the tough tackling and enthusiasm of the Broch had surprised Dundee. The clock seemed to have stopped as time was slipping by very slowly, but, when referee Syme finally blew for time it was absolute, "BEDLAM," with the Bellslea going wild. My one memory is of the lonely figure of Bill Brown standing in his goals, with a skull cap on, alone with his thoughts. (Hard to believe that, a few years later, he would be at Wembley lifting the F.A.Cup with Spurs.) As the result filtered through it must have sent shock waves through Scottish football. How could a team from the Highland League knock out a star-studded team from the Scottish First Division? That defeat changed the rules of the Scottish Cup forever. From the next season the elite teams in Scotland didn't enter the Cup until the 3rd round.

I couldn't wait to get the papers on Sunday to read all about the game. The Green Final headline was, "HAIL BROCH, DUNDEE ARE WHACKED"

The Sunday Express said, "A FLUKE," - don't you believe it!

The Sunday Post headline read, "FRASERBURGH WERE A TEAM INSPIRED."

The following are attendance figures for the cup ties played that day:

Fraserburgh	v	Dundee	4,500	£630
Babcock	v	Forres	250	£110
Dumbarton	v	Buckie	6000	£500
Celtic	v	Albion Rovers	27,000	£3,375

How times have changed in the price paid to watch football, as you see from the above figures. But, on a sour note, a press article on the Monday read: "They haven't a player from their home town, train 40 miles away from their ground and nine of the team train in a gym in Aberdeen." As we move on forty years nothing has changed, for money has ruined the game, but let's savour that moment as they don't come around very often.

The following Saturday we came down to earth with a real bump. Buckie Thistle were the visitors in the 1st round of the Aberdeenshire Cup and went through to the 2nd round with a 0-3 score. But, with the news that we had been drawn at home to Stirling Albion in the next round of the Scottish Cup, the Broch players had more on their minds than Buckie. Tom Ferguson, the Stirling Albion manager was at the Bellslea on Saturday, having a look at the Broch, but he couldn't have learned very much from that game. Broch Secretary Jimmy Duthie was at Pittodrie watching Albion. Could you imagine Charlie Duncan putting one of the club committee to watch the opposition nowadays? I don't think so!

As the game drew nearer, the Broch was at fever pitch. I managed to get a ticket at school from my gym teacher, Stanley Green. Every day there were headlines in the newspapers, "Would Bunny McCall be fit?" "Is Bobby Auld's ankle ok?" So it was on to the game, with the teams lining up:

Broch: Mowatt, McKenna, Aitken, Meldrum, McCall, Auld, Strachan, Bradford, Andrews, Smith, Brander.

Stirling Albion: Stewart, Hailstones, Pettigrew, McKechie. Sinclair, Kilgannon, Rice, Spence, Gilmour, Bennie, McPhee. Ref – W. M. Syme, Glasgow

Albion started the stronger. Rice had a shot that flashed past the post in the 1st minute, but, as time went on, the Broch were coming more into the game and forced the first corner, though Bradford headed high over. Bradford then had the ball in the net, but it was disallowed for a foul on the keeper. Brander floated another corner to the back post and Strachan hit the cross bar, what a cracker of a game. But disaster struck for the Broch in the 12th minute. Albion, who had hardly been in the game, so far, scored through

McPhee. The Broch hit back, with Brander's 25 yard shot well saved by the keeper. On 20 minutes the Broch appealed for off-side, but the ref' waved play on and McPhee chipped the ball over the keeper to make it 0-2, much against the run of play. Spence and McPhee were a thorn in the Broch defence and in 34 minutes, the Broch were 0-3 down, Spence scoring with a shot high into the net, as Albion threatened to run riot. The defence which had looked so solid against Dundee was now a bit of a shambles, but the Broch kept plugging away and finally got a break. Pettigrew tried to thump a clearance, but the ball hit Andrews and rolled into the net - game on! Stirling got their first corner only in the 43rd minute, and at half-time it was the Broch 1, Stirling Albion 3.

Any hope the Broch had of saving the game vanished just two minutes after the interval. McPhee hit a long ball to Spence who rolled the ball into an empty net to make it 1-4. The tough tackling of Albion was puting the Broch off their stride, but the home team were playing all the football and were rewarded in 66 minutes when Strachan netted from a pass from Smith to make it 2-4. The Broch were well on top now and Albion were resorting to just clearing their lines. Then Brander scored in 73 minutes to make it 3-4 and the fightback was on. Though the Broch fought to the bitter end they couldn't find that elusive equaliser. As the ref' blew for time a disappointed Broch team trudged off the Bellslea, but to the applause of their fans. Monday's headlines were,
"GALLANT BROCH GO DOWN FIGHTING."
"BROCH FATED TO GO DOWN."
Ref' ANGERS 5,000.
The Daily Express report said the most glaring thing of all, namely that a First Division half back line had wilted to a Broch forward line instead of dominating the game. The score in corners tells its own story, with the Broch winning 12 to Albion's 1, eight of them coming in the second half. Stirling Albion went on to beat Morton 1-3 at Cappielow

but lost to Celtic 1-3 in the 4th round. Aberdeen beat St. Mirren 3-1 in the final, while, for us it was, "Never mind, there's always next year."

So it was back to the bread and butter of the League business. Elgin City were on top,

P	W	D	L	F	A	PTS
19	11	3	5	64	34	25

while the Broch were in 4th place.

P	W	D	L	F	A	PTS
14	9	3	2	39	25	21

The Broch were at Lossie and found themselves 4-0 down at half-time, but in a rousing second half, managed to salvage a 5-5 draw with a late Brander penalty. Dark horses Rothes moved into second place as the Broch went to McKessock Park, but came home pointless after a 6-0 hiding. The Broch then went joint top of the league with a 3-2 win at Kings Mill against Inverness Thistle, Strachan heading the winner from a Brander corner. Fraseburgh moved to the top of the league with a 1-4 victory of Keith at Kynoch Park. Brander 2, Andrews, and Strachan got the goals.

The league positions then read:

	P	W	D	L	F	A	PTD
Broch	26	16	5	5	78	52	37
Rothes	25	16	4	5	76	45	36

The headlines were, "Photo Finish for the Flag." Broch beat Inverness Thistle 8-0 at the Bellslea with four goals in 12 minutes, while Rothes beat Buckie Thistle 6-1. In the final games the Broch beat Lossie 7-2 at Bellslea while Rothes drew 1-1 at Forres. So it was a play off and the arguments started. The Broch said they'd play Rothes at any ground any night, but Rothes chairman, Mr Enfield, said the match should be played at Borough Briggs, not very fair as Rothes is only 5 miles from Elgin. A toss of the coin for the venue seemed fair, but Rothes seemed to want things all their own way. They then wanted the game to be played the following season, but that was out of the question, so the Broch finally agreed to Thursday 14th May at Borough Briggs, with a 7.15 kick-off. This was Rothes' fifth game since the Wednesday of the previous week and the Broch's fourth. By way of contrast, it seems that todays superstars are tired by August or can't play two games a week. The teams for the play off were:

Rothes: Slessor, Peddie, McFadyen, Martin, Reddie, A Munro, Phillibin, Robertson, Grant, Marshall, Scott.

Broch: Mowatt, McKenna, Aitken, Simpson, McCall, Auld, Strachan, Meldrum, Andrews, Bradford, Brander.

Ref: - J. Allan, Inverness.   Att' - 4,200. (Rothes played in a blue and white strip.)
The game kicked off in sensational style when Marshal hit the underside of the bar for Rothes in 9 minutes, but the Broch's reply was a twenty five yard shot from Auld, on 30 minutes, which also hit the bar. Scott and Marshall (Rothes) and Brander (Broch) then got into an argument and within seconds all hell let loose with about nine or ten players getting into the act. The referee would have needed eyes in the back of his head to see all of what went on, but eventually peace was restored. Bradford and Marshall were taken aside by the ref (no red cards in these days) who pointed to the stand for Bradford - what a decision!
Marshall's name went into the book, so the Broch had to play the last 60 minutes with ten men. If you're a Rothes fan, 56 minutes is the most important time in their history. For the Broch, it was a death knell. Martin crossed from the right and Grant headed on to Scott who met the pass with his head as well. The ball hit the post, struck keeper Mowatt and rolled into the net for Rothes 1 Broch 0. The Broch kept on fighting, but to no avail and the clock was ticking on to the ninety minutes when the ref' blew for time.

What a season that was. A Qualifying cup final, beat Dundee, an unlucky result against Stirling Albion, and lost the League play off. But now, as the story continues, there are a lot of dark days ahead for the Broch faithful. We didn't know it then, but the glory days were passing.

What did all football fans do in the summer? As a young boy in the late1950s I wasn't into the football bug yet of kicking a ball morning, noon and night, that was still to come. When the summer holidays came round, it was spent down the harbour or over at the beach. Is it just my imagination or were the summers a lot warmer and sunnier when you were young?
We used to go down to the harbour and as the boats were unloading their catch we used to ask for a "sail." If you're a local loon you'll know what I'm talking aboot. You would ask the crew for a "sail," round to the Balaclava, where the boats tied up, and most said "yes." Some of the boats I remember were the, "Vesper," the, "Girl Pat," and, "A Pal of Mine." A skipper took us out to the mouth of the harbour one day when it was a bit choppy. I don't know if I enjoyed it, as I was hanging on like grim death. As the boats tied up we would run back to the market and start again. A couple of my pals, Jimmy and Johnny Colvin, became fishermen. Other days were spent fishing for podlies under the Wine Tower (there was a sewer that ran out there from Maconochie's.) You didn't need much, a line, a sinker (usually an old washer) and an old bit of loaf as podlies would eat anything. Our mothers weren't too pleased about the smell of our clothes when we got home, but that was another thing.

Season 1959 -60

As season 1959-1960 came closer there wasn't the same excitement as you usually got. A few of last season's heroes had left and, "Old Father Time," had caught up on others. Bunny McCall had signed for Elgin City but, on a brighter note, Harry Yorston (the former Dons star) had put pen to paper for us. On Saturday, August 10th, this Broch team lined up against Deveronvale in the League Cup: Mowatt, McKenna, Milne, Meldrum, McHattie, Auld, Davidson, Yorston, Russell, Smith, McDonald.

It was not a very impressive start, as we lost 0-1, but a 2-2 draw at Peterhead and a further draw at Huntly put our first points on the board. We really needed to beat Peterhead at home, but could only manage a 1-1 draw. Another 2-2 draw at home to Huntly made it impossible to win the section, so it was on to the Broch's last game at Vale, with nothing at stake. The weather was so bad, torrential rain and a howling gale, that, the with the light getting worse, the referee played just 35 minutes each way (there were no flood lights in those days.) Oh, by the way, the Broch lost 1-0.

Saturday August 29th turned out to be a really bad day for the Broch. The first league game of the season away, against Rothes, ended up in a 9-1 defeat. The following Saturday saw a 5-0 win against Ross County. Was the Rothes result just a "freak" score? A home tie in the Qualifying Cup v Caley gave us something to look forward to, but it wasn't to be. The final score was Broch 4 Caley 7. No more glory, for that season at least.

Saturday, October 17th saw the Broch defeat Huntly 2 – 0. Nothing strange in that, but it turned out to be our last win that season. A 1-1 draw at home to Inverness Thistle and the same again against Elgin City and a 4-4 draw to Buckie was all we managed that season, with just seven points won at home. Away, we managed a 1-1 draw at Peterhead and 1-1 at Keith. Only 9 points for the season, not surprisingly the team finished bottom of the league. On January 16th the last point the Broch won at home was that 4-4 draw with Buckie. When you're bottom of the league you never seem to get the breaks. Yorston scored to make it 5-4, but Buckie protested that the ball went through a hole in the net. The ref consulted the linesman and gave a goal kick.

Around that time a letter, addressed from Jersey and sent to the "Herald" from a shareholder, wanted the Broch to turn to an all local team.

On the bright side, Central Buchan beat Dundee 2-1 at the Bellslea. I wonder if you recognise some of these, "up and coming," stars of that time.

C. Buchan
(North)
1

B.Newlands　　　　　A.Mackie
(Central)　　　　　　(Central)
2　　　　　　　　　　3

P. Whicher　　R. Bain　N. Cameron
(Longside)　　(Central)　(Stuartfield)
4　　　　　　　5　　　　　6

N. Beaton　J. Noble　J. Connon　A Noble　G. Malley
(St. Fergus)　(North)　(Central)　(Longside)　(Central)
7　　　　　　8　　　　　9　　　　　10　　　　　11

J. Connon put the Broch 1-0 up in the 60th minute and Beaton made it 2-0 in the 70th. Dundee scored a late consolation to make it 2-1. Brian Newlands was the star man in keeping the defence tight. Last time I met J.C (Jimmy Connon, he used to frequent the Brewery) he reminded me he really was not a bad player, but he lost interest in the game.

The first diesel train to leave the Broch for Aberdeen left the town on June 15th. If you wanted a taxi in those days there was not much choice. It was either:

Charlie Parker   Phone 573 or Barbours Garage   Phone 55

I remember going with my uncle in a black Hackney taxi to the railway station on a Saturday night to collect the, "Green Finals" and drop them off at Johnny Walker's paper shop in High Street. I think it's where Rogers Electrical is now. It all seems like yesterday, does time accelerate as you get older?

Chapter Two

The not so Swinging Sixties

As we entered a new decade, when the Beatles and Rolling Stones would top the charts, the Broch were propping up the league, but things could only get better after the previous season. At the AGM, Secretary Mr F. Park appealed to the town to give the team more support. As so often happens in football, if you're not winning, people won't turn out. The line up for the new season was: Stroud, Husband, Milne, Auld, Bruce, Chalmers, Strachan Ogilvie, Fraser, Noble, Rollo.

The fixtures got under way with a 2-0 win at Princess Royal against the Vale in the League Cup. New signing Fraser from New Pitsligo made a scoring debut and Johnny Strachan scored late on to make it 2-0. New centre half Bruce had an outstanding debut, as did goalkeeper Arthur Stroud. We met the Vale at Bellslea on Saturday August 17th. The Broch went 1-0 up with a dodgy penalty, then Fraser made it 2-0 on 67 minutes after rounding the keeper and rolling the ball into the net to give us a promising start to the season.

A 1-0 win at Peterhead gave us 7 points, but not enough to get into the League Cup semi-finals. With a home tie to Lossie in the Qualifying Cup we needed to hit a bit of form, but it was not to be. Lossie went into the hat on a 1-2 score – looks like it will be a long time before the glory days return. A 2-2 draw at Peterhead, and a 3-1 victory at the Bellslea over the Xmas period, gave us a bit of cheer.

The Broch's away form that season was a disaster, with no-one knowing what to expect. Results like 6-3 at Huntly, 6-1 at Inverness Thistle and 8-3 at Caley didn't make good reading in the Green Final. On February 4th we were at Peterhead in the 1st round of the Aberdeenshire

Cup. Cumming made it 1-0 early on for the home side, before goals from that old war horse Strachan in 41 and 49 minutes put us in front, but Cumming struck again to make it 2-2. Simpson scored the winner for the Broch, on 80 minutes to earn a semi-final place. A home tie v Huntly followed on February 18th but, again, it was not to be the Broch's day with the final score Broch 1 Huntly 3.

Elgin won the League with a play off v Keith at Victoria Park, Buckie. The Broch finished 4th from bottom:

P	W	D	L	F	A	PTS
28	8	7	13	58	80	23

The last home game was on April 8th and the Broch gave a debut to a young goal keeper by the name of Bobby Forsyth (Spicy) who was later to become a legend in football folklore. The match ended with the result, the Broch 2, Rothes 2.

The sixties were in full swing. You could go along to the Dalrymple Hall and dance to Tommy Tucker and the Strangers for an admission of 3/-. A "Herald," cost 2d. The summer was spent down the harbour. Do you remember the pea-pod lorries? They used to stop at the weighbridge across from where Smith's Fish Shop is now. We would pinch a bunch of peapods from the lorry and head for the black sands and eat them till we were sick. The lorries were heading for Maconnachie's where the pods were processed into tinned peas.

Season 1961-62

By any standards, the 1961-62 season had to show an improvement. A change of format that year meant the League Cup was to be played at the end of the season. On August 12th the Broch kicked off v Elgin City at the Bellslea. The team that day was: Stroud, Milne, McHattie, McLean, Bathgate, Fraser, Yeoman, Pirie, Simpson, McBeath.

Willie Grant made it 1-0 for Elgin and former Broch star Bunny McCall made it 2-0 to secure the league points. Roy Ewan had signed from Forfar, but a mix up in registration held up his debut. I never knew who made up the fixtures, but a fortnight later we played Elgin at Borough Briggs and lost 1-0. Goals from Bathgate and Simpson away to Huntly put the first points on the board. But more was to come, and would you believe it? In the Qualifying Cup 2nd round we were drawn away to Elgin City! It didn't get any better, 3 goals in 7 minutes blew the Broch away. Ewan (67) and Bruce (87) pulled it back to 3-2, but it was too little too late. No Cup glory again so back to League business. 3 draws and 7 wins including a 6-1 away to Buckie set us up nicely for the Xmas derbies. A large crowd turned up at Bellslea against Peterhead only to be disappointed. The visitors took a 2-0 lead before Ewan pulled a goal back for the Broch in 72 minutes to end the scoring. Bad weather cancelled the return the following week.

That Xmas you could watch Dick Whittington at the Picture House on Mid Street for 2/6d (about 12p). A bottle of Grants Whisky was 42/-(£2 – 20p). A dozen bottles of Tennants Lager was 11/10d (round about 60p) . Changed days!

Back to football and to a home tie in the semi-final of the Aberdeenshire Cup v Keith (must have got a bye in the 1st round). A 2-0 win put us into the final against the Vale. The 1st leg was at Banff, and what a disaster! The final score was Deveronvale 5 Broch 1. Forsyth scored our consolation goal. The second leg on 12th May at Bellslea looked like a formality, as Vale were 0-2 up by half time. D. Forsyth made it 1-2 on 47minutes, then Simpson equalised in 59 minutes. Strachan scored to make it 3-2 on 65 minutes. Forsyth made it 4-2 in an amazing comeback. Vale missed a penalty late on. Final score Broch 5, Deveronvale 7. We played the Vale six times that season – won 2, drew 1, lost

3. We lost 21 goals and scored 19. Poor defending or great goal scorers, I'll let you make up your own mind!
Would you believe the Broch finished higher up in the League than Caley, in 7th bottom place!

P	W	D	L	F	A	PTS
28	12	4	12	51	60	28

Season 1962-63

"The Broch will continue," was the headline as season 1962-63 drew nearer. But what did the future hold for the club with no money and up to its eyes in debt? I remember two of the committee going round the Bellslea with a sheet for a collection and an appeal, over the loud speaker, asking for volunteers to go on to the committee. Would the stirring battles of the past pass into oblivion? Times were certainly getting tough. There were no new strips every season like we see today. The Black and White Strips back then had faded until they were cream and grey. There weren't even eleven pairs of socks the same.

The Broch team that turned out against Deveronvale in the League Cup at the Bellslea, on Saturday August 11[th,] was: Stroud, Noble, Third, Simpson. Robertson, G. Strachan, J. Strachan, Summers, Ewan, Forsyth, McBeath.

Final score was Broch 1 Vale 5. Ewan scored for the Broch. Next up was Peterhead with a final score of Broch 3 Peterhead 6 – OUCH!!

With no money, the Broch turned to an all local policy with guys like Doshy Noble, Brian McCann, Brian Third, Angus Taylor and Peter McDonald playing from time to time. It was reported that we need gates of 1200 people to keep going. The average gate was 300, hard times indeed. The Webster Tyre Co donated £5.5/-. A supporter named Sandy donated 5/-, a lot of money in those days, but it was getting to the stage of one man and his dog watching. A home tie –v- Keith in Qualifying Cup gained some vital

income, with the score Broch 2 Keith 2. The Broch took a 2-0 lead, with Ewan scoring in the 6th and 22nd minutes. Then Woodcock pulled one back from a penalty in 39 minutes and Fowler in 72 minutes earned Keith a replay. Dennis Forsyth was at centre for the Broch and his brother Bobby wore the number 11 shirt. (What, Bobby a winger?) The replay was all one way, with Keith winning 5-2. A 2-2 draw at home to Ross County and a 3-3 draw at Elgin on October 6th was some improvement. Sadly, this was not to last, four straight defeats came, followed by a home win (2-1) against Buckie on November 17th. There wasn't another win till March 2nd (4-1 against Keith.) Scores like. Keith 8 Broch 1 and Peterhead 6 Broch 1 were not uncommon, so if anybody from Fort William ever reads this, we've, "seen it, done it and got the T shirt!" A 2-0 defeat at Vale in the Aberdeenshire Cup saw the bad news resumed. The defeats kept coming, 7-2 away to Vale, 6-0 at Clach and 5-3 at Nairn. 1962 - 63 was a bad winter for the Broch. Our last game was played on May 25th, which we lost 0-1 to Inverness Thistle. Roll on the summer!
Elgin won the league, scoring 105 goals. It was no surprise that the Broch finished bottom.

P	W	D	L	F	A	PTS
28	3	3	22	34	93	9

Three wins at home and three draws away from home was all we had managed to achieve.

At the Playhouse you could go to see, "The Young Ones," with Cliff Richard, for 9d, less than 4p in new money. By this time I had joined the Boys Brigade and so it was off to summer camp at Echt. It was miles away. I had £2 to spend and £1 for accommodation, plus a palliasse full of straw to sleep on in a school gym. Football all day and bed at 10 o'clock. P.T. every morning – I don't think kids would appreciate doing that in this day and age.

Rangers beat Celtic 3-1 in the Scottish Cup Final after a 1-1 draw.
Man Utd beat Leicester 3-1in the F.A. Cup Final.
Jimmy Greaves of Spurs was top scorer with 37 goals.
Jimmy Millar of Rangers scored 27 goals.
Allan McGraw of Morton scored 30 goals.

Season 1963 - 64

The back pages at the start of season 1963-64 showed that there was still much uncertainty as to whether or not the Broch would continue. The Herald wrote, "What's a Town without a Team?" but just round the corner there came a saviour. Mr Peter Cameron, an Aberdeen businessman, was ready to back the Broch. Suddenly things didn't look so bad. A couple of big names arrived, Tommy Ring (ex Clyde) Jimmy Milne (not the carpet fitter - this Jimmy signed from Forfar and was at Hearts for a while) and Johnny Allen of Dunfermline and Aberdeen. Had the dark clouds lifted? Had the Broch turned the corner?

Another team was elected to the League, Brora Rangers from the far north of Scotland. With the Bellslea getting a makeover, we waited in anticipation for the start of the season. A 6-1 win in a friendly v Banks o Dee was a good start. The teams that day were:

Broch: Stephen, Russell, McLean, Brown, Milne, Smith, Allen, McDonald, Ingram, Christie, Ring.

Banks o Dee: Gray, Bremner, Hamilton, Gorman, Logan, Kirkland, Singer, Cumming, Brady, Finnie, Dawson.

This whetted our appetites and, on the following Wednesday, we put nine past the Toolies.

Toolworks team was: Muirhead, Yule, Noble, McGowan, Fraser, E Noble, Cardno, McDonald, Blair, Taylor, May.

The final score was 9-3, with Allen (4) and Ring (2) Brown (1) Summers (2) scoring for the Broch. Toolworks scorers were Blair (57) Taylor (63) and May (84)

FROM BELLSLEA TO BRORA THESE ARE MY HEROES

On Saturday August 10th we played at home to Huntly in the League Cup. I can remember this game as though it was yesterday. The queue to get into the Bellslea stretched along to the corner of the street, something that hadn't been seen for a long time. The game started in sensational style. Young of Huntly hit the byline and crossed to Christie who flashed the ball past Thom to put Huntly 0-1 in the lead - time - 30 seconds. A Ring free kick resulted in Christie heading in to make it 1-1. Allen made it 2-1 on 27 minutes, then Byiers equalised on the stroke of half time. There was no more scoring and the game ended 2-2.

The attendance was estimated at nearly 2,000, showing that the crowds would come back if we got a match winning team. At that time the Huntly shirts were gold with a black v-neck. I don't know where their nickname of, "Tigers," came from. I've never heard them called that in all the years I've watched Highland League Football.
A 4-0 defeat followed at Peterhead with Billy Weir hitting a hat-trick. The terracing talk was, "has Peter Cameron backed a loser or pit his money into a white elephant?" A 5-0 drubbing at Christie Park the following Saturday didn't do our confidence any good. Next outing was a 3-1 win at home to the Vale with a Ewen hat-trick. Strange game, football. Allen was our best forward at Peterhead yet he was dropped. Ring was non-existent and still played. Doshie Noble had a super game at left back. Next up was Vale at Banff. New signing George Kelly made a scoring debut to help the Broch to a 2-3 victory. Our final League Cup game was at home to Peterhead. Too much chopping and changing of the team doesn't do any good, and as a result the Broch were defeated 1-4. Too many ex pros came into the Highland League and didn't realise that you have to put in a decent shift and not stroll about. They should have taken a look at the local boys who played for the jersey. A young Peter McDonald had a reasonable game against Peterhead, and at least he didn't let his head go down. We finished bottom of the section with 4 points.

It was back to League business. I thought that the days of getting a tanking were past but then the score from Clach came through, Clach 8 Broch 2. Had the latest bubble burst? It looked like Tommy Ring and Co had seen better days. With a home tie the following week against Peterhead in the 1st round of the Qualifying Cup, it was a, "must win," to save our season. On September 7th Peterhead took the game to the Broch and were 0-3 up in 30 minutes. The Broch looked dead and buried, but Allen reduced the lee-way on 38 minutes and at the interval it was the Broch 1, Peterhead 3. Kelly made it 2-3 on 48 minutes and the Broch were awarded a penalty on 73 minutes, from which Meldrum gave Wood no chance. It was now 3-3 and all to play for. Wood put the Broch in the lead for the first time on 80 minutes, as the Bellslea erupted. It stayed this way to the end, with the final score the Broch 4 Peterhead 3, "come awa' the Burgh." It had been a long time since the fans had invaded the Bellslea pitch.

We were drawn away to Rothes in the 2nd round. The Broch took the lead on 31 minutes and Allen tapped the second into an empty net in 70 minutes to make it 0-2. A Rothes consolation goal came in 88 mins but the final score was Rothes 1 Broch 2. It was nothing to write home about, but it's the result that counts. I didn't know what happened to goalkeeper "Thom" but the Brochs new keeper, John Curran from Keith, had made the jersey his own. He played for Queens Park, Aberdeen and East Fife, but on some days "he couldnae catch a bus".

The quarter final draw was away to new boys Brora Rangers. What a journey! I wanted to go but my parents said it was too far and I was too young. At that time the bus would leave at 6am. There was no Kessock Bridge in those days, just up the Struie and keep on going. It was worse if you were up there in early December. No floodlights and a 2 o'clock kick off. What a nightmare!

The match day came and the Broch took the lead in 30 minutes through J. Allan, a new signing from Clach. Jackie

Kane added a second, on his debut, to put the Broch on easy street. Doshie Noble sustained an injury and, as was usual, moved onto the wing but added Broch's final goal. McRae scored a consolation goal late on for a final score of Brora 1 Broch 4. Scottish Cup here we come. Hibs, maybe Rangers, who cares! It was back to earth, however, the next Saturday, with a 1-4 home defeat at the hands of Caley.

We knew we would have to buck up our ideas for the semi-final the following week as we got a home draw v Forres. It was rumoured that the cameras would be at the match. True to the rumour, there was a camera perched in the stand. Every Saturday evening as Scotsport would start you would see a clip of the game, "in black and white of course." Forres, at that time, played in an all white strip, with a yellow and chocolate hoop on the shirt if my memory serves me well.

The teams that day were:

    Broch: Curran, Russell, Carroll, Brown, Milne, Smith, Davidson, Fowler. Allan, Kane, Meldrum.

    Forres: McDonald, Cochill, Noble, McIvor, Nisbet, Main, Shaw, Beveridge, Curmie, Roy, Dingwall.

Referee – Mr J P Barclay (Kircaldy)

Forres won the toss and elected to kick into a stiff breeze. The Broch hit too many long balls, which, with the wind, simply ran out out for goal kicks. Tragedy struck them in 7 minutes when a Russell passback slipped past the keeper's reach and rolled into the net to make it 1-0 to Forres. In the 18th minute, Dingwall made it 2-0, but Allan (my hero) pulled one back on 26 minutes, making it 1-2. Meldrum scored to make it 2-2 at half time. Roy put Forres 2-3 in front in 60 minutes, then Allan (what a player) made it 3-3 in 70 minutes. Shaw netted in 73 minutes for Forres to settle the issue. Final score, Broch 3 Forres 4, and what a game! Forres went on to win the Cup by beating Buckie Thistle 8-4 over two legs.

A season ticket for the Bellslea, at that time, was £2:5/-. You're lucky if you can get a pint these days for that money!

The amateur league also was in full swing. Sandhaven topped the league with Pittulie, Toolies, Lads Club, Inver St Cairn chasing, with a new, young and up and coming side, while St Modans were making heavy weather of it. One score was Pittulie 10, St Modans 3 with a young George Malley scoring. I had the pleasure of playing for them at one stage. There weren't many young teams willing to have a go in the amateur league but St Modans developed into a household name in the local game. A string of their players progressed to play for the Broch, e.g.George Malley, Nigel Hunter, Davie Anderson and Robbie McDonald to name just a few.

Back on league business, Brora, the league's new babes, were at the Bellslea on Saturday Nov 2nd. The teams that day were:

Broch: Curran, Forrest, Carroll, Brown, Smith, Milne, Smith, Ingram, Kane, Allan, Kelly Meldrum.

Brora: B.Sutherland, Mackay, Pryde, Macrae, Millar, J.Sutherland, Macleod, Patience, Reid, Gunn, Alexander.
Referee – J. Chivas Aberdeen

The pace of the game was too much for Brora. Broch went 1-0 ahead in 21 minutes, Allan added his second in 30 mins to put Broch 2-0 up. Jackie Kane made it 3-0 on 38 minutes and Ingram put the Broch on easy street when he made it 4-0 on 40 minutes. After half time, the Broch eased off and T. Reid reduced the lee-way. There was no further score. Brora number nine, Tommy Reid, went on to be a legend in the Highland League, with Caley, if I remember correctly.

The draw for the Scottish Cup was made and the Broch were drawn away to Dunfermline, whose manager, Jock Stein, was making a big impression in the old eighteen club first division.Not the best of draws but maybe we would make a couple of pounds!

The following week, after the Brora game, the headline in the paper was, "Broch sign ex Celtic star Fernie." I thought it was a mis-print, but, on Saturday, December 7th, he lined up in a black and white shirt at home to Keith.

Broch were 1-0 up at half time, and, after the restart, Fernie put through his own goal, but the Broch went on to win 3-2. Fernie only stayed on for a couple more games, as he was looking for a manager's job. I didn't think he would have signed for £1 a week and a fish supper!

The following week we were up at Keith. This was the first game I was allowed to go to myself. There was just the team bus, with no supporters' buses at that time. The Broch won 1-0. Eddie Noble (Ebbens to his friends) scored the winner. The Keith stand was brand new and I had never seen such a large bath in the dressing room before, especially with 11 players, all in the buff, in it, quite a shock for one so young! The next few games in the run up to the big game were a disaster. We lost five games including a 1-6 thumping at home to Nairn.

On Saturday, Jan 25th 1964, the Broch set off for East End Park with a prayer. The teams were:

Dunfermline: Herriot, Callaghan (W), Lunn, Smith, McLean, Miller, Wilson, Peebles, Dickson, Kerry, Callaghan (T)

Broch: Curran, McCann, Forrest, Bruce, Milne, Carroll, Davidson, Kane, Allan, Fowler, Ewan.

As everybody suspected, we were on a hiding to nothing. The final score was 7-0, with Dickson (5) Kerry and Peebles scoring. Brian McCann was a shock choice at right back as he had been out injured for a few weeks. Since both teams played in black and white a change of strip was required. As the Broch didn't have a second strip, they played in the Toolies' kit, white shirts with a blue collar and blue shorts. After the game, all the players were handed a brown wage packet with a £20 note in it. When McCann opened his, there was a 10/- note in it, that's the difference between playing for the shirt and the so called Superstars. It was decided, after this, that the Broch were to adopt an all local policy, so they put eleven players up for sale. Tommy Ring and George Kelly were among them.

The next game was at home to Keith in the Aberdeenshire Cup. This saw a 3-2 win with Eddie Noble crashing home a free kick. A home tie against the Vale followed in the semi-finals. With six local players in the team there seemed to be a bit more fight. On 25 minutes, the Vale took the lead. Curran kicked a clearance against McDonald and the ball rolled into the net. Allan (worth his weight in gold for the Broch) scored with a penalty to earn a replay. That replay started in sensational style, with the Vale scoring within 30 seconds. D Forsyth levelled on 16 minutes, then Eddie Noble scored a tremendous solo goal, after beating three players in a mazy run and crashing the ball into the net, to put the Broch into the final. Another hat-trick followed for Johnny Allan in a 4-1 win against Rothes to set us up nicely for the postponed game at Xmas against Peterhead, however, this game was abandoned after 45 minutes, due to the wind and lashing rain, with the score standing at 0-0. The only real highlight of the game was Johnny Allan hitting the bar with a free kick from all of 40 yards, with the wind behind him, kicking into the "Pole's garage" end.

The local lads were doing us proud, but a Wednesday night game at Lossie on April 22nd brought us back down to earth with a 7-2 defeat. Half an hour before the kick off there had been only six players stripped. The boys from Aberdeen had broken down somewhere (there were no mobile phones then.) When the game eventually kicked off it was always going to be a race against time to finish it because of the light, and play ended in semi-darkness. Our last home game was a 3-1 win over Ross County. The team that day was: Buchan, Milne, Jamieson, Forsyth, McCann, Carroll, Keith, Noble, Allan, Smith, Meldrum. The game brought another two goals for J. Allan and a 'pile driver' from Eddie Noble.

As for the final of the Aberdeenshire Cup, well that's a long story, but I'll try to keep it short. Buckie somehow scratched and the tie and the Cup were awarded to the Broch without kicking a ball. That was another season gone. We had made it, though with a struggle and continuing questions about survival. The Broch finished 13th, in other words 4th from bottom. Never mind, the 'Mogganers,' were 14th and 3rd bottom!

P	W	D	L	F	A	PTS
30	7	5	18	52	90	19

The music world was about to change as Radio Caroline set up house on board a ship and was the first pirate radio station. Now that the longer nights were in, it was football till it was dark. Everybody had their patch. The boys from Marconi played over where Doig Springs are now. Guys like big Dod Bruce, Ronnie Mennie and Johnny White all turned out to be decent players. Then there was St Modans, where the South Park School was built. There were a few Cup Finals won and lost there. Anyway, the law of the land was the big guys ruled so the young guns were always thrown off the pitch. One night a young Sandy Souter had had enough, so off he went for Big Bill to sort things out. Bill arrived and says, "I'm not moving till ma loon gets a game," so he said, "Sandy go hame and get ma jacket." A young Francie Connon shouted, "better get his coat as well, 'cos he's gaun to be a lang time." The last time Francie was seen was in the distance with Bill at his rear - those were happy days! Of course I shouldn't forget the boys who played on the old Hockey Park: Gordon Bissett, Mousie McRae, Billy Wardle, Johnnie Stephen to name a few of them. Mousie McRae was playing for Parkvale when he was 15, but he came back to have a kick about with us. He was so good we used to tell him to go and play with the big boys. At that time, everybody was interested in football. I well remember Alfie Summers and his two dogs. He was scout for Parkvale and took any of the Broch boys who had a bit of promise, like Brian Newlands, Bertie Bowie, Ian Williams, Baxter, Speem(Sandy Watt) and Gilbert Stephen. There was no junior football locally then, with Buchanhaven Hearts the nearest club, though not many people had a car in those days. Johnny Allan signed for Peterhead, stayed a while and was never heard of again(should have stayed at Bellslea!)

Season 1964 – 65 (Another season, but only just)

Highland League Secretary, Charles Fraser, issued a statement to the Press. He was delaying drawing the League Cup because of uncertainty surrounding the Broch's future. The Broch held a special meeting, and secretary John Buchan said this would decide whether we continued or not. It was that close. So next time you're having a moan at the present team, just think, if it hadn't been for those guys back then, there would be no senior football in the Broch.

It was not the best of starts that year, with a 5-0 drubbing at Recreation Park in the first game of the season, but we bounced back with a 3-0 home win against Huntly. With all the big names gone it was now up to the local boys. An Eddie Noble hat-trick was the highlight of that game. A double header against the Vale followed.The Broch got a 2-2 draw away but we lost 6-1 at home. Was this going to be a further sign of the times? We were 3-0 down to Brora at half time, but ran riot in the second half to win 5-3, Noble in 70 minutes, P. McDonald 72 minutes, Smith in 80 minutes, D. Forsyth 86 minutes and McDonald on 89 minutes finished it off, to the delight of the Bellslea crowd, "come awa the Burgh!" A sad note was the sudden death of former Broch star Johnnie Noble, better known as, "Katie's Johnny." He had starred for the Broch for seven years and was only 52 years old. He had two sons who both played for the Broch, Johnnie and Eddie (better known as, "Ebbens.")

With an away tie in the Qualifying Cup looming, the Broch had to hit a bit of form. A 4-3 defeat at Nairn and a 3-2 one at home to Caley didn't do our confidence any good and, when the tie came, it was not to be. We lost narrowly 1 - 2, so it was back to trying to pick up some league points. On Saturday, Sept 26th the Broch were up at Telford Street to play Caley. The next few lines do not make good reading! Reid put Caley 1-0 up in 4 minutes. Noble made it 1-1, then Smith made it 2-1. W. Smith equalised to make it 2-2 in 38 minutes. Caley missed a penalty but Stephen put them 3-2 up just before the interval then 3 goals in 3 minutes made it 6-2. The Broch then hit a quick double, from Noble and P. McDonald, making it 6-4. Smith, Stephen and Reid added further goals for a final score of Caley 9 Broch 4. I was sure the Green Final had carried a misprint, but the Sunday Post clarified the result. The Broch team that day was: Buchan, Reid, Milne, Fraser, McCann, Carroll, W. Smith, P. McDonald, Noble, A. Taylor, D. Forsyth. The following week at home to Inverness Thistle we lost 5-4, then 4-2 away from home to Clach. When was this nightmare going to end?

Two more defeats followed, 6-2 at home to Forres and 6-2 away to Rothes, giving a total of 30 goals against and just 14 goals for. Everyone must have been dying to play the Broch on this form. Next game up was at home to Lossie' and it was another high scoring game. The Broch gave a debut to local lad Alan Keith who opened the scoring in 27 minutes. He made it 2-0 in 33 minutes and Noble made it 3-0 before P. McDonald made it 4-0. Lossie hit back with a bizarre goal just on the stroke of half time. Mair scored from the touch line, but was it meant to be a cross? Reid made it 4-2, then Young made it 4-3 with a penalty. The come back was complete when Milne made it 4-4 seven minutes from time. Our next game at home was against Nairn who had Dave Johnston scoring goals for fun. Allan put Nairn 1-0 ahead in 19 minutes, but Noble made it 1-1 a minute later. McLennan made it 2-1 midway through the second half. Meldrum then went on a mazy run before crossing for Dennis Forsyth to head a spectacular goal. The final score was 2-2 and a creditable draw.

A bit of light relief now. Do you remember the half-time kick about? After the players went in at half-time all the young fans would have a kick about, usually about 15 a side, with one ball and one goalie, in the same goal. Bill Rennie, the groundsman, would come and chase them off and it was then a quick sprint up to the other goals, some on bikes as well. By the time the groundsman got up the other end the players were usually on their way back out. There was no tannoy at that time so the half time raffle was on a board written with chalk. One young lad (Charlie Crawford) (Sunty was his byname) used to walk round the park. His reward was a, "bradie," and a bottle of juice. It was not unusual for games to be halted when the local, "mutt," brought proceeding to a halt and the poor referee, to great applause, led it off to the side. Sorry, no red cards! On one occasion the dog that had come on spotted a rabbit, so the chase was on. That was the best entertainment we'd seen in a long time!

The Broch used to train on Tuesdays and Thursdays at that time. I probably spent more time at the Bellslea then than I did at home. I can remember John Cheil stoking the old fire, for hot water for the showers. Not many of the Aberdeen lads trained at the Broch so the numbers were made up with local amateur league boys. Forbes Bruce was a Gym Teacher at Fraserburgh Academy and he would train the Broch players. He was pretty hard on them, but, by fair means or foul, he got them fit. The only lights we had were up on the stand, so they shone from one end of the stand to the other and half way across the park. We only had a couple of footballs and they were kept for match days, so a plastic one was used for a practice game. Today's players don't know they're living!

Our next game after the two draws was away to Keith. Things weren't getting any easier as we lost 7-3. Carroll scored an own goal in the 4th minute, but two quick goals by E. Noble put us 1-2 ahead. This lead was short lived, as Smith made it 2-2. The Broch went 2-3 up 2 minutes later through Meldrum, but a Munro penalty, in the 50th minute, made it 3-3. The Broch were run ragged in the last 25 minutes, with four goals scored in that period, making the final score Keith 7 Broch 3. The last half hour of every game seemed to let the Broch down. I didn't think we would be able to hold on to Eddie Noble, whose goal scoring exploits must have been noticed by other teams. While we were at the wrong end of the table, Eddie was up there with the best in the scoring charts.

In those days it was not unusual to chop and change players' positions. For the game we lost 5-4 at Inverness Thistle, Spicey moved from goalkeeper to centre forward, Cliff Meldrum went from outside left to left back and Johnny Carroll shifted from right back to centre half. Speaking of changes of positions, Cliff Meldrum was at left back for the day against Peterhead when we played them. The Broch got a penalty in the first thirty seconds of the game and Meldrum took the kick, but the Peterhead keeper Thom saved it. Not many players miss a penalty with their first kick of the ball. By the way, Peterhead went on to win that game.

On Saturday November 28th the Broch travelled to Borough Briggs to play Elgin. Nothing strange in that, on the face of it, but the events of that day will live for ever, with a double hat trick for Willie Grant and a hat trick for Eddie Noble. Fraser scored in 4 minutes, then Grant made it 2-0 a minute later. Then followed a remarkable goal scored by Grant, standing in line with the back post, his header screwed in at the other post past a bewildered Forsyth to make it 4-0. Noble reduced the leeway to 4-1 then Noble in 50 and McDonald in 55 minutes made it 4-3, before two more for Fraser and another double for Grant made it nine. Noble hit a late counter for his hat trick but the final score was Elgin 9, Broch 4. I had the recent pleasure of meeting Willie Grant and he remembered that game vividly. The teams that day were:

Broch: Forsyth, Reid, Jamieson, Fraser, McCann, Carroll, Smith, Noble, D. Forsyth, McDonald, Meldrum.

Elgin: Low, Gerrard, D. Grand, Mair, McAll, McKenzie, McIvor, McIntosh, Grant, Fraser, Thomson.

The following Saturday December 5th we beat Huntly 8-0, with the scorers: Blair (2), Smith (2), Noble (2), D. Forsyth and Jameson, who went onto the wing when he was injured and scored the eighth goal. Just how bad must Huntly have been at that time, for we were no great shakes It was so dark at the end of the match that they put on the training lights attached to the stand. A roar arose from the crowd as someone shouted, "Is it tae let the players see far the tunnel is?" They were happy days!

A 4 - 3 win came at Buckie the following week, indicating that things were starting to look up. Dennis Forsyth put Broch 2-3 up that day. It turned out to be a milestone in the Brochs' history as it was the 3000th competitive goal the Broch had scored, (the 2000th had been scored in an 8-3 victory v Nairn County, in September 1954.) A 0-0 away to Rothes set us up nicely for the derby with the "Mogganers," on January 2nd. Carroll and Blair both had to go off with knocks. Carroll was worst off, but he resumed after five minutes, while Blair moved to the wing. In those days you just had to grin and bear it with injuries. Christie in 15 minutes, and Cormie in the 40th stretched Peterhead's lead before a penalty, in 86 minutes, by Jamieson made the final score 1-2.

Some atrocious weather over the next month meant we didn't play till February 6th at home to Ross County. A 2-5 defeat that day didn't help. 0-2 down we fought back to 2-2 but a Hosie hat trick settled the game. A 1-1 draw at Christie Park in the Aberdeenshire Cup was next, during which Broch centre half McCann collided with a post and was knocked unconscious. He was taken to hospital while the Broch held on for a replay.

What a corker of a game the replay was. Meldrum missed a penalty on 60 minutes and Huntly bombarded the Broch goal, but Spicey was having one of his better days. With the score standing on 0-0 the Broch moved Jimmy

Milne from right back to centre forward. He scored in the fifth minute of extra time but Sutherland made it 1-1 in 110 minutes before Smith put the Broch back in the lead in 113 minutes. The final score was Broch 2 Huntly 1 - how's that for tactics? Our next outing was a 2-2 draw with the Vale at home, followed by a right good old fashioned end to end game at home to Clach. Brett opened the scoring on 7 minutes then Clach got a penalty on 15 minutes, which Forsyth saved but the referee ordered a retake. Castell scored, to make it 0-2. Milne pulled one back on 30 minutes for 1-2, "Jimmy had got a new lease of life at centre forward!" Brett made it 1-3 on 37 minutes. Just after half time Donald made it 1-4. Three minutes later Smith pulled another one back to make it 2-4 and then scored again to make it 3-4. The Broch got another penalty on 82 minutes, but Robertson brought off a great save from Meldrum. The game finished Broch 3 Clach 4, showing once again that the one thing about following the Broch then was, from one game to the next, you never knew what to expect. The teams that day were:

Broch: Forsyth, Thomson, Jamieson, Reid, McCann, Carroll. Smith, McCall, Milne, Meldrum, McDonald.

Clach: Robertson, Lathem, Nudge, Smith, Rogers, Chisholm, Castell, Brett, Donald, Kane, Munro.

Referee – E. H. Pringle, Aberdeen.

What was I saying about what to expect? The 20th March that year was a very sad day for the Broch as the score came through, Ross County 13 Fraserburgh 2. Jim Hosie scored seven that day. I can't find it in myself to write about the game, but we took it on the chin and moved on. The teams that day were:

Ross County: Sutherland, Macleod, Vass, Mackenzie, Greig, McWilliam, Ross, Thomson, Hosie, McNeil, Clark.

Fraserburgh: Forsyth, Thompson, Fraser, Reid, McCann, Lamb, Smith, Burr, Milne, Carroll, McDonald.

Broch's two goals were scored by Billy Smith, but we should remember that those guys back then gave up their

Saturdays to pull on a black and white shirt. They played for nothing, and they got a fish supper on the way home, if they were lucky. "Come away the Burghy!"

Things didn't get any easier at home to Keith the following week though Jimmy Milne was still in good scoring form. He put the Broch 1-0 up in the first minute and netted his second in the eighth minute after Middler had levelled, but Keith went on to win 2-5. The away fixture to Brora Rangers never seemed to change in those days. Call-offs at the last minute like, "I'm working on Saturday morning," or a wedding, or any other excuse. Andy Lamb was not long married at the time when a knock at the door came at 6.45 on Saturday morning asking if he would like a game. I don't think his wife was too pleased! But those guys were the unsung heroes at the time, who, week after week, made sure that eleven shirts got on to the park. Brora won 3-0 that day, although they ended up with nine men, when two of their players went off injured. Our team that day was: Buchan, Williams, A Lovie, Forsyth, McCann, Fraser, Smith, Thomson, Anderson, A. Taylor, Lamb. Five of those players were amateurs.

Two more heavy defeats away to Peterhead (5 – 2) and Forres (8-1) didn't help club morale. For the game at Forres we had three brothers playing for the Broch, J. Robertson, N. Robertson and W. Robertson. We also had a, "Newman." He played for a few teams in those days.

Two weeks later we suffered another 8-1 defeat at the hands of Inverness Thistle. It was a continuing struggle to get a team onto the park and it was just as well we had so many keen amateur players to help out. The team v Inverness Thistle was: Buchan, Williams, Lovie, McGowan, McCann, Lamb, May, Smith, Taylor, Forsyth, Taylor. A 0-2 defeat at home to Elgin City, followed by 0-6 and 1-6 away to Lossie and Vale respectively, meant we had suffered twelve defeats on the trot, with the loss of 62 goals and only 12 scored. The last game of the season was the Aberdeenshire Cup Final v Peterhead. The 1st leg was a 0-0 draw on the 18th May. The only thing worthy of mention was Smith hitting the bar with 5 minutes to go. The 2nd leg wasn't much to write home about either, with Peterhead winning 4-0. The report made it fairly obvious that there was little prestige in winning this trophy, with Vale refusing to take part and the Broch as holders, because Buckie refused to play in the final the previous year. Funny old game, football! For a year it would be known as the forgotten trophy. Oh well, another season but, once again, only just. Elgin City were champions that season and, surprise! surprise! the Broch got the wooden spoon for being 16th in the League.

P	W	D	L	F	A	PTS
30	3	4	23	67	138	10

It was off to Arbroath and the B/B camp for me. One of the highlights of the camp was midnight dooking in the outdoor pool. If you dived in after midnight you got a certificate. The pool wasn't heated so you can imagine how cold it was at that time. One of my chums, John Anderson, thought he would dive in what he thought was the shallow end, "wrong," it was the deep end, so one of the officers had to dive in for him. Now John, for whom I have great admiration (for what he does with International Rescue all around the world saving lives) could not live down that wee mishap. We always have a laugh about it if I meet him. Does anyone remember Sgt Sim? Well, he is now retired from the Police, but, when we were kids, if we saw him we would run away even if we hadn't done anything wrong. That's the kind of respect you had for the police in those days. The TV on both channels stopped at 11.40 on a Saturday night. "Tommy Dene and the Tremors," were playing at the Dalrymple, 2/- (10p) before 9 o'clock, 3/- (15p) after 9 o'clock. Pubs closed at 10 o'clock and the dance finished at 11.30. The summer, "Kipper Barbecue," had the, "Jacko-beats," playing. I'm sure many of you have memories of that time and good ones at that.

Season 1965 -66

The reporter at the Herald at that time, Archie K. McTaggart, wrote before the season began, "Is it to be a Repitition of Last Season?" He, like most reporters, only travelled to away games when it suited. The Broch were still without Directors, so Jimmy Brown, "The Bomber," was appointed temporary secretary (nobody else would do it.) What had the Broch to offer a player coach? He would need a wage, a job and a house (not much chance of that with the financial difficulties involved in running a Highland League club.) The Broch were pressing on with team building and had drawn up a list of players they would like to sign. They were: Cormie (Forres) Cumming (Forres) Low (Elgin) Ellis (Rothes) W. Smith (Vale). One out of those five came. Then the headlines read, "Keeper Low joins Burgh." A real legend, he was dropped by Elgin nine games short of 500 appearances, so their loss was our gain. George Morgan (Duthie) and Nommie Robertson (Sandhaven Utd) also signed on. It was amazing also the number of players who crossed that dividing line and signed for sssh!! - Peterhead - then couldn't wait to come back. "Home is where the heart is."

A creditable 3-3 draw at home to Huntly in the League Cup, with Johnnie Low in inspiring form, keeping us in the game time and time again with some breathtaking saves. Murray put Huntly 0-1 ahead in 19 minutes. D, but Forsyth made it 1-1. Four minutes later. Murray made it 1-2 on 32 minutes. The lead was short lived as Bobby Forsyth brought the scores level a minute later (Spicy scoring, that was one for the record books!) Murray hit his hat trick on 44minutes, but we had to wait till 80 minutes for N. Robertson to score the equaliser. The team that started that season was: Low, Thomson, Carroll, Forsyth, McCann, Reid, Smith, Hall, N. Robertson, Duthie, R. Forsyth.

The following Wednesday it was off to Recreation Park to play Peterhead and back to our old ways with an 8-1 defeat. It was 1-1 on 32 minutes, but one way traffic after that. Dickie Ewen scored 5 goals that night and two more defeats, 4-2 at Huntly and 1-3 at Bellslea against Peterhead left us still looking for our first win. Two draws with the Vale, 1-1 home and 3-3 away, left us at the bottom of the section. The most disappointing thing was that three of those who played for Vale then, Doshy Noble, Brian Third and Eddie Noble might have been playing in a black and white shirt. From there things did not get any better. We went up to Forres and were 2-0 up in seven minutes with goals from Robertson and D. Forsyth, then pushed the self-destruct button for a final score of Forres 8, Broch 2. A Qualifying Cup game at home to Clach came the following week. We needed a good performance to get a bit of confidence back, but some of the team selections in those days never failed to amaze me. Take Nommie Robertson, who played at centre forward all his life, so where did he play on that Saturday? At left back! Did Jimmy Broon know something that we didn't? Anyway, it worked, because it was the Broch's first win of the season, 2-0. With the team up 1-0 and hanging on Denis Forsyth hit a 20 yard steamer past keeper Robertson to settle the issue. Don't know why the keeper bothered diving, but we were into the hat for the 2nd round draw and it was happy days again.

The 2nd round draw was made and we drew Wick Academy away (they were a non-league side at that time.) For most of the away games there was still never a bus, just cars to transport the team, but Wick was different. It was decided to stay overnight, so a collection was taken at the Bingo to help pay for the trip and a letter of thanks was sent to Mr Conner Kay, the manager of the Bingo, for his help. It wasn't an easy game. Broch went 1-0 up in six minutes through Peter McDonald but Wick equalised just on half time through Reid. After that it was all Wick, but the Broch held on for a final score of 1-1. The teams that day were:

Wick Academy: Davidson, Jack, McDonald, Webster, Campbell, Green, Allan, Macleod, Reid, Farquhar, Mackay.

Broch: Low, Thomson, Milne, Forsyth, J. Taylor, McCann, Smith, Macdonald, Robertson, Duthie, Noble.

There has been a story doing the rounds for years about this cup tie. It was said that Dave Caldwell played for Wick in the first game and then played for the Broch in the replay. I don't think either of the two teams would have risked that in the Scottish Cup. That was all right at the end of the season when, "new man," or, "trialist," played out the season just to get eleven players on the park. On Oct 16th, Caldwell signed in time for the replay against the Broch. The teams for the replay were:

The Broch: Forsyth, Milne, J. Robertson, McCann, Taylor, Reid, Smith, McDonald, D.Forsyth, Duthie, N. Robertson.

Wick Academy: Davidson, Caldwell, James Donald, Alexander Jack, Green, Findlay, Allan, Campbell, McKay.
Referee – F. A. Phillips (Inverness)

When the team lines were read out for the first game, neither Bobby Forsyth or John Low, who was away on business, would play, but then Johnnie Low just made it. He flew back up, something not many Highland League players did in those days. On to the replay, where, for the first 15 minutes of the game, the Broch laid siege in the Wick half, but keeper Davidson was in superb form. Against the run of play Wick broke away and Findlay scored the opening goal on 37 minutes. Nerves were getting the better of the Broch but two goals in two minutes from Smith and Reid put them 2-1 up, till Wick hit back with an equaliser on 65 minutes. With extra time looming, Davidson made his only mistake of the afternoon, when he let a shot from Duthie slip through his hands and roll over the line for the winner, much to the relief of all at the Bellslea. Scottish Cup here we come! A semi - final followed against Caley, which we lost 5-0, but a good write up from Jim Lornie helped boost our confidence. It had been a long time since we got such a big write up. It was usually a small report away in a corner of the paper.

It was now the end of October and with all the excitement of the Cup we were bottom of the league with no points on the board.

P	W	D	L	F	A	PT
4	0	0	4	4	14	0

Our next home game was against Huntly. Only the Broch could pick up their first league points in the fashion they did. We went 1 – 0 up, through Robertson, but Huntly then hit a quick double to take the lead. The Broch's keeper, Low, went off with a dislocated finger, but returned five minutes later to change jerseys with Taylor. Low went to centre forward and crashed in two cracking goals in the 85th and 89th minutes to put the Broch 3 – 2 up and win our first points of the season. An away tie to high-flying Ayr United was our reward for reaching the Scottish Cup draw.

A young, up and coming, star from the Broch, Brian Newlands ("Tonto," to his friends) was off for a month's trial with Cardiff City. He played for Parkvale and was in his second season with them. Aberdeen were also reported to be interested in him. He was probably one of the best players ever to come out of the Broch, but he took a long time to get to the Bellslea. Brian was a good friend of mine and a real legend as you'll read later on. The Broch had installed Alex Beattie as trainer to get the fitness of the players up to scratch and he was a hard task master. Training back then was on a Tuesday and Thursday and I can still see old John Cheil, a real character at the Bellslea in those days. There was an old stove in the home dressing room and it needed a lot of wood to heat the water for the showers. Cheil would fill the fire and then settle down for a game of dominoes with his cronies. I probably still spent more time at Bellslea at that time, than I did at home!

Another story from that time was how Dennis Forsyth used to work in the Bakehouse on Friday night, then went out with the Baker's Van after that. On the Saturday, he was serving a customer about 2.15, who asked why he wasn't playing that day. "I am," Dennis replied. Turning the corner of the Bellslea, Jim Broon was waiting patiently and pacing back and fro. The time was 2.40 but Dennis was in, changed, and on to the Park at 2.55, not bad after working all night! That's what they did in those days. On training nights when the Bellslea was covered in snow they would play on the old hockey park, borrow the roller from the cricket park, mark a pitch and play under the street lights.The new all weather playing surface is only a few yards away from there, but back then only teams like the Real Madrids and Manchester Uniteds of this world trained on them. How the world has changed.

Gorgie Morgan remembers the time they went to Brora and the bus stuck in the snow, so they all got out and pushed it, some preparation for a game! By the way, the Broch lost 4-0 that day. Brian McCann was carried off again, so they played the last twenty minutes with 10 men. On one occasion they went to Keith, and were sitting in the dressing room at twenty to three when Broon came in, shouting to them.

"Come on then, get stripped," but alas, the strip hadn't arrived, so they had to rush out and borrow a second strip from Islavale. The proper strip eventually arrived just before half time. The guy with the strips thought we were playing Rothes so he had gone there - just another wee mishap.

It's funny how some games stick in your mind. The Broch were home to Forres on 4th December that year. Smith put us 1-0 in the lead, then Dennis Forsyth went on one of his mazy dribbles before hitting a teriffic drive from all of 30 yards to put the Broch 2-0 up. A McIntosh goal reduced the leeway just after half time. Then that man Forsyth was on the mark again with a free kick from 25 yards out (kicking into the Poles Garage end of course) which left the keeper rooted to the spot to make it 3-1. Duncan in 65 and Roy in 71minutes made it 3-3, but N. Robertson netted the winner with 5 minutes to go for a final score of Broch 4 Forres 3. It all seems like yesterday. The following week we played Elgin at home. We got another big write up in the paper from Jim Lornie, though I didn't think he knew where the Bellslea was. In those days Elgin were the king pins of the Highland League, but we lost only narrowly 4-3 to them. The teams that day were:

Broch: Forsyth, Crighton, Caldwell, Milne, Taylor, Reid, Smith, Forsyth, Robertson, McDonald, Duthie.

Elgin: Connell, Gerrard, Laing, Ralph, Sanderson, Grant, Graham, Douglas, Mackintosh, Cowie, Gilbert.
After we were out of the Qualifying Cup, the Broch finally signed Dave Caldwell who went on to star for them, as did big Dod Crighton, a rugged centre half, who was a prison warder and had been around in the Highland League for a while.
Another home derby against Peterhead resulted in a high scoring match. What a ding-dong game it was. Smith put Peterhead 0-1 up on 44 minutes, but Robertson equalised with the last kick of the half for 1-1. Duthie put the Broch 2-1 ahead in 50 minutes, then Sim made it 2-2 with a penalty. Two quick replies from Smith in 53 and Robertson in 60 minutes, put the Broch 4-2 in the lead. Then another penalty from Sim made it 4-3. Christie for Peterhead then made it 4-4 and Fraser settled it with 4 minutes to go for a final score of Broch 4 Peterhead 5. They don't seem to have games like that now. I'm sure some of the older Peterhead supporters would like this kind of excitement nowadays instead of watching some of the rubbish served up in the Scottish League. The return match was played in atrocious conditions with patches of snow covering a sodden park, but it was the same for both teams. Peterhead ran out 5-2 winners to complete the double. Another two defeats at the hands of Keith, 1-0 away and 3-1 at home didn't help matters before the big game against Ayr United in the Cup came around. It was nice to be centre of attention for a change, with the Press turning up at a training session for a photo shoot. That Saturday morning

the headlines in the Daily Express were, "Broch list 13 for the Cup."

"We're all set to shock em again, remember Dundee," Hamish Black wrote, so the Broch set out, at 4.30 in the morning, for Ayr and a 450 mile round trip. First stop would be Glasgow for breakfast, where the officials would pick the team. They only just made it in time, as they got lost going through Glasgow. The teams that day were:

Ayr United: Millar, Malone, Murphy, Oliphant, Monan, Moore, Grant, McMillan, Coburn, Hawkshaw, Paterson.

Fraserburgh: Low, Milne, Caldwell, Duthie, Crighton, Reid, Smith, McCann, N. Robertson, Forsyth, G. Robertson.

If it hadn't been for an inspired display of goal keeping from John Low, it would have been a cricket score, with all the action in and around the Broch box. It took Ayr 44 minutes before Paterson netted to put them 1-0 in the lead. The second half was much the same, with Ayr hitting the woodwork three times. A very tired Broch team trooped off at the final whistle. Johnnie Low got a standing ovation from the Ayr crowd, with the final score Ayr Utd 1 Fraserburgh 0. The crowd was 4,726 and gate receipts were £569.

After the excitement of the Cup it was back to league business. On a snowy day at the Bellslea we entertained Caley. The game was held up for 20 minutes as the Caley team bus went off the road at Tyrie, though, luckily, there were no injuries. It was end to end stuff, but the condition of the pitch was getting worse. Kerr put Caley 0-1 up on 12 minutes. As the half wore on Dennis Forsyth went on one of his mazy runs, only to be chopped down, but the referee waved play on, much to the home crowd's annoyance. As he blew for half time, the referee was hit by a pie thrown from the stand. Quick as a flash someone shouted, "Di ye like a cup o' tea with one of Dennis's pies?"(He was a baker!) Caley went on to win the game 0-4.

A surprise 3-1 win followed at Peterhead in the Aberdeenshire Cup with goals from McCann in 40 minutes, McDonald in 42 and Robertson on 50 minutes. The semifinal was lost 1-3 to Vale. Low had to go onto the wing as he injured his hand. Spicy took over in goal, but he wasn't a substitute, as they weren't invented yet. Not many goal keepers had played in outfield positions on every ground in the Highland League. That honour was left to Spicy, as I'm sure he's told me or you a few times over the years. On April 9th, the Broch beat Inverness Thistle 2-4 at Kingsmill. It would be 18 years till the next victory there in League or Cup. Speak about bogey teams.....

On a rainy night in May we beat Buckie 7-1 and that was followed by a 4-4 draw with Lossie, exciting stuff. The last game of the season was away to Caley, who had just finished runner's up in the League to Elgin City. The day didn't get off to the best of starts as, at that time the players travelled in cars. Nommie Robertson had two punctures on the way up. He had the strip in the boot of his car, so the match was delayed. If you were ever at Telford Street, you'll know how long a walk it was to the stand. When the players arrived, the crowd was waiting for a 3pm kick off. They trooped in carrying the hamper, much to the delight of the home support. It was to get worse - the Broch had only 10 players. An appeal went out over the tannoy for someone to play for the Broch. One brave lad, Willie McLean, a local Welfare player, volunteered so at 3.15 the game kicked off. With 86 minutes gone Caley were cruising 3-1, but then the Broch were awarded a penalty. Smith reduced the leeway but the Broch weren't finished, Nommie Robertson scoring on 90 mins to make it a 3-3 final score. Spicey refers to that game as Caley 3 Ragged Rovers 3, as they did not have a full strip. The teams that day were:

Caley: Mackie, Lazenby, Presslie, Patience, Mair, McInnes, McDougall, Allan, Cumming, Simpson, Smith.

Broch: Low, Wallce, Milne, D. Forsyth, Taylor, McCann, Smith, McLean, Robertson, Duthie, R. Forsyth.

Referee – E. Bent, Kinloss.

So, for another season, the Broch hit the dizzy heights of 3rd bottom in the league and, with Huntly losing 147 goals, it had been an exciting season..

Broch:	P	W	D	L	F	A	PTS
	30	8	3	19	58	93	19

Season 1966 - 67

With a bit of stability returning, things were looking brighter for the fast approaching 1966-67 season. Walking past the Bellslea the smell of new cut grass set the pulse racing as the season got closer. I left school and started as an office boy in the CPT, better known as "The Toolies." There were eleven hundred and fifty people employed there at that time. Having to work overtime at nights, especially in the summer when all your mates are out playing football, was no fun. I felt a bit caged in, on looking out of the window, when the sun was shining. Never mind, it would soon be Saturday. By the way, my first wage was £4:3:4d for a 40 hour week!

The first games of the season used to be in the League Cup, but that year, instead of sections, it was played as home and away legs. We started off at home to Vale. A Mair hat trick for Vale, with the Broch getting two late goals, set the Vale up nicely for the second leg, but a 2-4 win up at Clach on Saturday was just what we needed before the return match at Vale. We won 1-0 to take the game into extra time, but with the weather getting worse and the light fading, the referee had no choice but to abandon the game. I was sitting in the bus waiting for the players to get changed and saw Jimmy Brown come onto the bus with a big grin. They had tossed a coin for the replay and guess who guessed right? Well done Jimmy! Alas, the following Monday night, after a six o'clock kick off, we were beaten 6-2. Vale's two Mair brothers destroyed the Broch that night. The teams were:

Fraserburgh: Low, Henderson, Milne, McCann, Forsyth, Reid, Smith, Caldwell, Robertson, Duthie, Wright.

Deveronvale: Thom, B. Third, G. Noble, E. Noble, Smith, Calderwood, F. Mair, Grant, Fordyce, Robertson, K.Mair.

Referee – D.C. Haynes, Lossiemouth.

Three players who would feature in the future Broch line up arrived around this time. They were: Mike Wright (Ellon) Ian Johnston (Cuminestown) and David Whicher (King Street A). We hoped that trio could form the basis of our forward line and, with their pace, score a few goals into the bargain. On September 10th a 5-2 win at home to Brora took us up to the dizzy heights of seventh in the league - mind you we'd only played five games.

Long serving full back Jimmy Milne had a benefit game v Aberdeen A. It turned out to be a real classic with Sandy Fraser notching a hat trick and John Low pulling off some inspiring saves to keep the Broch in the game. Two goals from Watt put the Dons 0-2 in the lead and it looked all over as they went 0-3 up. But young Whicher reduced the leeway to make it 1-3. Fraser then made in 2-3 from the penalty spot before Carroll made it 2-4 on the stroke of half time. The second half started with the Broch getting forward with renewed vigour and determination. On 74 minutes, their hard work paid off and Fraser made it 3-4. In spite of constant pressure the Broch kept battling away and were rewarded when a cross from Henderson was headed home by Fraser to make it 4-4. I know it was only a friendly, but it's always nice to get one over on Aberdeen. A pitch invasion by young fans saw them mob Fraser at the end as the home support roared their approval. It was nice to see that fighting spirit return and maybe it could set us up for the 1st round of the Qualifying Cup at home to Caley. The teams that night were:

Broch: Low, Caldwell, Milne, Duthie (Forsyth), Crighton, Reid, Smith (Henderson), Fraser, Robertson, Wright (Duthie), Whicher.

Aberdeen: McGarr, Hermiston, Kirkland (Carroll), Buchan, McAbe (Robb), Kennan (Cummings), Noble, Robb (Sandison), Taylor, Watt, Carrol. Crowd - 800.

Jimmy Milne spent eleven seasons at the Bellslea. A real local hero, he saw some good times, and bad times as well. Sadly, he is no longer with us, but his kind of spirit kept the Broch going through those bad times. A funny story he used to tell was of once when the Broch were away to Inverness to play Caley. On the way home they were all starving, so someone shouted, "come on Broon, what about stopping for something to eat," so, stopping the bus at Fochabers, Broon told them:
"You lot stay here, I'll get the fish suppers because its sixpence (6d) dearer to sit down and eat them. I'll get them and take them onto the bus." As they were almost at Tyrie, Jimmy was elected to go down to the front of the bus to ask "Broon" if there was any chance of wages that day. Broon's answer was quick:
"You don't get supper and paid as well." There was no answer to that!
The Herald published an appeal, urging all fans to turn up in numbers for the Qualifying Cup tie against Caley, but the game itself was a big let down. The headline on Sunday was, "A Forward Would Never Have Scored." Chic Allan, who wore the number six shirt, hit a screamer past Low that took the Inverness men into the next round on a final score of Broch 0 – Caley 1. As I remember, it was around about this time that the substitutes rule arrived in the Highland League.

At Telford Street in the League the following week, Caley turned the screw and hammered us 6-1. But things were not that bad after that, with three wins on the trot, a rare occurrence at that time. We won 3-1 at home to Keith, 1-2 away to Buckie and 2-0 at home to Vale, with Mike Wright and Ian Johnstone in good scoring form. By mid-October the Broch were 3rd in the League, not bad. Then, out of the blue, Johnnie Low put in a transfer request (better find Spicey) but the club turned him down. On Dec' 19th it was the 1st v 2nd clash in the League, Broch v Ross County. In a bad-tempered match County won 0-2 with goals from brothers Ian and Gordon Davidson. Another Brocher making a name for himself was Brian Newlands, who scored the winner for Sunnybank in the Scottish Junior Cup in an exciting game v Banks O' Dee. He scored the winner in 84 minutes to make it Sunnybank 4 Banks O' Dee 3. Brian was top scorer in the Juniors, with 20 goals, and, as a result, Arbroath were reported to be interested in him.

It was not often we came to the Xmas derby with the Broch above Peterhead in the table, so would it be another classic? Well, I've been to some derby games but this one is still being talked about. Leighton put the visitors 0-1 up in 14 minutes, with Forman making it 0-2 on 21 minutes and it stayed that way till half time. After the restart, Forman made it 0-3 and Peterhead were in complete command. Whicher pulled one back in 60 minutes, then the fun began. Brian McCann punted the ball over the dyke. The referee signalled for a second ball, "I didn't know the Broch had two match balls". Turner of Peterhead was waiting to take the throw with the second ball that had arrived at his feet, when the ball that went over the dyke came back. Georgie Morgan took the throw and started a Broch attack. The Peterhead players stopped, Fraser of the Broch kept going and planted the ball beyond keeper Innes. "Goal!" or was it? The referee said yes and the linesman agreed. Bellslea became bedlam. The referee was being pushed and shoved, losing his whistle, and having to borrow another one to restart play. It was now the Broch 2 Peterhead 3. Forman made it 2-4 in 80 minutes, but it was all Broch now. Robertson made it 3-4 in 86 minutes and then Forsyth had one cleared off the line. The final score was Broch 3 Peterhead 4. Oh how I miss those games! The following week we reversed the score with Mike Wright hitting a hat-trick to dump Peterhead 2-4, Nommie Robertson scoring the other goal. The teams were:

Broch: Low, McCann, Milne, Fraser, Crighton, Reid, Robertson, Forsyth, Wright, Duthie, Whicher

Peterhead: Innes, R.McNeil, G. McNeil, Sim, McDonald, Anderson, Turner, Ewen, Leighton, Forman, Summers, Bruce.

Referee – W. Miller, Aberdeen

After the New Year we went up to Dingwall to meet the League leaders. The game was abandoned after 55 minutes with the pitch waterlogged. Duthie had put Broch 0-1 up in 10 minutes before McMillan made it 1-1, but after half time the ref had no option but to call off the game as the pitch was in such a mess. How's this for a shock? Broch 5, Caley 1. Doubles for Wright and Duthie while Nommie got his usual goal, plus we had the luxury of missing a penalty. Dennis Forsyth told me it was the best save he's ever seen. The last game of the season was the match that had been abandoned at Dingwall. It was played on Friday night, April 28th. County won 3-0 to win the League for the first time. The reason the game was played on the Friday night was to let everyone go to the Scottish Cup Final next day where Celtic defeated Aberdeen 2 – 0. That concluded another season. We finished 7th in the table.

P	W	D	L	F	A	PTS
30	12	5	13	55	56	29

Rothes lost 104 goals but didn't finish bottom. That honour went to Huntly.

Scotland defeated the world champions in their back yard. You know, them from the other side of Hadrian's Wall! If you still haven't got a clue, it was England! Did that make us world champions? Morton won the old 2nd division scoring 113 goals and only conceding 20 after 38 games. Sadly, this was to be Third Lanark's final season. Ron Davies, Southampton, was leading scorer with 37 goals in the English 1st division. Steve Chalmers, Celtic, led in Scotland with 21 goals but Joe Mason of Morton took him with 35 goals.

Season 1967 - 68

New signings Summers (Peterhead) Notman (Huntly) and Chalmers (Turriff) were in the line up for the opening game of the season up at Telford Park where we lost 6-0. It was not a great start. The following Wednesday we beat Deveronvale 3-2, at the Bellslea in the League Cup, with goals from Georgie Duthie in 7 minutes, Charlie Whyte on 57 minutes and Notman, with Vale snatching two late strikes from Bruce and Eddie Noble. A Dennis Notman double the following Wednesday put us through to the semi finals with a final score of Deveronvale 2, Fraserburgh 5. I couldn't remember when the Broch had last been in a semi-final. George Malley was on the bench for Vale for that game. The number of trialists who came and went at the beginning of the season wasn't real. Some of the names I can't remember myself. The Broch team that night was: Low, Murray, Reid, Summers, McCann, C. Low, Smith, Johnstone, Chalmers, McKay, Whyte, A. Young.

By the time we met Peterhead in the semis, John Low had moved on and Johnny Massie from Mintlaw had taken over in goals. He went on to give sterling service in a line of great keepers who have played for the Broch. It was about this time that Kenny Rogers, "Dodger" to his friends, made his debut. He went on to be a real Broch legend, but not on the wing where he started. The semi final turned out to be a real blood and thunder affair, with personal feuds all over the field. Broch were reduced to ten men after half time, Georgie Duthie being sent packing for complaining about an offside goal. Peterhead's Christie scored to make it 0-2. It was so far off side that Stevie Wonder would have seen it! The ref was clearly having a nightmare. McCann was next in the book for kicking the ball at Grant as he was lying injured. The final score was Broch 0 Peterhead 2 and the referee for that game was W. Christie, of Aberdeen.

A home draw against Rothes in the Qualifying Cup was good news. We could look to progress in the competition as they were anchored at the bottom of the table. We were beaten 6-2 up at Ross County the following week. The score would suggest an easy win, but with the score at 1-1, Notman, Chalmers and Low all had efforts blocked on the line with the County defence all at sea. But if you don't take your chances you pay the penalty. County ran out worthy winners. A late goal in the Qualifying Cup from Kenny Rogers saw us through to the next round, with the score Broch 2 Rothes 1. Here's a score you don't see every day, Qualifying Cup 2nd round, Ross County 9 Lossiemouth 6. At the time I wondered if they were playing five half time, ten the winner?

Lady luck was on our side, with another home tie in the Qualifying Cup v Clachnacudden. Chalmers netted the only goal as the Broch held on for a win. Was this to be our year? You couldn't ask for anything more than a home tie against Elgin City in the semi-finals and the Bellslea had its biggest crowd for years as the Broch kicked off and opened the game in determined style. Elgin keeper Lawtie did well to dust a D. Forsyth effort round the post, while at the other end, Broch keeper Massie was keeping Elgin at bay with three wonder saves. Graham put the visitors in front and at half time it was 0-1. Massie came to the Broch's rescue, again denying Graham. Then came the turnaround and Notman scored for the Broch to make it 1-1. Thomson in 83 minutes made it 1-2, but the Broch were not to be denied and Forsyth equalised in 85 minutes. Thomson sealed the tie with a goal 30 seconds from the end. The final score was Broch 2, Elgin 3. We never seem to get a break against Elgin. The teams were:

Broch: Massie, Milne, Reid, Summers, McCann, Duthie, Forsyth, Johnston, Chalmers, Notman, Rogers.

Elgin: Lawtie, Gerrard, Laing, Smith, Grant, Middleton, Thomson, Douglas, Graham, Dalziel, Gilbert

Referee – D W Robb, Arbroath.

The Broch were making heavy weather of the season after the defeat in the semis v Elgin. Six defeats on the trot and a home tie v East Stirling in the Scottish Cup was not far away. We had to borrow a strip as East Stirling played in black and white hoops. The rule then was that the home team changed if they clashed and another rule said that you had to supply a new ball. Nothing strange in that, but the Broch didn't have any new match balls so they decided to whitewash an old ball. It looked alright before the kick off, but with drizzle coming down, the ball was gradually changing colour and players were going around with white circles on their shirts and foreheads, and, at half time Broch asked their opponents for a loan of one of their match balls. The game itself had got off in sensational style with a Broch goal in the 1st minute, I. Chalmers scoring direct from a corner at the Clinic end, but Shire equalised in 28 minutes through Mitchell. Two minutes after half time, the same player put Shire in front. It was nip and tuck then until Ross made it 1-3 for Shire in 85 mins and Mitchell completed his hat-trick two minutes later for a final score Fraserburgh 1, East Stirling 4. The teams were:

Broch: Ross, Milne, Reid, Summers, McCann, Wright, Forsyth, Johnstone, Nutman, Duthie, Chalmers: sub Rogers

East Stirling: Davie, Miller, Nulston, Ross, Craig, Anderson, Gillespie, Hammel, Borland, Mitchel, Jones: sub J. Anderson

Referee – I K Brines, Bankhead   Attendance - 850

Prior to the game, the Broch fixed up Charlie Ross, the ex Stenhousemuir goalkeeper, as regular keeper because Massie was unavailable. Any time I meet Bobby or Dennis Forsyth we always have a laugh at some of the incidents that happened back then. I don't know how the Broch got away with some of them.

It was off to Recreation Park for the first of the Xmas derbies. Duthie put Broch 0-1 up in 2 minutes with B. Third equalising in 14 minutes to make it 1-1. Charlie Duncan hit a 25 yard screamer that Massie couldn't hold and Christie netted easily, while Third made it 3-1 in 22 minutes. An own goal by Murray then made it 4-1. The Broch were falling apart as Christie scored his second and Peterhead's fifth to make it 5-1, then Forsyth was unlucky with a shot that hit the bar. Third completed his hat-trick, just on half time, to make the score Peterhead 6, Fraserburgh 1. After half time we hit the bar again and then Wright reduced the leeway when he made it 6-2. Peterhead then rattled the Broch cross bar before Forsyth made it 6-3, with a direct free kick. Third however was not to be outdone. He added his fourth and the Blue Toon's seventh to make the final score Peterhead 7, Fraserburgh 3. Santa had come early for the home side.

A large crowd turned up at Bellslea hoping to see the score reversed. Again the Broch took the lead, Chalmers opening the account in 31 minutes, but that man, Third was at it again making it 1-1 in 36 mins. A minute later, the Broch regained the lead with a cracking drive from Wright, before Third levelled in 44 minutes. At half time it was 2-2, but McCann didn't appear after the interval and Milne replaced him. Rogers made it 3-2, but the lead was short-lived. Anderson made it 3-3 from the centre. The Broch then lost possession and Third scored to complete his hat-trick and make it 3-4. Keeper Massie was carried off and Milne took over in goal before the end. The final score was the Broch 3, Peterhead 4. That's what I called a real old fashioned derby for the old firm, "come awa the Burghy." Sorry Thirdy, but I was glad to see the back of you from the Highland League. The teams that day were:

Fraserburgh: Massie, Reid, Murray, D. Summers, McCann, Wright, Forsyth, Johnstone, Notman, Duthie, Chalmers: sub Milne

Peterhead: Thomson, R. McNeil, Thornton, C. Duncan, Anderson, Calderwood, Simpson, Christie, Third, Beaton, Buchan

Referee – W. D. Reid, Aberdeen

A bad run of results followed the derby games, with another four defeats, 0-2 (h) to Ross County, 2-0 (a) against Clach, 1-3 (h) to Caley and 2-3 (h) against Clach. About this time, the Broch gave a run to another local loon, Johnnie Whyte, who later made the number 2 shirt his own and went on to captain the team. With guys like Sydney Reid and Kenny Roger establishing their position in the team, things seemed to be looking up. The season was drawing to a close and, with the usual late call offs, a host of trialists from the amateur league were used. These included Lewis McKenzie, Charlie Whyte and Peter McConachie. Big John Cruickshank made his debut in a 4-1 defeat at Keith. The team finished a disappointing 2nd bottom finish with 14 pts with Elgin champions.

P	W	D	L	F	A	PTS
30	6	2	22	51	99	14

"The Facelles" were playing in the Legion (tickets 3/- before 9 o'clock, and 5/- after 9pm.). You got a stamp and went to the pub for a pint till 10 o'clock and then went back to the dance, showed the stamp and walked in. At the pictures you could watch "The Great Escape" again. It was 16/5d for council rent (82p in new money). In the charts –
Puppet on a String – Sandie Shaw
Then I Kissed Her – Beach Boys
Silence is Golden – Tremeloes
A new Vauxhall Viva was £675, but few folk could afford one.

Season 1968 - 69

Former Aberdeen and Caley full back, Jimmy Hogg, signed for the Broch along with local loons, Nigel Hunter and George Bruce, "Dod" to his friends. Hogg was probably past his best, but he added that bit of steel that the Broch needed. We didn't get off to the best of starts, losing 4-1 to Peterhead in the 1st leg of the League Cup. The Broch team that began the season that day read: Massie, Whyte, Hogg, Bruce, McCann, Notman, L. McKenzie, Forsyth, Mair, Chalmers

Lewis McKenzie gave the Broch an early lead on 15 minutes, but that man Third was at it again with goals in 20 and 44 minutes, for Peterhead to go in at the interval 2-1 up. After the break, Massie saved a Christie penalty and then Third completed his hat-trick to make it 4-1 at full time. Buchan replaced Notman for the 2nd leg at the Bellslea the following Wednesday. Thornton scored early on to put the visitors in command, but Mair made it 1-1 before Reid put the Broch in front on 30 minutes. The lead was short-lived. Christie made it 2-2, three minutes later and once more the visitors took the lead through Thornton, for 2-3. Further goals from Christie and Thornton, who completed his hat-trick, made the final score Broch 2 Peterhead 5. Agg 3-9. One thing about those derbies in the sixties was that you could normally be assured of a few goals.

An away tie to Lossiemouth was up next in the Qualifying Cup. New signing Gordon Davidson from Ross County made his debut that day and, in a hard fought first half, the Broch got the goal they were looking for with Chalmers scoring in 29 minutes. It stayed that way till half time, but McHardy made it 1-1in 48 minutes though the Broch held on for a replay at Bellslea park. The replay was a classic and was talked about for a long time after. With the Broch 0-3 down after 50 minutes played, it looked like, "the tatties were over the side." McHardy, after 5 minutes, Boyd, in 44 minutes, had the visitors in a comfortable lead at half time at 0-2. McHardy made it 0-3 after 50 minutes and, by then the the Broch players were looking at each other, trying to figure out who was to blame. The home support was getting restless, with the natives howling at the bench for changes. George Bruce replaced John Whyte and, within two minutes, he slammed in a free kick to open the Broch's account at 1-3. Rogers then punted a 40 yard chip to the back post and the dozy defenders and the goalkeeper, Norris, let it fly into the top corner to make it 2-3 as the Bellslea erupted. A minute later Dennis Forsyth dummied a couple of Lossie defenders before slamming a low drive into the bottom corner for 3-3. It was all Broch now and the winner was straight off the training ground. Reid flicked on a free kick, for Davidson to steal in at the back post and smash it into the net in the 80th minute to complete a remarkable fight back. The game finished Fraserburgh 4, Lossiemouth 3. The teams were:

Fraserburgh: Massie, Roger, Hogg, Whyte, (Bruce) McCann, Forsyth, Hunter, Johnston, Chalmers, Davidson, S. Reid.

Lossiemouth: Harris, Fotheringham, Stewart, McKenzie, Richmond, Smith, Tulloch, McHardy, Allan, Campbell, Bruce, Boyd

Ref' – J. Shanks, Elgin

The quarter-final draw was another away tie at Huntly, on Oct 12th, and what a marathon this turned out to be. The first game was a 1-1 draw, with Sherriffs scoring for Huntly and Bruce replying for the Broch. The replay finished 0-0 at the Bellslea, but, the following week at Elgin, the Broch won 3-0 with goals from Forsyth, Bruce and Reid. A home draw came at last, against Ross County in the semi-final. With County not having lost a game that season, it made them firm favourites and disaster struck the Broch after only 7 minutes. Whyte tried to clear a loose ball for a corner, but it hit McLellan and flew into the net to put County 0-1 in front. The Broch got back on level terms when Reid crossed for Bruce to head home, with keeper Morrison rooted to the spot. Davidson then put the Broch in the lead on 38 minutes. Sydney Reid then went on a mazy run, drew the keeper, but over-ran the ball and it went out for a goal kick. The Bellslea atmosphere was electric. Every time County won the ball, the crowd started booing and when the Broch retrieved it a great, "Hurrah!" went up from the front of the stand. The ball went out of play and when the second ball arrived, some one shouted, "Bring on the Dundee ball." Another time, when both balls were over the dyke and play was held up, another fan shouted out:

"Never mind the ball, get on with the game." That kind of thing was what made the front of the stand at Bellslea extra special, on big match days, especially. The second half however became a, "backs to the wall," job, with Hogg and McCann never putting a foot wrong (where do referees find all those extra minutes from?) A big sigh of relief came as he finally blew for time up with the score Broch 2 Ross Co 1. A Qualifying Cup Final, who would have believed this a couple seasons ago? Well done Jimmy Broon. The teams that day were:

Fraserburgh: Massie, Roger, Hogg, Whyte, McCann, Davidson, Hunter, Johnston, Bruce, Forsyth, Reid. Sub - Clark

Ross Co: Morrison, Borley, Brett, Lornie, Greig, Mackenzie, Horne, Davidson, Lynas, McMillan, McLellan. Sub - Murray

Referee – R Garside, Lossiemouth

It was to be Nairn County in the final and, at that time, finals were two leg affairs, with the 1st leg at the Bellslea. What a let down it was. Gone were the off the cuff moves and, by the time Stephen had opened County's account in 20 minutes, the Bellslea roar was reduced to a whimper. Further goals, from Smith, in the 31st and 63rd minutes, left the Broch shell-shocked. Every time we played a ball forward, it went to a red shirt. The sheer determination of Dennis Forsyth brought reward with a goal in 86 minutes, but it was too little, too late. The final score was Broch 1, Nairn County 3.

The Broch looked smart in their new kit. It was changed days from a few seasons earlier when they lined up for a photograph at the start of a season. Ten of those old shirts had become a kind of grey and cream instead of black and white. Dave Caldwell had worn the one new black and white strip and he stuck out like a sore thumb. Nine players had worn hooped socks, which were black and white, and the other two wore white with black tops, embarrassing to say the least, but now those days were over. The teams that day were:

Broch: Massie, Roger, Hogg, Whyte, McCann, Hunter (Chalmers), Johnstone, Bruce, Forsyth, Reid.

Nairn: McKenzie, McFadden Young, Smith, Cadenhead, Stapleton, Clark, Stephen, Thom, Murray, Sim (Smart).
Ref – R D Henderson, Dundee

The 2nd leg at Station Park was a pretty poor affair, with both teams very nervy. Dennis Forsyth then brought the game to life. Whyte sliped a nice pass through for him to round Young and hit a low shot into the corner of the net in 43 minutes, to put the Broch right back in the game. Tragedy struck again for the Broch in 54 minutes. A seemingly harmless cross hit McCann and rolled into the net to put Nairn 2-3 up on aggregate, and that was the final result. Nairn won the Qualifying Cup for the first time.

The Broch's last league game was a 0-3 defeat at home to Inverness Thistle on September 21st. The final v Nairn was on November 16th, so we played 8 cup ties on the trot. No wonder we were bottom of the league. It was top versus bottom the following week, with high fliers Elgin City at the Bellslea. A Bryan Thomson goal was all that separated the teams, as we waited in a state of anticipation for the Cup draw. Our reward was an away tie at Montrose in the Scottish Cup, but first there was the matter of a derby match against old foes Peterhead. Bruce opened the scoring in 8 minutes, then former Broch player, George Duthie, equalised in the 35th minute. Reid put Broch back in front on 40 minutes but tempers were getting frayed as the ref blew for half time. After the restart, Lewis Duncan squared the game at 2-2, on 62 minutes. Broch Keeper Massie was having an inspired game but he was finaly beaten when G. Duthie hit the winner in 80 minutes. The final score was Broch 2, Peterhead 3.

The Broch had fixed up Jimmy Noble from Caley. Jimmy played for Parkvale, and was signed up by Aberdeen before joining Caley. In the years to come he was to become a real star. "Sneaky," as he was known by his friends, was worth the entry fee just to watch his skills. Much later, I talked to Georgie Morgan about his fallout with the Broch, at that time, but the least said about that the better. After a couple of weeks deciding about his future, Peterhead came calling and offered him £100 to sign, but he refused. A fortnight later they upped the offer to £200, which was a lot of money in those days, so he signed on the dotted line. Peterhead wrote to the S.F.A. to cancel his registration with the Broch, but the reply said there had never been a G. Duthie on their books, though George had played for the Broch for at least four seasons!

Next up was Montrose on 4th January, not the best of times to play Scottish Cup ties, especially so soon after Hogmanay. The gap was too much on the day. The Broch were 3-0 down at half time, though the hard working Forsyth got his reward with a goal in 64 minutes to make it 3-1. Further goals from Thomson in 74 minutes, Michie in 77 minutes and Livingstone on 81 minutes, brought the final score to Montrose 6, Fraserburgh 1. The teams were:

Montrose: Stewart, Martin, R. Smith, Michie, Munro, Thomson, McDonald, Livingstone, Welsh, Craig, Finn.

Fraserburgh: Massie, Whyte, Hogg, Roger, McCann, Davidson, Noble, Johnston (Chalmers), Bruce, Forsyth, Reid
Referee – W. Balfour, Inverness   Crowd -1,400
Receipts £156

With a home tie v Buckie Thistle in the Aberdeenshire Cup to play, we were anchored at the bottom of the table at the end of January.

P	W	D	L	F	A	PTS
13	2	1	10	19	37	5

Sydney Reid gave us an early lead against Buckie and then Davidson made it 2-0. Grant pulled one back for the visitors, but Reid made it 3-1 after half time. Grant then got his second of the day, but here was no further scoring, so the game finished Broch 3, Buckie 2. The semi final was at home to Huntly. Massie was injured so the Broch fell back on Bobby Forsyth again, but Huntly ran out comfortable winners 0-3. The following week, with Massie still injured and Spicey unavailable, Georgie Duncan made his debut in a 3-2 win at home to Rothes. It was now April and the Broch still had 10 league games to play. My mate Robbie McDonald made his Broch debut away at Lossiemouth where we lost 3-0. He went on to play for another season. He said, joking, the only way he got a game was because he used his car, but didn't claim petrol money. A 2-0 home win v Forres, saw Robbie score his first goal. I thought the only time Robbie crossed the half way line was when the teams changed round at half time!

We rounded off the season with five defeats and four wins, finishing 5th bottom. Elgin were champions.

P	W	D	L	F	A	PTS
30	7	6	17	47	87	20

It was off to Butlins for me in the summer holidays (£22 a week) with the boys, George Malley, Brian Newlands, Alex Barclay and Charlie Whyte, who sadly is no longer with us. On the way down it started pouring with rain and the wipers weren't working, so we tied a piece of string to them, put it in both side windows and started pulling back and forth. Don't know how we got there! Everybody must remember the Pig and Whistle Pub. That's where I first came into contact with Charlie Duncan and we've remained friends ever since. It was Alex Barclay's birthday on the Thursday, so we had a big party for him, but that turned out to be a disaster. While tidying up afterwards, security saw the boys putting all the empties into the waste buckets. In those days you weren't allowed drink in the chalets, so they were told to pack their bags and get out. It was about 1.30 in the morning. I was otherwise engaged somewhere else at the time, so when I arrived back at the chalet, about 7 o'clock in the morning, what a shock I got to find the chalet empty. A loud knock came at the door and, when I opened it, this guy said.

"Where the "………." have you been. Get your bags packed and get out." So when I arrived at the car park at the top of the hill, the lads were out for the count in the car waiting for me, HAPPY DAYS! The funny thing was we went back next year and got in with no problem. We were not the only Brochers asked to leave - Sandy Souter and his mates slept in a field under a combine harvester!

Season 1969-70

If you're like me, can't stand the cricket, don't play golf, and hate watching it on TV, the new season can't come quickly enough. With Johnny Massie finished playing, we were on the lookout for a goalie, but, "there's always Spicey." Brian McCann had gone off to Peterhead (traitor), so we were short in numbers. As the season drew closer, Ally (pop) Fordyce was signed from Caley and Charlie Ogston from Deveronvale and finally John Pirie, a former Keith goal keeper arrived.

When the Broch ran out for the first league game v Rothes, what a shock! Gone were the famous black and white strips, replaced with a white shirt with two black circles round the neck, black shorts and red socks. It took a bit of getting used to. The team that lined up that day was: Pirie, Roger, Hogg, McDonald, Milne, Morrison, McRae, Noble, Fordyce, Davidson, Reid. A 1-1 draw was not the best of starts. The only highlight of the match was from two dogs who disrupted the game, much to the delight of the crowd.

It was back to Recreation Park again for the 1st leg of the League Cup. The Broch were well on top and it was no surprise when Fordyce put us 0-1 in front after 25 minutes. Duthie made it 1-1 after 29 minutes and then Christie put the home side in front four minutes before the break. After half time, Bruce hit the woodwork, as did former Peterhead winger Malcolm McRae, before Davidson scored a deserved equaliser. McNeil made it 3-2 in 80 minutes and that's how it finished. The feeling in the Broch camp was that they had a great chance in the 2nd leg, but the Committee decided to change the team around and, when it was announced, Jimmy Hogg shouted out, "Hey Broon, did ye pick the team out of a hat?" A large crowd turned up for the 2nd leg, hoping to retrieve the score, but Brian Third made sure there was no shock with a double in 15 and 29 minutes to put the game beyond the Broch. Christie added a 3rd goal and our only reply was from Ogston in 71 minutes. That put Peterhead into the semi finals on a 3-6 aggregate score.

Next up were high flying Inverness Thistle at the Bellslea and what a result - 6-0. Big Dod Bruce had one of his days with a hat-trick and McRae, Fordyce and Reid were our other scorers. The only disappointment was that Charlie Duncan wasn't playing. What a boost, as we drew Nairn County away in the 1st round of the Qualifying Cup. It turned out to be another marathon. Sim put Nairn 1-0 in front. Fordyce made it 1-1, in 72 minutes, to take the game to a replay at the Bellslea. Davidson, in 12 and 14 minutes, put the Broch into a comfortable 2-0 lead at half time, but Nairn hit back, through Munro, in 52 minutes, and Thom in 88 minutes, to take the game to another replay at Elgin, on the following Wednesday night. There was a sensational start to that game. Hogg brought down Munro to give away a penalty, and Smart made it 0-1. Then Bruce left three defenders trailing before sending a screamer from 18 yards into the top corner, before Fordyce made it 2-1. Big Dod smashed another rocket that hit the woodwork with the keeper rooted to the spot but there was no more scoring and it ended up the Broch 2, Nairn 1. There's nothing like doing it the hard way. Next was a difficult away tie to Brora Rangers and what a disappointment. A Tommy Reid hat trick sent the Broch packing, with the final score Brora 3, Broch 0.

It was another sad time as another Broch legend passed away, John (Cheil) Duthie. He was 66. He spent ten years in English football with Hartlepool, QPR, Crystal Palace,

Norwich and Crewe before becoming our trainer. A bucket of cold water and a sponge was all he used and I can still see him yet, giving the players a rub with the pipe still in his mouth. On windy nights, when I'm at the Bellslea alone and there's something blowing in the stand, I still say to myself, "that's Cheil checking that everything is all right."

Another goal-keeping crisis erupted that season, when Pirie was set to leave, due to work commitments, so where do we find a keeper in the middle of the season? I suppose we'd have to scan the amateur league or the juniors. My mate Gordon Bissett was playing for St. Modans at the time, and he didn't realise the Broch were watching him. After a match, he was approached by a Broch official and asked if he would sign, so he signed a form at the back of the changing rooms and was told to report for training the following Tuesday. He stayed for a season, but he had to choose between badminton and football as he was one of the top players in the North East. He chose the latter, but went back to playing amateur again. By this time, we had signed Bob Elrick from the Mintlaw area. Another couple of young players Bellslea bound were Willie Bruce and John Duthie, no other than "Tosie," a real hell raiser and the Gazza of the seventies, who always wore his heart on his sleeve.

Brian McCann didn't last long at Peterhead. They were on their way to play Brora one week when he found out he wasn't playing, even though they had been thrashed the week before. He got off the bus at Elgin, saying he was unwell, when it just so happened the Broch were at Nairn that day, so he went to watch them and got a lift home. He was spotted by a reporter, so Peterhead found out and he was soon on his way back into the local fold. (There's no place like home).

I thought the bad old days of cricket scores had gone, but a 9-0 drubbing up at Ross County, was followed by Inverness Thistle getting their revenge for that 6-0 hiding with a resounding 9-1 scoreline. At this time we were still unable to field the same eleven players every week. There was always a strange name on the team lines. Johnnie Buchan from, "Belgar," was asked to play at Buckie on a Wednesday night 31st March. Just as we thought the weather was improving, the rain lashed down like bullets just before the kick-off and it didn't get any better when the game got started. The referee asked both teams to abandon the game, but they decided on half an hour each way to finish the fixture as the light was getting bad as well. The Broch won 3-0 and the team that night was: Elrick, Roger, Stephen, McCann, Milne, Malley, L.McKenzie, Noble, Fordyce, W. Bruce, Buchan. W. Bruce, Fordyce and L. McKenzie got the goals.

It really was a harsh winter that year, with no games between mid-December and mid- January. On one Saturday at that time, the weather wasn't too bad up north whereas this corner was snowed in. Everything came to a halt. The Broch were due to play at Inverness but it was impossible to get as far as the, "Broad Mile Steen," at New Pitsligo, and Parker, the bus operator, wouldn't let them go. The Broch presumed the game would be off, but they didn't bother to find out and, as it turned out, the game was still on, but no Broch, so they were called to a special meeting to explain. This is how it went. Jimmy Brown stood up to explain.

"Parker" said, "there's no way my driver's taking you to Inverness and Parker said, "I've another bus stuck in a snow drift". Then Charlie Fraser brought the meeting to a halt and queried:

"Mister Brown, who the hell is Parker?"

"He's the bus driver," Jimmy replied. The Broch were severly censured.

On a sadder note on 21st January, tragedy struck the whole community of the Broch, when the Fraserburgh lifeboat, "The Duchess of Kent" was lost with only one survivor. I remember that day, when the lifeboat rockets went off. The weather was not that bad onshore, but out at sea, a real storm was brewing and the boat hit a lump of water and capsized. If you're a Brocher, every person knew one of the crew, even if it was just a nod of the head or a, "fit like," in the passing. It was a very sad time. At the end of the season, Celtic agreed to come to the Bellslea to play for the lifeboat disaster fund, just before they were due to play their second European Cup final against Feyenoord in Milan, which, incidently they lost. One European Cup win is enough to put up with in a lifetime. So it was all systems go for this game. At that time it was 2/6d (25p) or 3/6d (35p) to watch the Broch, but for that game the prices were: ground 7/6d (35p) stand 15/- (75p). The attendance was 6.000, a throwback to the glory days. I still have my ticket, no 1058. Celtic ran out worthy winners with a final score of 7-0. Ian Stephen remembers the game well. He told me he was chasing shadows all night and never felt so knackered in his life after a game. The teams that night were:

Broch: Elrick, Roger, Stephen, McCann, Milne, Malley, Fordyce, Duthie, Noble, W. Bruce, Reid. Subs: G. Bruce, D. Forsyth, R. McDonald, D. Anderson.

Celtic: Williams, Craig, Hay, Murdoch, McNeil, Brogan, Johnstone, Lennox, Wallace, Auld, Hughes. Subs: Hood, Callaghan, Chalmers.

Referee – L. K. Bain, Bankhead

The scorers were: Milne, 16 minutes, o.g. Wallace, 26 minutes, Craig, 53 minutes, Hughes 55 and 67 minutes, Auld 61 minutes and Hood 71 minutes.

I remember Jock Stein standing on the steps of the Royal Hotel, looking at his watch just before 10 o'clock, with the players arriving from all directions, like doos returning to a doocot. That was the influence the Big Man had. As the season drew to a close, we were still leaking goals and a 5-1 drubbing at Brora in the final game didn't help. (On the team lines that day was a certain W. Ritchie (Baxter) who had a spell at the Bellslea.) We finished the season 5th bottom. Caley were champions, but what about Buckie Thistle, they never won a game, managing only five draws!

	P	W	D	L	F	A	PTS
BUCKIE	30	0	5	25	22	146	5
BROCH	30	9	5	16	47	87	20

Celtic were champions. Falkirk won the old 2nd division. Chelsea won the FA Cup 2-1 against Leeds Utd at Old Trafford, after a 2-2 draw at Wembley. Aberdeen, surprisingly, beat Celtic 3-1 in the Scottish Cup. Here's a name from the past. Bradford Park Avenue were relegated from the old English 4th division and never regained admission.

Chapter Three

The Seventies (So Near & Yet so Far)

As we head into another decade, the pace of life was getting quicker. The music scene changed. Glam rock was the scene. Garry Glitter, Alvin Stardust and Status Quo hit the charts. Flair trousers, kipper ties and platform shoes were all the range. Everybody wore a three piece suit to the dance on a Saturday night.

My mate Brian Newlands signed for Peterhead from Arbroath, boy did he get some stick from me. Newlands – Peterhead - it didn't have a ring to it. At the Bellslea, youth was given its fling. In a blaze of glory a young 16 year old school boy, David McKenzie, broke into the team. He had spindly legs and was in need of a hair cut, but boy could he play. It was unusual for a young lad not to play amateur league or junior for a year or two but he was that good. Another promising player was Brian McCombie who was also still at school. The bus taking the team to games would leave Bellslea and sit outside the Academy waiting till the schoolboys finished their match before heading on to where the Broch was playing that day. With goalkeeper Elrick gone, Spicy (Bobby Forsyth) was back between the sticks (again.)

It was a much changed line up for the 1st leg of the league cup at Christie Park, but a 2-1 victory there followed by a 1-1 draw at the Bellslea took us into the quarter finals. A 25 yard free kick from Kenny Roger was the highlight of that second leg. In an exciting quarter final, we lost 5-4 at home to Deveronvale. Milne made it 1-0 in five minutes, but a Robertson double put Vale 1-2 in the lead. Fordyce then made it 2-2. After the break, two strikes from Millar had Vale 2-4 in front before Hunter pulled one back for 3-4. Millar completed his hat-trick in 80 minutes but McCann then scored the goal of the game, taking on the Vale defence before slipping the ball past the keeper to end the scoring. The result was Broch 4, Vale 5. A subsequent 4-1 defeat in the qualifying cup at Ross County meant that we had gone out of both cups in a fortnight.

Saturday Oct 31st was a bad day for my mate George Malley. At Victoria Park, Buckie, he had just come on as sub when he clashed with keeper Simpson and broke his leg. At that time there was only one substitute allowed, but a late strike from Rexy Hunter squared the game at 2-2. On a Saturday night a bunch of us used to meet in the Station Hotel lounge and discuss the results from the matches they were involved in. When Big Dod Bruce came in that night, he told us George had broken his leg, but he hadn't come home with the rest of the team, so Dod thought he was still in hospital in Elgin. Not a lot of people had house phones at the time, so we went around to tell his parents what had happened. George spent eleven days in hospital before he was released. The team that day was: Forsyth, Roger, Sim, Duthie, Milne, Bruce, McKenzie, Noble, Fordyce, Hunter, Bissett. Sub: Malley.

A few weeks later Broch went up to Rothes and were thrashed 10-2, an unbelievable result, but, to make matters worse, Peterhead were sniffing around the Broch players (again.) Rexy Hunter and Doug Milne were their targets and a bizarre transfer then took place. Peterhead were going to offer £400 for them both, but the Broch jumped the gun and told them, "we're not letting them go for less than £250," so Peterhead just smiled and said, "deal." They were both back at the Bellslea, a few weeks later, for the Xmas derby. It was a typical Broch v Peterhead game, all blood and thunder. The Broch's new signing, Bert Innes, was showing up well. He thought he'd scored that day, only for the flag to go up for offside. Jimmy Noble finally scored the winner at the Clinic end with ten minutes to go as the Bellslea crowd went wild. The teams were:

Broch: Forsyth, Whyte, G. Noble, Duthie, McCann, Bruce, Roger, Noble, Fordyce, Innes, McKenzie

Peterhead: Connell, Duthie, Ross, McKen, Anderson, Milne, Hunter, Christie, Third, Newlands, Morris
Ref – W. D. Reid, Aberdeen.

There was only one player in the Peterhead line up that day who was actually from Peterhead. The police were kept busy and they went into the stand to interview supporters about a few cans (empty of course) that had landed on the pitch, while, off the pitch, someone was being interviewed about putting the matchball into the boot of his car. Fast forward thirty years. Now where have I heard that story before? Some things never change!

The following week was the return game at the Recreation Park against Peterhead. Could we do the double, which we hadn't managed for a while? It was looking good when Roger put us 0-1 up in 8 minutes and then a shot by big Dod Bruce beat keeper Connel but stuck in the mud on the line and was cleared. We were still looking good, until Newlands struck with two headers, in 53 and 77 minutes for Peterhead, and two late strikes, from Hunter in 88 and Ross in 89 minutes, sealed the win for the Blue Toon. The final score was 4-1. I was sitting in the stand when Newlands scored. He raced up the park with his arms aloft and then smiled at all the Brochers with his fist clenched. As I was waiting on the team bus, the news was filtering through about the Ibrox disaster where 66 people were killed. Things like that put football and life into perspective.

On December 26th the Broch beat Peterhead at home, but did not play another game until Elgin City on February 6th, which we lost 3-1. Another new goalkeeper appeared for the club, Andy Beattie, a local lad whose father owned the Royal Hotel in the town. I lost count of the keepers we had over those few years. A 1-0 defeat away to Keith in the Aberdeenshire Cup 1st round and three straight defeats in the league made for an early finish to our cup and league campaigns. April 3rd, at home to Clach, was our last game, but we lost, with a score of 0-1. About that time though schools football in the Broch was really taking off. The Academy team lifted everything they entered with players like:

```
                        1
                   Ritchie Burnett
          2                              3
       J. Crawford                   S. Crawford
      4              5                   6
   D. McKenzie    J. Anderson       R. Hutcheson
   7          8           9          10          11
 R. Fraser  B.McCombie  I. Sharp    A. Sim    J. Stephen
```

Six of that team went on to play for the Broch and even the amateur league was strong at that time. There were no pub names for sponsorship back then. It cost the players £1 to get a game; that was for washing the strip and paying the referee. These were the names from the past.

	Played	Points
Maud	17	29
Youth Club	14	24
Toolworks	15	23
Invercairn United	18	22
Swifts	18	22
St. Modans	14	22
New Pitsligo	14	22
Parkhill	17	22
Ship Builders	17	15
Rosehearty	17	9
Gray & Adams	18	6
Blue Bird Rangers	14	6

Caley won the highland league title with Inverness Thistle second, but Thistle scored 23 goals more than Caley. We finished 5th bottom.

P	W	D	L	F	A	PTS
36	7	6	17	47	77	20

Celtic were champions, while Rangers were 4th. St Mirren and Cowdenbeath were relegated and Partick Thistle (again) along with East Fife, were promoted.

No more Butlins holidays for the boys. It was off to Majorca for a fortnight, £96 and flying from London. No bad eh!!! Chirpy Chirpy Cheep Cheep was the holiday song, sung by, "Middle of the Road." It couldnae be thirty five years ago, but how time flies when you're enjoying yourself!!!

Season 1971-72

With Brian McCann taking on the role of Player/Manager, things were looking up. The team that began that season was probaby the strongest squad we'd had for a long time, with the arrival of Bertie Bowie from the Youth Centre and William Ritchie (Baxter), a prolific scorer with the Youth Centre. Johnny Massie also was available again, but disaster struck early in the season, at Elgin. With the Broch down 1-0, to a Gerry Graham strike, Baxter was carried off with a broken leg on 40 minutes with G. Catto replacing him. Gilbert made it 2-0 after half time and Thom added another two to make it 5-0. It was a bad day all round and, sadly for Baxter, he never fully recovered from that break and returned to playing amateur.

The 1st leg of the League Cup at Christie Park ended in a 4-2 defeat, with Fordyce and Innes the Broch scorers. A 7-1 win at home to Rothes however was just what the doctor ordered, with Bertie Bowie scoring four. The Broch then played Huntly the following Wednesday in the return League Cup tie. The Broch had all the possession, but all we had to show for it was a Bert Innes strike just on the final whistle. The final score was Broch 1 Huntly 0, but the aggregate score was Broch 3, Huntly 4. A home tie to Caley in the

Qualifying Cup was next, but we got a 0-4 drubbing with Jim Lynas hitting a double. The teams were:

Broch: Massie, Whyte, G. Noble, McCombie, McCann, Duthie, McKenzie, Noble, Fordyce, Innes, Bowie.

Caley: McKenzie, Bennet, R. Noble, Neild, Pressley, Anderson, Park, Allan, Johnston, Lynas, Fyfe.

With guys like Donald Park, Chic Allan, Dave Johnston and Allan Pressley in the Caley team that day, it was like men against boys.

The following week we beat Clach 6-4, with Bowie scoring another hat trick. Bell and Gilles put Clach 0-2 up before Bowie made it 1 – 2 in 30 minutes and after 40 minutes, Fordyce made it 2-2. Bowie scored again in 42 minutes to make it 3-2, then Fordyce and Billy Thomson made it 5-2. Billy Thomson (Ellon) from Clach scored from the spot for 5-3, before Bowie made it 6-3. Gilles then finished the scoring, at 6-4. Oh for a few games like that now!

The referee that day was Billy Christie. When he ran the line at the Bellslea stand side, any decision that went the Broch's way had someone shouting, "that's your "fry" safe this week." By the way, a fry is a parcel of fish. A few weeks later we were beaten 5-3 at Keith, but the goals kept on coming. On December 4th, the Broch had Freddie O'Brian playing up front in the number 10 shirt. With the score tied at 1-1, Freddie put the Broch 2-1 up with a diving header. After half-time goalkeeper Massie was injured and O'Brian returned to his rightful place. The Broch went on to win 3-2. The following week at Buckie, Freddie played in goal and saved a penalty, helping the Broch win 1-0. A player profile in the Green Final at that time read, "Freddie has a bright future," but, the following week, he was lifted for fighting out at Rosehearty! It was nice to get a bit of recognition in the Press, but for the right reasons, like, "Hail the Bellslea Babes."

A 12 minute hat-trick for Bertie Bowie, against Nairn was his third of the season, and it was only November. It meant teams were starting to look over their shoulder at the Broch. When Jimmy Noble (Sneaky) left Aberdeen, he went to Caley. They found him a job in Inverness, but that didn't last long, as he was homesick. At that time, he was on £14 a week, plus bonus. When he came to the Bellslea, £4 was all they could offer, but he was glad to be back home. With the derbies not far away, the Broch were in good nick. The festive period arrived in the form of a 0-2 win at Recreation Park, with goals from Noble and Bowie and keeper O'Brian outstanding in goal. The teams for that Xmas Day game were:

Peterhead: Connell, Duthie, Ross, McRae, Anderson, Pirie, Duncan, Hunter, W. Miller, Newlands (Morris), Kerr.

Broch: O'Brian, Whyte, Noble, Sharp, McCann, Duthie, McKenzie, Noble, Fordyce, Roger, Bowie, sub: Catto.
"a 3-1 win at Bellslea, with Willie Miller netting two, was revenge on the old enemy. "Can ye hear the Peterhead sing?" Brian Newlands was on the bench that day.

Another tragedy hit the people of the Broch that year, when the fishing boat, "Nautilus," sank with the loss of seven crew members. All of them were local lads. It puts life into perspective doesn't it?

Bertie Bowie's goal scoring exploits were attracting the attention of a few other clubs. Inverness Thistle, Dundee Utd and Cardiff City were having him watched. Another starlet was Jim Crawford (Craffie). He made his Broch debut v Caley, a game that ended in a 4-1 defeat, with Dave Johnson scoring a double. Dave McKenzie was the Broch's scorer. Bertie Bowie was off on trial with Cardiff City, but returned for the trip away to Inverness Thistle.

The match started in sensational style when McCann collided with a barrier. With the sub Catto acting as trainer, he couldn't replace McCann, so the team had to play on with ten men for the next 10 minutes, till McCann recovered and returned to the fray. The Broch were soon back down to ten men however when Rogers was ordered off after an off the ball incident. Then, with the Broch trailing 2-0, Stephen crossed a ball that was a yard over the byline, from which McDonald headed home. All in the Broch team assumed the ball was out, so the keeper placed it for a goal kick, only for the ref to point to the centre spot. The final score was Thistle 3, Broch 0.

A 2-1 win against Keith followed, in the Aberdeenshire Cup 1st round, Bowie hitting the winner for his 20th of the season. The semi-final was away to Peterhead, who were trying to win the trophy for the fifth season in successsion. The Broch led 0-1 until the 83rd minute, with Kerr then hitting two late goals to put Peterhead through to the final. The Bell's Cup was next, bringing a 3-1 win against Aberdeen University. The next round brought a home tie v Deveronvale, with a goal that keeper O'Brian will want to forget. Sandison crossed to the back post in 70 minutes, O'Brian had it covered and was about to move to collect the ball from the back of the goals for a goal kick, when it dipped and dropped into the net, a bad goal to lose. Then a poor goal kick was directed to Sandison who hit it first time over O'Brian's head for Vale's second goal. Freddie shouted over to the bench and the trainer thought he was injured, but Freddie replied, "I'm needing off." It was not his day!

Saturday 11th March saw another classic, with the Broch 4-0 down at half-time to Brora, but what a fight back they staged to earn a 4-4 draw. The usual call-offs came when we played Brora. The team that day was: Forsyth, Catto, G. Noble, Roger, McCann, Duthie, B. Massie, J. Noble, Fordyce, McKenzie?. Bowman?. (I don't know if it was meant to be Bowie in the match report.) Sub: Watt. Scorers were: Bowman (50), Fordyce (57), McKenzie (68) and McCann (73). A 3-2 defeat followed, at home to Huntly, when McCann gave a substitute debut to local Youth Centre lad Sandy Souter. However the amateur league had a stupid rule, that, if you played more than three games for the Broch, you couldn't return to play amateur, which spoiled it for a lot of promising players. There were some arguments at amateur meetings about this rule that took so long, you would have needed a flask and a piece to sit through it all!

Kenny Rogers told me about the time back then when the car he was in broke down just five miles from Rothes (it was always just cars for this distance of games) so they started walking. They managed to hitch a lift and arrived with a quarter of an hour to spare, going on to win 5-1. The Dryburgh Cup was up next, which involved the eight teams that had scored the most goals. The Broch beat Keith 1-0, with an Ian Sharp goal late on, to give us a semi-final at home to Brora Rangers. It had been a long time coming, but we finally signed Brian Newlands from Peterhead. What a class act he was, with the final piece of the jigsaw a 2-0 win. It was, "welcome home," for Newlands, with him scoring the second to the delight of the home support (the crowd that night was 1,200.)

What was it with the Broch and cup finals? We were due to play Elgin in the final and they decided to play it at Borough Briggs, what happened to common sense? As usual the Broch took a big support through for the match and it was a cracker of a game. Bowie was causing Elgin all sorts of problems, at one point rounding the keeper and rolling the ball towards an empty net, only for Gerrard to race back and clear off the line. Elgin took the lead on 19 minutes through Graham, but that was short lived. Lawtie couldn't hold a McKenzie cross and it fell to Bowie, who slammed it into an empty net to make it 1-1. Then a powerful header from McIntosh, which Duthie was helpless to stop, flew into the net so at half-time it was 2 – 1 to Elgin. The second half started in sensational style, with Elgin getting a penalty for a handball incident, from which Graham made it 3-1. Both teams were then reduced to ten men, when McCann and Nicol were sent off for squaring up to each other, before Fordyce pulled one back for the Broch. Then the referee halted the game and had a word with Jimmy Brown for a remark made to the stand side linesman. The final score was Elgin 3, Broch 2, but could you imagine the Old Firm agreeing to play a Cup Final at either of their stadiums? I don't think so.

Money was never the be all and end all of playing for the Broch, but, before the game, Brian Newlands had been speaking to Keith Nicol of Elgin, who asked if the Broch were on a win bonus as Elgin were on one (of £50 a man.) Brian got together with a few players to see if the Broch could manage a win bonus. Jimmy Brown's reply was, "We're no a rich club but we could manage £5." That said it all.

So that was another season over. Charlie Duncan's Inverness Thistle were champions, scoring 114 goals in the process. The Broch were in 8th place,

P	W	D	L	F	A	PTS
30	14	2	14	69	63	30

while Vale got the wooden spoon with just nine points. Derby County were champions in England, with Leeds Utd runners up. Celtic won the league in Scotland with Aberdeen runners up. St Mirren and Cowdenbeath were relegated (there was no Premier League yet.) Partick Thistle and East Fife were promoted. Arsenal beat Liverpool 2-1 to lift the FA Cup and Celtic won the Scottish Cup 2-1 against Rangers after a 1-1 draw.

Season 1972-73

We waited in anticipation for the new season, could we hack it at last with the big boys? Once again a goalkeeper crisis had arisen. John Massie's shifts at Peterhead Prison, where he was a warder, had changed and he couldn't be available every Saturday. Aberdeen trialist Freddie O'Brian had decided to sign for Buchanhaven Hearts, after a misunderstanding with the Broch. He thought they weren't interested in him, so we started where we had left off the last season with a 1-1 draw at Elgin followed by 0-0 at home with Caley.

That set us up nicely for the League Cup, which had changed its format to a knock out competition. Our first tie was against Vale, at Princess Royal Park. Brian McCann was serving a suspension and Jim Crawford was farmed out from Aberdeen. Two goals apiece for Newlands and Bowie, a Noble penalty and a Fordyce goal completed a comfortable 6-0 win. Next up was a home tie with Huntly. Crawford opened the scoring in ten minutes, but then Simpson made it 1-1. A minute later Noble missed a penalty, Huntly keeper Ogston making a fine save, but Bowie restored the Broch lead in 23 minutes. Then it was Huntly's turn to miss a spot kick when Thom hit the bar. Bowie made it 3-1 in 62 minutes only for Bruce to reduce the leeway a minute later. The final score was Broch 3 Huntly 2. The teams were:

Broch: Massie, Whyte, G. Noble, Duthie, Rogers, Newlands, Fordyce, J. Noble, Crawford, McKenzie, Bowie. Sub: Sharp.

Huntly: Ogston, Reidford, Lamond, McKenzie, Finnie, Chalmers, Forsyth, Simpson, Bruce, Sandison, Thom. Sub: McGregor.

Ref - W. D. Reid, Aberdeen

Massie was unavailable for the trip to Brora so Charlie Marioni, from amateur club Cairnbulg, wore the goalkeeper's jersey for the day. Not a great debut, with Brora winning 5-0 and Tommy Reid scoring four goals.

The semi-final draw was away to Elgin (again.) Like they say, every doggie has his day and this was the Broch's finest day for a long time. A 2-0 win, with goals from Fordyce (51) and J. Crawford (88) sent us into the final v Inverness Thistle. Before the final the headlines were, "Broch declare War on Tappers." It was reported that one of the Inverness clubs was the culprit, but we never knew which one. Was it Caley or Clach? Charlie Duncan was training with the Broch at that time and it was decided he should find alternative accommodation for a while. Buckie Thistle then failed in a bid to sign out of favour centre half Brian McCann who instead said, "I want to stay and fight to regain my place." John Massie, who pulled a muscle in his back, was fit again for the final and ex-Broch player, George Malley, was the Broch's new trainer and, knowing, "Dod," he'd have them fit, that was for sure!

The game started in sensational style. Newlands put the Broch 1-0 up in the third minute only for Stephen to make it 1-1 in 8 minutes. Back came the Broch and Newlands made it 2-1 but then McLaren scored to make it 2-2. Back came the Broch once more and Fordyce scored in a goalmouth scramble, for 3-2. Just before half time, Cowie made it 3-3 and a minute after the interval, Bowie was brought down in the box only for Noble to miss the resulting penalty. After that Thistle took command and Stephen goals made it 3-5. McCann came on as substitute and scored in the final minute for a final score of Broch 4, Inverness Thistle 5. The teams were:

Broch: Massie, Whyte, Noble, Duthie, Roger, McKenzie, Fordyce, Noble, Crawford, Newlands, Bowie. Sub: McCann

Inverness Thistle: Reilly, D'Arcy, Cumming, Bremner, Lazemby, McLean, Stephen, Cowie, Duncan, McLaren. Sub: Morrison.

Ref – D Smith , Elgin.   Crowd 1,820

It was a very quiet bus on the way home, but we hadn't time to feel sorry for ourselves. Would you believe we had to play Inverness Thistle away the following week in the Qualifying Cup? A decision was made that the situation with Johnny Massie was unacceptable, so the Broch signed up Bobby Forsyth (again) and he went straight into the team v Thistle on the Saturday. "Mr Reliable and never lets you down," he was a real legend. Doshy Noble dropped to the bench and McCann was at left back. Cowie put Thistle 1-0 up in 23 minutes, but the Broch fought back, and Fordyce netted in 36 minutes. We were level for only two minutes, before Cowie scored to put Thistle 2-1 up at half time. Morrison in 84 minutes sealed it for Thistle for a final score of Inverness Thistle 3, Broch 1.

November 18th and it was back to Borough Briggs to haunt Elgin, and what a game it was. Bowie opened the scoring in 29 minutes and Graham equalised. Then Falconer, in 38 minutes, made it 2-1 and Crawford scored in 50 minutes. Then Bowie made it 2-3, but Falconer made it 3 – 3 in 83 minutes. Ian Sharpe came on as sub in 90 minutes. His first touch was a header into the Elgin net for 3-4, in that final minute with no time for a come back. I can remember little Brucie Buchan and me dancing on the roof of the dug out. Those were happy days!

The Broch were getting good press for their all local policy and the team spirit was good as most of the players were good mates as well. The usual card school on the way to away games was very serious, but good crack. I used to think there were only 50 cards in a pack and I never knew where, "Tosie," (John Duthie) hid the other two, but every time he opened, everybody would pack. One time at Portsoy, Craffie came on the bus with a bottle of whisky for the boys, but he told Tosie it was his turn at the next away game, so he obliged a fortnight later. The only thing was I didn't know they sold whisky with an optic on the bottle, very strange, but there you go!!

A derby double was up next. A Davie McKenzie strike after half an hour at Recreation Park was all that separated the teams for a final score of Peterhead 0, Broch 1. That game was brought to a halt for two minutes while spectators fought on the park. In the return game at the Bellslea, Bertie Bowie hit the winner after 80 minutes, for a "Happy New Year!" The teams were:

Broch: Forsyth, Whyte, Newlands, Roger, McCann, Duthie, Fordyce, Noble, Sharp, McKenzie, Bowie.

Peterhead: Connell, Ewen, Pirie, Anderson, Rennie, Christie, Duncan, Forsyth, Ross, McMaster, Gordon.

There was a shock in store for Broch fans as Inverness Thistle swooped to sign John Duthie for an undisclosed fee, but at least there would be 52 cards in a pack the next time we played cards. We wished all the best to John.

Buckie Thistle were due at the Bellslea in the 1st round of the Aberdeenshire Cup and what a game it turned out to be. Dod Simmers put Buckie in the lead in the first minute. It was 0-2 in 16 minutes, again through Simmers and it looked all over when Christianson made it 0-3 in 20 minutes. But Bowie in 25 and Fordyce in 36 minutes made it 2-3, but, just as the Broch were getting on top Winton scored for the visitors in 43 minutes to make it 2-4. Newlands brought it back to 3-4 in 60 minutes and McCann in 70 minutes made it 4-4. Disaster followed, when Simmers scored in the 87th minute to make it 4-5 and completing his hat trick, but the Broch were not finished. I remember the equaliser as though it was yesterday. Newlands hit the underside of the bar with a header that crossed the line at the Clinic end to make it 5-5. All hell broke loose as the referee, surrounded by Buckie players, blew for time. The replay was a quieter affair with the Broch running out 0-3 winners.

An easy 2-0 win in the semi-final against Peterhead at the Bellslea, with Sharp in 10 and Bowie in 24 minutes the scorers, saw the Broch into the final. That game was at Banff against Deveronvale on Saturday April 7th, where we broke our duck. The town was buzzing. Every pub had a bus going to the big game for, when they were successful, the Broch had the largest away support in the league. The game started at a hectic pace. Bowie had the ball in the Vale net in 14 minutes, but was ruled offside. Then Forsyth came to the Broch's rescue with the save of the season, as he blocked Wilson's shot from three yards to keep his goal intact. At half time it was 0-0. A minute after half time, Princess Royal Park went wild as Bowie put the Broch 0-1 in the lead. Police were called to cool down the crowd after an outbreak of fighting, then Newlands made it 0-2 in 58 minutes, but Vale hit back, with Chalmers in 63 and then Wilson in 69 minutes levelling the score. "Oh no, not a repeat of Elgin!" Newlands on 78 minutes put us back in front, and completed his hat trick in the 81st minute, to make it 2-4 and it looked all over for the Vale as Bertie Bowie slotted home his second goal from the penalty spot. The final score was Deveronvale 2, Fraserburgh 5. A huge roar went up from the away support as Broch skipper Kenny "Dodger," Roger received the famous old trophy and a great night was had by all. It was some job trying to lift the cup to get a drink out of it, changed days from the doom and gloom of the sixties!

There was the new, end of the season, trophy to play for that year, from sponsors Bell's Scotch Whisky, which was better known as the Bell's Cup. The Broch were drawn away to Buckie Thistle in the 1st round. A comfortable 1-5 win, with three goals in the first 15 minutes, from McKenzie and new signing Gibby Stephen, set us up for a trip to Peterhead in the semi- final. McKenzie and Bowie ran Peterhead ragged and with two goals in a minute midway through the first half from Bowie, and Sharp adding a third after half time, to make the final score Peterhead 0, Fraserburgh 3. At that time, the price to watch Highland League football was 33p for adults and 16.5p for children, a far cry from today's inflated prices.

Ross County were top of the league and they beat Inverness Thistle at Kingmill to force a league play off in front of a crowd of 3,000. The final of the Bell's Cup was between the Broch and Huntly, in a two leg affair. In the first leg at the Bellslea, former Dons goalkeeper, John Ogston, broke the hearts of the Broch forwards with some super saves. For all the Broch's pressure, it was Huntly who took a precious lead back to Christie Park, scored by another ex-Don, Lewis Thom.

On Thursday May 10th, the Broch ran out on a rainy night at Christie Park for the 2nd leg. Ally Fordyce scored on 15 minutes to put the Broch 0-1 in the lead and square the tie on aggregate at 1-1. Bertie Bowie made it 0-2 and then scored again in 53 minutes to make it 0-3, before Bruce netted for Huntly for 1-3. Bowie completed his hat trick in the 75th minute to make it 1-4 and Gibby Stephen netted the fifth goal in 85 minutes to make the final score Huntly 1, the Broch 5. Aggregate score Huntly 2 Broch 5. Two trophies in one season and runners up in a third. Things were really looking up at the Bellslea. Jimmy Brown wrote a letter to the Herald thanking the Broch fans for their tremendous support over the season. It's true that a successful Broch team has the best support in the Highland League. With the Social Club up and running, it looked as though money problems were going to be a thing of the past also. On a Saturday night if you weren't in and seated by 7:15pm you couldn't get a seat. Entertainments like, "Two for the Road," or, "Question Mark," really packed them in.

Inverness Thistle were champions, beating Ross County 2-1 in the play off at Telford Street with Charlie Duncan netting the winner, but, despite a successful season in cup competitions, and with Bertie Bowie having scored 32 goals, the Broch were 6th bottom of the league.

P	W	D	L	F	A	PTS
30	11	5	14	46	52	27

Sunderland won the FA Cup beating Leeds Utd 1-0 while Rangers won the Scottish Cup, thanks to a Tom, "Jaws," Forsyth tap in. The summer holidays were upon us, and it turned out to be a real adventure. A group of us including: Bertie Bowie, Gibby Stephen, Ian Sharpe, John Duthie, Johnny Whyte, Roy Beattie and myself, bought a tent for £50, hired a dormobile and headed north. Our first stop was Aviemore, then we headed for Fort William and took a ferry to somewhere. All that was there when we arrived was a few houses and a pub, not so bad! A pint and a pie, then back onto the ferry to head for Oban. Let's just say a good time was had by all. After the holiday we sold the tent for £40, which was not a bad bit of business.

Season 1973-74

As the new season drew closer, there were a couple of new faces at the Bellslea. Raymond Cardno arrived from Buckie

Thistle and Bobby Fraser from the Youth Centre (with the one and only Rexy Hunter soon to follow.) Rexy left the Broch and came back again so many times. I don't know how long he played, but he was a prolific goal scorer and a real character. Another new strip arrived, this time with a black patch down the middle.

A 4-1 defeat at Clach in the first league game was followed by a 4-0 defeat at home to Huntly in the League Cup. It was not the best of starts. Next up was Forres at home and the final score that day was 7-2, with our new local hero Bobby Fraser notching a hat trick. What a difference a week makes. With Doshy Noble retired, Cardno slotted in at left back, but Raymond will be remembered for his party piece on the bus away from home with a few choruses of, "The Rattlin Bog," and Rexy's favourite, "I am the Music Man." Nice one lads! The team that started the season was: Forsyth, Whyte, Cardno, McKenzie, Rogers, Newlands, Hunter, Noble, Fraser, Stephen, Bowie. Sub: Fordyce.

With a home tie in the Qualifying Cup v Vale, we had a chance to progress, but what a shock! Goals, from Chalmers in 10 minutes and Wilson in the 47th, put Vale in a commanding position. Noble however pulled one back in the 55th minute and then Newlands saved the day with the equaliser in the the 85th minute making the final score Broch, 2 Vale 2. The replay turned out to be a formality with goals from Bowie 2, Stephen, Noble and Fraser for a final score of Vale 1, Broch 5.

A place in the Scottish Cup was up for grabs, with a difficult away tie to Inverness Caley. The game started with the Broch in command, but they scorned chance after chance to take the lead, only for Caley to hit us, with two sucker punches just before half time. McKinnon struck in 41minutes and Elder in 43 to give them an undeserved 2-0 lead, but it was a different story in the second half. Goals from McKenzie in the 51st and Bowie in the 55th minute put the game in the melting pot. Then, in 65 minutes, Fraser put the Broch in the lead for the first time. A long 25 minutes followed as Caley threw everything but the kitchen sink at us. What a relief when the ref finally blew for time. The final score was Caley 2, Broch 3. This must have been the biggest upset in the Qualifying Cup for many a year, as Caley were expected to be in the Scottish Cup every season. The best memory of the game was when Bobby Fraser netted the winner. All the Broch fans were behind McKenzie's goal singing, "butter fingers," to Wizards hit, "Angel Fingers." I won't forget what his reply was that day! The teams were:

Caley: McKenzie, Gerrard, Beatson, Carroll, Presslie, Brankine, Makinnon, Elder, Bell, F. Neild, Fyfe.

Broch: Forsyth, Cardno, Newlands, McKenzie, McCann, Roger, Fordyce, Noble, Fraser, Stephen, Bowie.

A Bobby Fraser double away to Keith in the League the following week set us up for the semi-final at the Bellslea v Ross County. There was a good atmosphere in the ground as the teams ran out to the biggest crowd of the season and a great escape came for the Broch after just 15 minutes. Garrow hit the post and the ball rolled along the line, with Forsyth just a spectator, before it was cleared. All was square at half time 0-0, but the Broch were kicking downhill towards the Pole's Garage in the second half. Bowie went on one of his mazy runs and, with a trail of County defenders chasing him out, he still brought the best out of keeper Pryce. Hunter came on for Fordyce and hit a terrific shot which the keeper tiped round the post. It looked like a replay at Dingwall as the clock ran down the minutes until a last gasp attack by County led to the winner with Fleming netting in the final minute. There was no way back for the Broch. Final score Fraserburgh 0, Ross County 1.

Just when you thought the Broch were getting their act together, calamity struck. Saturday, November 3rd was just another Saturday, until Spicy injured himself in the warm up. What could they do? Someone then spotted Freddy O'Brian heading for the Station Bar for a pint. He was just ordering his second pint when Jimmy Brown collared him.

"Come on Freddie, we need a goalie," so it was over to the Bellslea and onto the park with ten minutes to spare. The score that day finished Broch 1, Deveronvale 1.

Bertie Bowie, for all the publicity of his scoring feats, was a real down to earth guy. Jimmy Brown came in at 2.40 and announced the team, but no Bowie in the line up. He didn't say much. Most players would have brought the house down, but not Bertie. Brucie Buchan brought to Jimmy's attention that he had missed out Bowie's name from the team lines. Quick as a flash, Jimmy shouted,
"There's been a change in the team selection." "We're going to play a more attacking game." Pointing to a member of the team he said, "you'll be on the bench." Bertie put on the No 11 shirt to Jimmy's favourite saying, when the ball wasn't played forward quick enough.
"No tippy-tappy the day."
With the disappointment of the semi-final in the past, the draw for the Scottish Cup paired us with Lossiemouth away. That's the last thing every Highland League Club wants in the cup, but they all just had to get on with it.

On Saturday December 15th at a frosty Grant Park, the Broch ran out to a huge roar from their large travelling support. Bowie put them into the lead in 9 minutes and added a second on 42 minutes. Lossie hit back, with two goals in 3 minutes from Dunnet and Collie and, at half time it was 2-2. Bowie completed his hat-trick to put the Broch back in the lead in 53 minutes, at 2-3. Three minutes later it should have been all over, but Rogers blasted a penalty over the bar (it was so high he nearly hit an oil rig). Lossie kept plugging away and Collie made it 3-3 before Forsyth saved the day for us with a super save. The Broch went on to hit the post, but the game ended as it started, all square, at 3-3.

There was a real rumpus about the replay. Under SFA rules, Saturday replays can only be permitted if clubs are more than 100 miles apart. As both clubs were nearer than that, it was a costly business getting players off their work for a Tuesday replay.

The teams that day were:

Lossie: Fraser, Scott, Machray, B. Fraser, Dunnett, Souter, McDougall, Wood, Gordon, Collie. Subs: McKnight, Kellas.

Broch: Forsyth, Cardno, Newlands, McKenzie, McCann, Roger, Fordyce, Noble, Fraser, Hunter, Bowie. Subs: Whyte, Gammack.

Ref – F. Phillips, Inverness

The Broch and Lossie appealed to the SFA, but they said no. The stand roof at the Bellslea had a large hole in it as sections had been blown off in a storm that hit the town, and it was touch and go if the game went on. It was dangerous to get onto the roof to make any repairs, due to the bad weather, but the SFA ruled that if the game didn't go ahead on Wednesday, it would be the following Monday. This tie then took another twist when SFA Secretary, Willie Allan, sent two telegrams demanding a pitch inspection, but you had to have a referee, on the SFA list, for this purpose. As there wasn't one in the area within 42 miles, they had to take the Broch's word that the game would go on. With the north east of Scotland covered in snow, Lossie just made it. There was even a light cover of snow on the Bellslea as the game went ahead with a 1.30 kick off. It was probably the worst day of weather I've ever watched football in, with a gale force wind and sleet that carried on throughout the game. Still, it was good to see the Broch back to playing in the famous black and white strips.

Three goals in the first 15 minutes, from Hunter in 4, Bowie in 8 and Newlands in 13 minutes gave luckless Lossie no chance of finding their feet. Further goals from Bowie in 55, Hunter in 57 and Fraser in 73 minutes, it made a miserable day for the visitors. The final score was 6-0 and, just when you they thought that things couldn't get any worse, the Lossie players returned to the dressing room to find water running down the walls and onto their clothes. Don't mention Scottish Cup glory! The tie produced gate receipts of £114. The Linesman's expenses came to £48 and Lossie had to fork out £100 in broken time payments.

Another prodigal son was about to return to the Bellslea. John Duthie (Tosie) was allowed to leave Inverness Thistle. Peterhead were sniffing about, but he chose to come home where he belonged. A blunder, in not registering him within the fourteen day limit, meant he was signed, but couldn't play against Lossiemouth.

There was no time to relax. The festive derbies were upon us, with the first game on December 22nd at Recreation Park v Peterhead. The Broch started where they left off and scored in the 1st minute. Fraser squared the ball to Hunter, who shot into the empty net for 0-1. It stayed that way, although Christie hit the post and Ewen and Noble were ordered off in 82 minutes, for a final score of Peterhead 0, Broch 1.

The return at Bellslea the following week was another classic. As the Broch came onto the field, they were lifted by the crowd singing.
"Fraserburgh, Fraserburgh, We'll support you ever more."
The Broch struck early again and were 1-0 up in four minutes as Fraser made no mistake with the chance. They went 2-0 up in 41 minutes when Duncan brought down Fraser in the box and Bowie made no mistake from the spot. The half time and final score was Broch 2, Peterhead 0.

Peterhead: Connell, Ewen, Rennie, Pirie, Sievewright, Milne, Campbell, Duncan, Christie, Summers, Gall. Subs: Horn, Buchan

Fraserburgh: Forsyth, Cardno, Newlands, McKenzie, McCann, Roger, Fordyce, Noble, Hunter, Fraser, Bowie. Subs: Stephen, Sharp

The following Saturday, it was off to Cowdenbeath for the next round of the Scottish Cup. The Broch took around 500 supporters to the match, the biggest away support they had seen for a long time at Central Park. When we arrived at the ground, it was like going back in time, you would have thought that the war had just finished. The game itself turned into a nightmare. McKenzie had a shot cleared off the line, but the home side took the lead in 21 minutes through Laing. Bowie then had the ball in the net, but the referee gave a penalty, which Bowie then missed. Cowdenbeath went 2-0 up in 28 minutes, Thomson hitting a 20 yard shot into the net, but Hunter reduced the leeway one minute before half time. In the second half, the Broch had the ball in the net twice, but both goals were disallowed. The game remained open until Cowdenbeath hit two late goals in 80 and 86 minutes for a final score of Cowdenbeath 4, Broch 1, not a true reflection of the game. E. H. Pringle was a referee I won't forget in a hurry! What a nightmare he had. The attendance at that game was1352, with gate receipts of £272.

It was back to League business, with two home games against Huntly and Brora. Both teams caught the Broch at the wrong time with a 7-0 win v Huntly and 7-1 v Brora, but the headlines at the time were, "Dons fail in bid to sign Bowie."
Buckie were next to be put to the sword with a 5-1 defeat, but a 0-3 defeat at home to Keith in the Abedeenshire Cup brought us back down to earth.
On Feb 2nd 1974, the League table read:

	P	W	D	L	F	A	PTS
1 Inverness Thistle	22	13	6	3	55	28	32
2 Elgin City	23	13	6	4	50	23	32
3 Fraserburgh	19	13	3	3	54	23	29

In those days it was still two points for a win.

With a double header against Inverness Thistle coming up, we were in with a shout of the Championship. A 3 - 3 draw in Inverness and 1-1 draw at the Bellslea didn't help us, but a 5-2 win up at Ross County brought us back into contention. There was no Bobby Forsyth in goal. He was replaced with former Don, John Ogston, very strange! A subsequent 2-0 defeat away to Rothes and a 1-1 draw with

Ross County at the Bellslea all but put paid to any hopes of the championship.

What was it with the Bell's Cup, for our love affair with it continued? A 0-5 win away to the Vale, was followed up with a 6-1 win at home to Buckie, with Jimmy Noble scoring a hat trick. Next came a 2-0 win up at Keith, with Newlands and McKenzie scoring. Does anyone remember the Bell's miniatures? Every sixth person who went through the turnstyles received one, so all the boys made sure they were 6, 12, 18 and so on. Not being a whisky man, you would swap it for a tin of lager. They too were happy days.

Elgin City finished as champions and the Broch finished third.

	P	W	D	L	F	A	PTS
Elgin	30	19	7	4	71	30	45
Inverness Thistle	30	14	12	4	66	39	40
Fraserburgh	30	16	7	7	72	43	39

Scotland beat England 2-0 at Hampden, Leeds Utd were champions of England's divison 2 and Denis Law scored that famous back heel to relegate Man' Utd. In the European Cup, eight man Athletico Madrid held Celtic to a 0-0 draw at Parkhead, but lost the second leg 2-0.

Now here's a right romantic story. Bobby Forsyth was in goal for Broch v Cowdenbeath that season. Six years before he had played in midfield v East Stirling, both games in the Scottish Cup. He also played in the Junior Cup, in goal and outfield, for Parkvale and Buchanhaven Hearts, not to mention the fact that he played in goal and outfield at every Highland League ground. For good measure, he played at every Junior ground, in goal and outfield as well, he was up there with the best.

Season 1974-75

As the summer passed, the Broch made only one new signing, Charlie Esslemont was released from Aberdeen, but he lived locally and signed on. Jimmy Brown got the recognition he deserved with a star pic in the Green Final. "Jim puts Broch back on the Soccer Map," the headline said. His own comments were, "I think the Broch are on the brink of a major breakthrough in north of Scotland soccer."

Away to Rothes, in the first league game, we were 2-0 down after 30 minutes, but Hunter and Esslemont (pen) made it all square at half time, 2-2. After the turn round, the Broch ran riot with goals from Hunter (2), Fraser and Noble. The final score was Rothes 4, Broch 6. Wednesday August 14th remains etched in my memory, for as long as I continue to follow the Broch, and if you were there that night, at a rain soaked Recreation Park to watch the Peterhead v Broch League Cup match, you'll know what I mean. The Broch ran out worthy winners by 10 goals to nil. Yes 10 – 0!!! As I sat in the stand with my father, he turned round to me after eight goals and said, "Are we going now?" My reply was "We're staying till ten." The teams that night were:

Peterhead: Connell, Ewan, Rennie, D. Summers, Sievwright, Coutts, McKenzie, English, Watson, Cheyne, Beattie. Sub: Cameron.

Fraserburgh: Forsyth, Cardno, Newlands, Stephen, McCann, Duthie, Fraser, Noble, Esslemont, Hunter, Bowie. Subs: Gammack, Sharp.

Hunter opened the scoring in 13 minutes and Duthie added number two in 26 minutes. It was 0-3 with Hunter scoring again, before Bowie made it 0-4 in 34 minutes. Esslemont then scored, to make it 0 – 5, in 39 minutes, with Noble adding a sixth just before half time, and the Broch fans chanting "Easy, Easy, We Want More." The Broch obliged when Noble made it 0-7 in 50 minutes, then Bowie, in 56 and 82 minutes made it 0-9 before Hunter made it a magic 10 four minutes from the end for a memorable final score of Peterhead 0, Fraserburgh 10. I often have a laugh with Robbie Coutts, the local butcher, saying, "there's not a lot of folk ken you were in the Peterhead team that lost 10 – 0."

Well, there are more now! George Ritchie didn't mention this game in his book, though I thought he would.

Despite a 2-1 win away to Huntly in the Qualifying Cup Quarter-final, with goals from J. Duthie and Brian Newlands, two goals in six minutes, away to Keith in the semis, put paid to a Cup Final appearance again. But, no sooner were you out of one Cup when you started out on the next one. For us, it was a difficult away trip to Buckie Thistle in the 1st round of the Qualifying Cup. With the game goalless well into the 2nd half, Broch's Esslemont missed a penalty, but two late strikes from Hunter and Bowie put the team into the 2nd round again, away to Elgin City. The headline in the Sunday Post was, "The Miss of a Lifetime."

Hunter put the Broch into an early lead, only for Gray to make it 1-1. Nine minutes after the interval Gray struck again to give Elgin a precious lead 2-1, but the Broch hit back through Esslemont (64). The next incident turned the tie on its head. With quarter of an hour to go and the game finely balanced, Fordyce pushed a through ball to Hunter, who looked a mile offside. The linesman's flag stayed down and the referee waved play on, so Hunter rounded Lawtie, but he too had thought he was off, as everybody else had stopped. He chipped the ball over the bar instead of rolling it into the empty net and the ref gave a goal kick. With five minutes to go, Sandison made it 3-2 and put Elgin into the next round.

Our first league defeat was a 0-4 loss, at home to Ross County on Nov 2nd, but our overall form was good, with eight wins, two defeats and a draw leading up to the derby games. With Peterhead out to avenge their 10-0 defeat earlier on in the season, this was billed as a Xmas cracker. Watson drew first blood for the, "Blue Tooners," with a crazy goal. He took a pot shot that seemed harmless, but it squirmed through Forsyth's legs and rolled over the line. The Broch got back on level terms when Noble slammed an 18 yarder past the helpless McHattie in 23 minutes, but our recovery didn't last long. A few minutes later Watson put the visitors in the lead again at 1-2 before Fraser squared it just before the interval for 2-2. The Broch hit the woodwork a couple of times, but couldn't get that elusive third goal. Grant hit the winner for Peterhead on 87 minutes and there was no time to reply. The final score was Broch 2, Peterhead 3. The teams that day were:

Broch: Forsyth, Roger, Newlands, Hunter, McCann, Duthie, Fraser, Noble, Esslemont, Stephen, Bowie. Sub: Fordyce.

Peterhead: McHattie, Rennie, Rhynd, Krukowski, Sievwright, Beattie, Watson, Styles, Grant, Horn, Cheyne. Subs: Summers, Park
Ref – L. J. S. Officer

The game the following week was just as controversial. Peterhead had three shots cleared off the line in the first twenty minutes and then, against the run of play, the Broch took the lead through Esslemont in the 25th minute. The same player thought he had put Broch 0-2 in front, scoring from a free kick 25 yards out, but the ref ruled that it was indirect. Then Fraser scored the simplest goal of his career. A through ball to McHattie was left to him, but he left it to Sievwright. With Fraser lying handy, he side-footed the ball into the net, to the delight of the large travelling support. At half time it was Peterhead 0, Broch 2. Summers then hit a 30 yarder to pull Peterhead back into contention, but Esslemont made it 1-3. Grant, with a penalty in 79 minutes, ended the scoring for a result of Peterhead 2, Fraserburgh 3. We never got fed up with winning at Recreation Park!

On Saturday the fourth of January, the Broch went to the top of the table with a 1-2 win away to Elgin. Gibby Stephen and Bobby Fraser were the Broch scorers.

P	W	D	L	F	A	PTS
19	14	2	3	58	27	30

A 2-2 draw with Ross County and 1-1 with Caley kept us in the lead at the top. A 3-0 win v the Varsity in the

Aberdeenshire Cup 1st round followed, but a shock home defeat by Deveronvale came in the cup semi-final, McBain being the scorer for Vale. The following week however we thumped them 5-1 at Princess Royal, with top scorer Bowie hitting a double. But, game by game, the league pressure was getting to the Broch and they kept looking over their shoulder. The fans were not helping either on match days, with rumours travelling around of how the other games were doing.

The top scorers that season, so far were -

Wilkie	Ross County	32
McKintosh	Ross County	28
Chrisite	Keith	28
Hunter	Broch	23
Bowie	Broch	19

Up and coming striker, Bobby Fraser was on 15 goals. He had scored 25 the previous season, which was not a bad striking rate for a young lad who stepped up from the amateurs. Bobby got the nickname, "the road runner" because he was so quick off the mark.

A 1-2 defeat, at home to Elgin City, all but ended the Broch's title hopes, while a 3-0 defeat had put Keith to the top of the league. Then, with five games to go, we were due to play Inverness Thistle at the Bellslea. A certain C. Duncan put Thistle on their way, with a blistering drive in 33 minutes. A McCann own goal and a strike from Fraser completed a miserable afternoon at the Bellslea for a final score of Broch 0, Inverness Thistle 3.

Keith went top again with a 5-0 win over Brora Rangers, but we bounced back with a 2-6 win at Brora, with Rexy Hunter scoring four goals. Then a 3-3 draw with Clach at the Bellslea meant that we wouldn't even be runners up and a 2-1 defeat at Caley on the last day of the season put us in overall third. It was so disappointing after leading for so long. That's the joy of being a Broch supporter, they always have to do things the hard way. That same day, Saturday 29th March, the Rothes v Buckie match was postponed because of snow. Clach became champions and Keith were runners up, maybe next season.

	P	W	D	L	F	A	PTS
Clach'	30	19	8	3	72	32	46
Keith	30	20	5	5	90	41	45
Broch	30	18	5	7	86	48	41

I'll finish off the season the way I started. Broch supporter, Jim Docherty, wrote a song especially for Jimmy Brown. It goes something like this, to the tune of, "For These are my Mountains:"

"FOR FAME AND FOR FOOTBALL WE'LL TRAVEL A' OWER
WE FOLLOW THE BURGHY WHATEVER THE SCORE
WE'RE SELDOM DEFEATED THOUGH FAR DO WE ROAM
IF WE LOSE WE THRASH THEM AT HOME
FOR THESE ARE OUR HEROES AND THIS IS OUR TEAM
FROM SPICY TO BERTIE THE FINEST WE'VE SEEN
WE'LL CARRY OUR COLOURS FROM EAST COAST TO WEST
TO FOLLOW THE BURGHY THE TEAM WE LOVE BEST
ONE WEEK UP IN ELGIN WE WATCHED WITH DELIGHT
WHEN THEY WERE DEFEATED THEY WANTED TAE FIGHT
WE BROUGHT BACK SOME PRISONERS BUT WAS BROUGHT TO MIND
KIDNAPPING'S ILLEGAL THE CLUB COULD BE FINED
FOR THESE ARE OUR HEROES AND THIS IS OUR TEAM
FROM SPICY TO BERTIE THE FINEST WE'VE SEEN

WE'LL CARRY OUR COLOURS FROM EAST COAST TO WEST
TO FOLLOW THE BURGHY THE TEAM WE LOVE BEST
WHEN THE GAME'S OVER AND THE LEAGUE HAS BEEN WON
WHEN WE'RE CELEBRATING THE FINE DEEDS THEY HAVE DONE
WE'LL ALWAYS REMEMBER WITH PRIDE AND WITH JOY
THOUGH THE TEAM THEY PLAYED MAGIC
THE BOMBER'S THE BOY"

The amateur league was still going strong and this is how the table stood on May 17th.

	P	W	D	PTS
Broch Centre	14	12	1	25
Redburn	14	8	1	17
Invercairn	14	8	1	17
Sandhaven	14	6	4	16
Toolworks	14	6	4	16
St Combs	14	5	2	12
Rosehearty	14	2	1	5
Parkhill	14	2	1	5

A bottle of Bacardi was £3.10p then. Dewar's Whisky cost £2.35p. It was 11.5p for a can of Tennent's lager. The, "Moon Shadow," disco was playing in the middle lounge of the Royal Hotel with the D.J, at that time, no other than Kenny King, who later went on to host Waves Radio. For me it was off to Lorret de Mar in Spain, for a holiday with the boys, for a bit of sun and a few beers.

The news that surprised everyone in that close season was of Brian McCann hanging up his boots and becoming manager. With three new faces in the squad, the team would now almost automatically pick itself. Goalkeeper Charlie

Gray (Rothes), Murdo Watson (Peterhead), Billy Massie (Youth Centre) took the squad up to 18 players. However a query from the committee was, "do they all get paid if they're not selected?"

Season 1975-76

A crowd of nearly 2,000 witnessed Brian McCann's last game, in his testimonial against Hearts. Hearts won 2-1, but we went on to beat Arbroath 2-0.

A shock 4-3 defeat at home to Vale in the League Cup wasn't the best of starts, especially as we were 2-0 up after 14 minutes. But Vale pulled us back until, with the final whistle due, we were 2-4 down. Billy Massie then scored, in the last minute, to make it Broch 3, Vale 4. We bounced back after that, on four straight wins, to go top of the table, with Rexy Hunter in fine scoring form, but another shock was in store. We lost to Forres in the 1st round of the Qualifying Cup, when the length of the table separated the two teams. Bowie and Hunter had shots that hit the woodwork, but then D. Fraser, in a rare Forres raid, hit a stunning 30 yard shot into the top corner of the net. Forres held on after that to go into the next Monday's draw, with the final score Broch 0, Forres 1.

October wasn't a good month, with defeats from Inverness Thistle (4 – 0) and Elgin City (2 – 1) followed by Ross County (0 – 3.) However, a change in fortune was about to take place. A 1-1 at title challengers Keith, was followed by a 1-3 victory away to Caley, with Newlands, Hunter and a late Fraser strike counting for the Broch.

On Saturday November 18th the top of the league table stood like this:

	P	W	D	L	F	A	PTS
Inverness Thistle	15	8	4	3	43	22	20
Fraserburgh	15	8	3	4	25	16	19
Nairn	13	8	2	3	23	15	18

Now came that time of year again, the Christmas derbies. Our all local side v Peterhead's Aberdeen select. There seemed to be a larger support from the Broch that year and they weren't disappointed, with Duthie and Roger solid at the back and Bowie, Newlands and Hunter not giving the home defence a minute of peace, this game was a classic. Newlands put the Broch in the lead on 29 minutes then Hunter hit an 18 yarder, with McHattie clutching fresh air, for 0-2. O'Hara pulled one back on 60 minutes, but the day belonged to the Broch with a final score of Peterhead 1, Broch 2.

Following an incident at Christie Park, Huntly, when referee George McRae (Fraserburgh) was pushed to the ground, the S.F.A. announced that it would be closed for two months. The Club was also fined £100, but on to a game that I'll remember for a long time, well the last 20 minutes of it anyway! This was the return match with Peterhead on Saturday 27th December. Peterhead strolled 0-1 up, with an O'Hara strike on 61 mins, but the Broch put on Massie and Crawford for Fraser and Watson and put Tozy up front. Kicking up the hill to the Clinic end, Tozy ran on to a through ball and crashed a shot into the roof of the net to make it 1-1. The Bellslea went wild. Three minutes later Tosy hit a poor shot at McHattie only for it to hit the goalkeeper on one leg and squirm under his body into the net. There was no wall in front of the stand at that time, and the force of the crowd pulled the fence down, with Tozy already in the crowd celebrating. The referee, Larry Officer, just stood and looked on in amazement and the game finished Broch 2, Peterhead 1. The teams that day were:

Broch: Gray, Gammack, Cardno, McKenzie, Roger, Duthie, Watson (Crawford), Stephen, Fraser (Massie), Newlands, Bowie

Peterhead: McHattie, Rennie, Smith, Krukowski, Sievwright, Pirie, Ross, Fraser, Third, O'Hara, Noble, Lawson, Horne.

Ref – L.J.S. Officer, Aberdeen

It was a merry Christmas season for us and six wins after New Year made all the league's big guns sit up and take notice. A 5-1 away win over Vale, was followed by 3-2 up at Clach, with an 88th minute strike from Ian Sharp securing the points. Then came a must win, game against Keith at the Bellslea, with Rexy Hunter scoring the only goal. We then hit Lossie for seven before the next game at home, against our bogey team Inverness Thistle. With the crowd still flocking into the Bellslea, Bowie put the Broch ahead in 11 seconds and Watson sealed the victory in the 80th minute. In between, Kenny Rogers got his marching orders after pushing Charlie Duncan, who had fouled keeper Gray. I was speaking to Kenny long afterwards and he said it was a waste of time him playing against Inverness Thistle, as he was sent off three times in three years. Most of the incidents involved Charlie Duncan, as he could fairly wind up, "the Dodger."

All of that good work halted with a shock 2-1 defeat at Brora on 21st February, though after that hiccup, we won the next six games on the trot. 1-0 at home to Buckie Thistle, and then an impressive 2 - 4 win at Ross County. Fraser (8), Hunter (22 & 30) had the Broch in easy street, before Urquhart hit back for 1-3. An own goal from Brett for 1-4 meant the points were finally heading the Bellslea's way though a late strike by County made the score more respectable. A big blow then came for the Broch, when Eddie Gammack broke his leg up at Forres in a game the Broch won 1-2.

At that time, Rexy Hunter was hitting the headlines for his goal scoring plaudits.
"A Reject Hits Goals Jackpot."
"Mintlaw plumber finds Leaks in Highland League Defences."
He had scored 20 goals so far that season, but his first spell had only lasted half a season when Peterhead came calling. Over the years this, 'must have,' thing with Peterhead was like a little boy at Xmas. Dennis Forsyth, Peter McDonald,

Jimmy Noble, Charlie Esslemont had all been lured from Bellslea, but why didn't they give some of their local lads a chance?

A 1-0 win against Buckie Thistle in Aberdeenshire Cup semi-final was a light relief from league business, with that man Hunter again providing the goal. Saturday March 20th was our last league fixture, a 4-2 home win v Forres, as our remaining games were cup ties. Next up was Huntly in the final of the Aberdeenshire Cup at the Bellslea. Two goals from McKenzie and one from Bowie had the 1500 crowd on their feet. Finnie scored a late consolation for Huntly, but the game was over by that time. What a change it was, winning a trophy at the Bellslea! Final score Broch 3, Huntly 1. The teams were:

Broch: Gray, Sharp, Cardno, McKenzie, Roger, Duthie, Watson, Hunter, Newlands, Stephen, Bowie. Subs: Fraser, Massie.

Huntly: Cooper, Gerrard, Barzoni, Raffan, Finnie, Watson, Chalmers, Laws, Simpson, Donald, McBain. Subs: McKenzie, Johnston.

Ref W. D. Reid, Aberdeen. Attendance -1500

A Bertie Bowie goal was then enough to see off Buckie Thistle in the semi-final of the Bell's Cup, with a final score of Broch 1, Buckie 0.

The date was May 8th, six weeks since our last league game, but we had to wait to see if Keith or Nairn dropped some points as the weeks passed. Some Broch supporters went to Rothes on the day they met Nairn, to add a bit of support for the home side, but they had to leave early as the visitors' support were upset at dropping a point, especially since, if Nairn had won at Rothes, that would have clinched the championship. There were provisional arrangements made for three play off ties: Nairn v Fraserburgh, Keith v Fraserburgh and Nairn v Keith. It turned out to be Nairn v Broch, on Monday 27th May, at Borough Briggs, Elgin. The Broch was at fever pitch and it was reported that 2,000 supporters from the town travelled to Elgin that night.

The team left far too early for the match. I travelled on the club bus that day and we left Bellslea around 3pm and then stopped at Portsoy around 4.30, which meant that the players had too much time to think about the game. The only team shock was that Ian McKay, better known as, "Cup tie," from East End Juniors, would be on the bench that night. The kick off was delayed to allow the crowd in, with the tension becoming almost unbearable. When the game began, both teams were making mistakes. Charlie Gray was having an uncomfortable night, with Nairn's high ball tactics, but theBroch couldn't seem to put two passes together. Duthie hooked a certain goal off the line with Gray beaten, but then disaster came just a minute from the interval when Nairn took the lead with Gordon heading into the roof of the net. At half time it was Nairn 1 Broch 0, but the Broch started the second half brightly and, on 50 minutes, when a Rogers free kick was only half-cleared, Gibby Stephen calmly shot into the net as Borough Briggs erupted! It was all Broch after that and in the last minute Mitchell kicked the ball off the line just as the referee blew for time. In extra time, disaster struck again when Tozy and Sharpie went for the same ball, just in front of the stand, and the ball broke kindly for Robertson. Gray raced from his goal, but the Nairn man chipped the ball inside the post, to make it Nairn 2 Broch 1, and it was all over. The teams that night were:

Broch: Gray, Sharp, Cardno, McKenzie, Roger, Duthie, Watson (Massie), Hunter, Newlands (McKay), Stephen, Bowie.

Nairn Co: Konczak, Forsyth, R. Mitchell, Cochrane, Brown, Wilson (W. Mitchell) D. Robertson, Gordon (Hendry) MacIldownie, P. Robertson.
Ref – L. J. S. Officer   Attendance - 3,367   Receipts - £1.040
Gordon Bissett and I had taken a couple of bottles of champagne along to celebrate, but they came home unopened. We stopped at Portsoy on the way home, but most of the players just wanted to get home. The next day headlines were:

"It's Nairn's Title After Extra Time"
"Broch a Gloomy Town After Title Defeat."
Every time I go to Elgin, I can see Tozy and Sharpie going for that same ball. At Nairn the league flag still flies, but I still say to myself, "That's oor flag."
Before the play-off the table top read:

	P	W	D	L	F	A	PTS
Nairn County	30	19	6	5	75	35	44
Fraserburgh	30	20	4	6	67	35	44

At the other end, Deveronvale collected the wooden spoon:

P	W	D	L	F	A	PTS
30	3	4	23	29	105	10

On the following Thursday, we had a Bell's Cup Final to take care of. It must have taken a great deal of motivation from the players to be up for this game and a Kenny Roger 35 yard free kick was all that eventually separated the teams. The final score was the Broch 1, Peterhead 0. Well done lads! It was going to be a long summer. A couple of weeks in the sun and a couple of beers might help.

Season 1976-77

The Bellslea was due for a facelift. My good friend Arthur Buchan and his mate put a new roof to the stand. (He is still waiting to be paid, but can be seen, to this day, doing jobs at the park.) It was a vital matter, getting the stand sorted out after the winter storms, or there would be no senior football played at Bellslea, at least that was the warning from the S.F.A.

The players all mucked in to put up a set of training lights, with borrowed parts made at the Toolies and Mitchell's. The lights were not good enough to play games under, but it was better than training under the street lights at the old hockey park. The young guns of today don't know they're living with the facilities now at Kessock Park. The shock news over that summer was Brian McCann submitting his resignation, after fourteen seasons with the Broch, saying football was taking up too much of his time. He said that, with training twice a week, the phone never stopping ringing on a Friday night and people stopping him in the street when all they wanted to talk about was football. It built up a lot of pressure. But, as the start of the season drew nearer, being the kind of guy he is, Brian was persuaded to return with George Malley as his assistant. Gibby Stephen's dodgy knee was playing up and it was with regret that he hung up his boots. His replacement was Allan Scott from Deveronvale and Ian McKay also arrived from East End. They would bolster the squad. The P & J wrote at that time, "It is still hard to credit that the Broch's attacking style in the last three seasons has not taken the league flag to Bellslea." But would the Broch's fantastic support get their reward in the new season?

Another milestone in football then was the recognition of Fraserburgh United, and in their first season, they just missed out on promotion. Broch Centre lost out in the final of the North of Scotland Cup with guys like John Stephen (Spike), Sandy Souter, Ian McKenzie (Zeek) and the Redburn boys, Ian and Jimmy Duthie all stepping up to the Juniors. I don't think you could take sixteen players from the amateur league these days and play in junior football. No disrespect to the amateurs of today, but football has changed.

The Broch fixed up glamour friendlies, at home to Motherwell and Airdrie. It made a change from Banks o' Dee every year. We lost 1-4 to Motherwell. They had guys like Jimmy O'Rourke (ex Hibs) Vic Davidson (ex Celtic) and Willie Pettigrew on display. Airdrie fielded a strong side as well and we lost 1-2 to them. The teams that day were:

Broch: Gray, Sharp, Watson, Duthie, Rogers, McKay, Fraser, McKenzie, Styles, Hunter, Bowie. Subs: Massie, Scott

Airdrie: McWilliams, Jonquin, Anderson, Black, March, Whiteford, Wilson, McVeigh, McCulloch, Walker, Clark. Subs: Colins, Cowan, Cairney.

A Rexy Hunter strike, against Huntly at the Bellslea, was enough to see us through to the 2nd round of the League Cup. Doubles from Hunter and Bowie the following Saturday made for an easy 6-0 win at home to Forres. Next up were Deveronvale in the 2nd round of the League Cup. The Broch left it late that day, with Hunter scoring the only goal of the game on 89 minutes. Then it was Caley, in the semi-final at Inverness on a Wednesday night, with only the diehard fans there. After an even first half, the Broch took the lead in 60 minutes through Hunter, but Penman made it 1-1 with a dodgy penalty. It was 1-1 after 90 mins, but Fraser had Broch 1-2 up in the second minute of extra time only for McIntosh to make it 2-2 and then score the winner in 112 mins. The final score was Caley 3, Broch 2, but the Broch got their revenge the following Saturday, beating Caley 2-1 at Bellslea with a double from Hunter. Keeper Charlie Gray was injured, so local lad Richard Burnett took his place. I wondered where Spicy was? A difficult Qualifying Cup tie lay ahead at Brora where D. McKay didn't take long to find the net. He put Brora 1-0 in front in 4 minutes and added a second just before half time. McKay made it 3-0, before McKenzie and Fraser scored for the Broch, to make the final score 3 – 2.

McCann was running the football side of things and he let the committee get on with other simple things like ordering a bus, but's it was not that simple. Picture this, the players standing outside the Bellslea Park on a cold dark morning, supposed to be to heading to Brora. Then Jimmy Brown remarked, "what time did you order the bus for, Dodie?"

"I never ordered it, you said you would do it." So, after some, "discussion," they phoned the bus company to find that all the buses were booked. As a last measure, it was recalled that Dodie's son's pop group, "The Power Vane," used the Bellslea to make a racket (I mean practice) They had a dormobile parked outside with all their equipment in it, so they emptied out the drums, speakers and guitars and told everyone to pile in, by the way, the dormobile was painted all over in flowers. I don't know what they must have thought, when they eventually arrived at their destination!

Aberdeen had asked for a friendly, to have a look at a few of Broch's young players. They said they would play a young side, but decided to give some first team players a game. They won 11 – 0 and the less said about that the better! Then a 4-0 defeat from our bogey side, Inverness Thistle, knocked us off the top of the league. A 4-2 win at Buckie, with Rexy Hunter hitting all the goals, was better. Brian Newlands was set to make a come back, after packing up in the summer, but it wasn't the same second time around. Jim Crawford was released from Aberdeen and went straight into the team v Elgin City, but it was a disappointing debut, which we lost 3-0.

Then came a lengthy spell of bad weather. We beat Forres at Mosset Park on Saturday 27th November and didn't play again until Dec 18th in a 1-1 draw v Lossiemouth at the Bellslea. Next it was Xmas derby time again and the first game at Recreation Park was played in arctic conditions. Peterhead won the toss and decided to kick with the wind. The Broch's defence held firm and turned around at half time with the score 0-0. After two minutes had gone in the second half, the Broch's Hunter made it 0-1 and Duthie added a second in 57 minutes, but Peterhead hit back with two goals in two minutes from Donald and McIntyre and an off the ball incident then saw McIntyre and Newlands sent off. McKay and Scott were certainly getting the hang of this derby thing (get into them) but Hunter had to leave the field after being kicked all over the shop. The Broch were well on top at this stage with Bowie running Rennie ragged until, with fifteen minutes to go, Rennie tipped a shot with his hand over the bar. Everybody in the crowd saw it except referee Cheyne. He consulted his linesman and then gave a penalty, McKenzie scoring with ease to make it 2-3. The Broch support went wild and not with joy, but the final score was Peterhead 2, Fraserburgh 3. There was still no love lost in this game, and a few windows of the supporter's bus were smashed on the way home, but, as the old Greeks used to say, "Let them hate, so long as they fear"

For the return on January 3rd, after a nice Hogmanay, the Bellslea was bursting at the seams, but what a let down. McIntyre put the visitors one up on 17 minutes, with Sievwright adding a second ten minutes later. It stayed like that till half-time and after the interval, it got worse, when McIntyre added a third. Back came the Broch and a superb shot from Hunter made it 1-3, but McIntyre then added a fourth to make it 1-4. Fraser and Sharp came on as substitutes and Fraser scored with his first touch for 2-4, but, with three minutes left, McIntyre added his fourth goal and Peterhead's fifth. The final score in a disappointing game was Fraserburgh 2, Peterhead 5. The teams that day were:

Fraserburgh: Gray, Cardno, Newlands, McKay, Roger, Duthie, McKenzie, Crawford, Hunter, Scott, Bowie. Subs: Fraser, Sharp

Peterhead: McHattie, Rennie, Smith, Pirie, Sievwright, Krukowski, Donald, Grant, McIntyre, O'Mara, Esslemont, Lawson .
Referee – L. Officer
A name missing from the Peterhead lines was former Broch star Jimmy Noble. It was obvious that he was out of favour, and not happy, so why didn't they just let him come home to the Bellslea where he belonged? Rexy Hunter was being tipped for Highland League Player of the Year, with headlines like "Rex Worth his Weight in Gold." With 23 goals that season, he wasn't a bad bet.

Three draws and two defeats, after the New Year, put the league beyond us. Then came a 5-0 win v the University in the Aberdeenshire Cup, but two goals in five minutes away to Keith in the semi-final meant we had only the Bell's Cup left to play for and we drew old foes Peterhead away. "Newman" put the home side 1-0 in the lead, but McKenzie made it 1-1 in the 77th minute with a penalty. The score, after 90 minutes, was 1-1, but then the home side failed to hit the net with four penalties, and, with the Broch scoring with two of theirs, it was away to Keith, on Saturday 21st May, for the final on a scorcher of a day. The Broch lifted the Bell's Cup again by defeating Keith 2-1. Crawford put Broch 0-1 up in 13 minutes and Fraser added a second, against the run of play, on 37 minutes, but Winton pulled one back for the home side in the 43rd minute. It was all Keith in the second half and it looked like an extra half hour when Duncan was tripped in the box. The referee, however, changed his mind and, after consulting a linesman, gave offside. The Broch held on, but only just, for a final score of Keith 1, Broch 2. Don't know how my old friend Sandy Stables would have taken that result!

Caley were champions,

P	W	D	L	F	A	PTS
30	21	4	5	80	31	46

with a disappointing 6th spot for the Broch,

30	13	8	9	71	45	34

while Forres collected the wooden spoon

30	2	4	24	34	113	8

It was off to Wembley then to watch Scotland v England, the old enemy. We'd fairly gone up in the world, flying down to London and staying in a hotel for two nights, instead of roughing it on the train. My good friends Peter and Sandy Cowe, who ran the Aberdeen supporters club, organised the trip. I'm sure there were a lot of guys out there who appreciated the super job they did. We put £2 a week away for it and saved for two years to cut the cost. All we had to go was turn up with our carry oot, nice one lads, but, even better, who could forget that afternoon's result of England 1, Scotland 2. I did manage to get on to the park after one of the policemen turned his back and that made up for a disappointing season.

Season 1977-78

As the eighties drew nearer, there were a few fresh faces, such as Alfie Crawford, Graeme Cruden and Graeme McDonald (pigeon) at pre-season training. With no youth system however, it was a matter of waiting your turn. Graeme McDonald and Graeme Cruden never really got a chance, so they decided to go back to amateur, but Alfie Crawford went on to play in the first team and scored a few goals on the way.

First up were Aberdeen, in Kenny Roger's testimonial, and what a turn up for the books, as the score ended 3-0 for the Broch. The headlines were, "McNeil's Red Army Routed." Fraser put the Broch 1-0 up in 18 minutes. Duthie made it 2-0 just after half time, with a surging run that left the Dons defenders in his wake, before sliding the ball past McLean. Then Hunter dispossessed Cooper, raced in on goal and tucked the ball in the net to make it 3-0, not a bad start. The teams were:

Broch: Gray, McKay, A. Crawford, McKenzie, Roger, Duthie, Massie, J. Crawford, Gammack, Hunter, Fraser, Bowie. Sub: McDonald

Aberdeen: McLean, Glennie, Mclelland, Smith, Gardiner, Cooper, Gibson, Rougvie, Davidson, Fleming, Campbell. Subs: Grant, McLeigh, Brown. Attendance - 900

A 2-0 win at the Bellslea v Peterhead in the League Cup followed, with goals from Hunter and McKenzie (pen) to set us up for an away tie at Christie Park v Huntly. The home side won that one 2-1, but a good 2-4 win at Forres in the Qualifying Cup, with Alfie Crawford on the mark, was some consolation. But then, oh no, would you believe it? We drew

Inverness Thistle away in the next round, but what a game it turned out to be. A.Crawford put the Broch 0-1 ahead in the 32nd minute, but Gibb made it 1-1 a minute later. Gibb scored again in the 42nd minute to make it 2 – 1, with Hunter equalising a minute after that. Gibb got his hat trick in the 52nd minute, to make the score 3 – 2, but, with time running out, Rogers made it 3-3 in the 89th minute. It was nice to see Kenny playing for the whole 90 minutes as, at Kingsmill, he usually had an early bath! The replay was a bore, with Thistle grinding out a 0-1 win. The only goal was scored by Ernie Drews. The Broch keeper, Charlie Gray, was taken to hospital with a fractured cheek bone, after clashing with Thistle centre half Bremner and after that he considered quitting the game. Rexy Hunter went in goal for the last 20 minutes and did well.

The Broch beat Rothes 1-2 the following week, with Freddie O'Brian replacing the injured Gray. Some good news arrived, that Jimmy Noble was on his was back to Bellslea. With Broch having no money to seal the deal, Arthur Buchan paid the transfer out of his own pocket. Jimmy made his debut in a 1-1 draw at the Bellslea v Inverness Thistle on the same day that Charlie Gray returned from injury. Saturday 10th December would be remembered as the "Battle of Dingwall." With Broch 1-3 in the lead, County fought back to win 5-4, with Kenny Roger and George Urquhart sent off. Then a tunnel bust up took place, with both sets of players getting involved. The ref, Sandy Roy, was then attacked by a County fan. It was just another Saturday in the Highland League. Hunter had put Broch 0-1 up, but Urquhart pulled County level at 1-1. Duthie, 24 & 30, made it 1-3. Broch, before Creany scored just before half time for 2-3. Sokolowski, Fleming and Nicolson added further goals for County, while Hunter got his hat trick to make the final score Ross Co 5 Broch 4. "Broch had too Many Santas," was the headline as Broch lost 0-3 in the Xmas derby at the Bellslea with Charlie Duncan starring for the visitors. Goals from O'Hara 2, and Christie, were all too easy for them and, with half the Broch team sporting beards, I could see where the, "Santas," idea came in. Before the return game, the Broch signed Alfie Smith from Peterhead. The tough tackling full back immediately made his debut, against his old club, and he wouldn't forget it in a hurry. The floodlights were on from the start, due to the poor light conditions, and it wasn't long before the home side took the lead, O'Hara making it 1-0 in the 3rd minute. Midway through the half, McKenzie made it 1-1 with a penalty, before Crawford punched a net bound shot over the bar and a further penalty was awarded. Gray saved O'Hara's spot kick and Donald then put the home side in the lead two minutes before the break. Peterhead then ran riot in the second half, with goals from Christie (2) O'Mara (2) and Duncan. The final score was Peterhead 7, Fraserburgh 1. Gray was carried off three minutes from time and Hunter went into goal. I had visions of Peterhead avenging their 10-0 defeat that day. The Broch fans disappeared like, "Sna' aff a dyke," as the goals rained in, but I stood there to the bitter end. Charlie Duncan loved every minute of that game. The teams that day were:

Peterhead: Cooper, Andrews, Rennie, Sievwright, Krukowski, Donald, Duncan, Hamilton, O'Hara. Christie. Subs: Lawson, Grant

Fraserburgh: Gray, McKay, Smith, J. Crawford, Rogers. Duthie, Noble, McKenzie, Hunter, A. Crawford, Bowie. Subs: Fraser, Massie.

Brian McCann was sensationally sacked for trying to strengthen his squad. The committee said there were no funds available, but the supporters club funded the signings of Alfie Smith and Jimmy Noble, much to the annoyance of the committee. McCann said "I will still give full support to Fraserburgh F.C. but from now on it will be from the terracing."

George Malley took charge of team matters for the Aberdeenshire Cup tie v Deveronvale. In an entertaining game, both keepers were in top form, Gray for the Broch

and a young man named Jim Leighton, for the Vale, who was on loan from Aberdeen. A 1-1 draw was just about right, with J. Crawford scoring for the Broch and Reid scoring for Vale. More shocks were in store before the replay, when it emerged that Rexy Hunter was on his way to Peterhead with a fee of £1,500 rumoured, but with the secrecy around the Bellslea then, we never knew. The next shock came when the Broch appointed Tommy McMillan, the former Aberdeen and Falkirk player, as our new team manager. In the replay against Vale, Duthie made it 1-0 in the 73rd minute and McKenzie scored to secure the game with a final score of the Broch 2, Vale 0. Huntly beat us 3-1 in the semi-final, with Bowie scoring a consolation goal for the Broch, but, with only one win, four draws and two defeats in the last seven league games, things didn't look good for the future. A 2-0 win against Peterhead in the Bell's Cup, with goals from Roger (33) and Bowie (51) saw us through to meet the Vale at Bellslea. This time however it was not to be, with Vale running out comfortable 0-3 winners. That was it for a very indifferent season. As they say, you can change your house, car, even the wife, but not your team. What would 1978-79 have in store?
The champions were Caley

P	W	D	L	F	A	PTS
30	23	3	3	85	40	49

with a disappointing 9th place in the table for the Broch,

| 30 | 9 | 6 | 15 | 55 | 65 | 24 |

while Forres again got the wooden spoon.

| 30 | 4 | 0 | 26 | 42 | 111 | 8 |

Season 1978-79

Former Aberdeen and Falkirk centre half Tommy McMillan made a shock return to Highland League football when he was appointed manager of Fraserburgh F.C. Tommy McMillan's contacts in football saw a change in policy, with a host of new faces at Bellslea. It was funny how money became available for him, though it had not been so for Brian McCann when the Broch were previously in need of new faces. Charlie Gray had gone and Ron McDonald took over in goal, while Ian Taylor, Billy Mitchell and Jim Oliver were also added to the squad. Oliver in particular was to become a fans' favourite.

After a comfortable 3-0 win at Deveronvale, we had a two leg game with Huntly, with the first leg at Christie Park, but what happened before we reached Huntly was unbelievable. On the way I looked out of the bus window and thought, "this is the road to Keith," so the committee folk, who were sitting at the front of the bus, were informed. Their answer was, "are we not playing Keith?" The Aberdeen lads were sitting in the Huntly dressing room, with half an hour to kick off, wondering what had they taken on in coming to the Broch. It was a Wednesday night, and, at that time, Huntly didn't have lights. We had made kick-off time, but only just, but the Broch took the lead on 17 mins and Gammack then added a second. New boy Mitchell made it 0-3 with a diving header, before Raffan (73) and Reid (85) minutes scored for Huntly to give them a chance at the Bellslea on Saturday. The final score was Huntly 2, Broch 3. At Bellslea, the Broch had the chance to put the game beyond Huntly, but Humble saved McKenzie's spot kick and, two minutes later, Reid scored for the visitors and made it 3-3 on aggregate. The second half belonged to the Broch, but we had to wait until the 83rd minute before Mitchell scored to put us into the semi-final. The teams were:

Fraserburgh: McDonald, Crawford, Smith, Gammack, Rogers, Duthie, Taylor (Oliver), McKenzie, Mitchell, Bruce, Bowie

Huntly: Humble, Raffan, Chalmers, Gerrard, Watson, Henderson, Buchan, Shearer, Reid, Cormie, Nicol.

The semi final was at McKessack Park against Rothes on a Wednesday night, but was another let down. An Allan header for Rothes (28th minute) was all that separated the teams and the game ended Rothes 1, Fraserburgh 0. Broch had Ally Christie as a trialist, but he did not sign, though Willie Donald, from Peterhead, put pen to paper. Willie's fame was more of the small ball, as he played cricket for Scotland.

The Qualifying Cup 1st round drew us away to non-leaguers Fort William. Goals from McKenzie, Taylor, Mitchell and Oliver, with Majec replying for Fort William, gave a final score of Fort William 1, the Broch 4. "Fort," had been trying to gain entry into the league for years and the Monday headlines were, "Fraserburgh to Support Fort Move," with Jimmy Brown commenting that he had been very impressed by their facilities and hospitality.

The events of the next few weeks however put Fraserburgh F.C. into sheer turmoil. It all started with comments, after a drink, from Tozy (John Duthie) which were passed on to manager McMillan. He then fined the player £30 and suspended him for a month. With a money-spinning Qualifying Cup tie looming, at home to Peterhead, the Broch committee did a u-turn, fining Duthie £60, but allowing him to play against Peterhead. McMillan then handed in his resignation and Ian Taylor followed. I think that, with the Broch having been all local for some years, it was sometimes a case of, "us and them," with the Aberdeen lads. Bobby Forsyth was appointed as manager before the Qualifying Cup tie.

I'm sure John Sievwright will remember this tie, as he scored with a cheeky back heeler, which he had been practising all season. Mitchell made it 1-1 to take the game back to Peterhead for a replay. A Lawson penalty there was all that separated the teams. Final score Peterhead 1, Fraserburgh 0. The teams were:

Peterhead: McHattie, Andrews, Rennie, Taylor, Sievwright, Krukowski, Christie, C. Duncan, McIntyre, Lawson, Hunter. Subs: Porter, Masson.

Fraserburgh: McDonald, Crawford, Smith, Gammack, Roger, G. Smith, McKenzie, Duthie, Mitchell, Donald, Bowie. Subs: Leys, Noble.

It looked like the end of the road for fans favourite, Jimmy (Sneaky) Noble, as a change of job made him unavailable. He would be sadly missed. Tommy McGuire came on loan from Aberdeen, and scored the winner in a 1-0 win over Ross County. Controversy surrounded the game as the Broch had fielded Neil Clark in goal, but County claimed he was still signed by Dundee Utd. They wanted the game replayed and their expenses for travelling refunded, "somebody give them their dummy back." The Broch were fined £250, but the result stood. A 2-1 defeat followed in the Xmas derby at Peterhead, with a young Brian Sim on the bench that day. Ian Duthie was on the bench up at Caley in a 4-1 defeat. Tozy was in the wars again, when he tried to break up a fight one Saturday night and the Press got the wrong end of the story, resulting in the headline, "Broch Player Goes Berserk." He was fined £10, but Ivor Lovegrove, another of the local characters, was up in court at the same time. He'd been up so many times, that the judge knew him by his first name. He was fined £5, so Tozy asked him how he managed to get off with a smaller fine than he had. Ivor's reply was, "I didn't go berserk".

A 0-0 draw with Elgin at Bellslea gave us a look at a Scottish legend, Jimmy Johnstone, even though he was maybe, "past his sell by date," by then, he still had the touches though. Our love affair continued with the Bell's Cup. We beat Peterhead 2-1, then Keith 1-0, after exta time, with Bowie netting the winner.

The final was at the Bellslea v Buckie Thistle. Oliver put the Broch 1 – 0 up in the 7th minute, but Cowie levelled the scores in the 20th minute. Cowie put Buckie in the lead in the 75th minute, but that was short-lived. Oliver scored his second goal in the 79th minute and the game went into extra time. Bowie then made it 3-2 in the 93rd minute and two more from Oliver and Donald made it 5-2, with another from Donald making it 6-2, to complete Buckie's collapse. That was five Bell's Cup wins in eight seasons. Spicy never got fed up telling anybody who wanted to listen about that game. Jim Oliver won the Supporters Club Player of the Year. After all their greetin', Ross County never won the league, they finished fifth and Keith were champions.

	P	W	D	L	F	A	PTS
Keith	30	21	6	3	67	25	48.
Broch	30	10	7	13	45	50	27
Lossie	30	3	4	23	24	109	10

Season 1979-80 (A Wind of Change Blows through the Bellslea.)

The Broch's appeal against the £250 fine (over the Neil Clark signing) was rejected, and there was another shock in store after an A.G.M. (In all my previous years of watching the Broch, I can never remember there having been an A.G.M.) The news was, "Broch Boardroom Shock," as Jimmy Brown and Doddie Gray were ousted from their positions, with Jimmy Adams put forward to take over as Chairman. Jimmy Adams was to give sterling service and he dug the Broch out of a few holes that they got themselves into. Furthermore, he became a well-respected official all over the Highland League and, better still, he was a "Real Broch Supporter." On a sad note, former Broch player Ally 'Pop' Fordyce passed away. He was only 35 and a real gentleman. He didn't drink, didn't smoke, and was a good, "all rounder," playing badminton, and cricket also, for Turriff. Jimmy Brown and Doddie Gray's appeal to the S.F.A, against their removal, was then rejected, so Jim Adams was officially the Broch's new Chairman. Jim Oliver was transferred to Montrose but in came Ian Sharp, Alex Crawford, Martin Buchan and Davy Robertson to bolster the squad.

Bertie Bowie was given a benefit match against Aberdeen. Bertie had scored more than two hundred goals, in eight seasons with the Broch, and had probably been the most exciting winger to grace the Highland League in that decade. A crowd of over 1,200 saw an exciting game with the Dons scraping through 2-3. D. Robertson had opened the scoring for the Broch only for McMaster to make it 1-1. J. Oliver put Broch 2-1 in front, but McMaster scored again, making it 2-2. McLeish then scored a late winner for a final score of Fraserburgh 2, Aberdeen 3. The teams that night were:

Fraserburgh: Clark, A. Crawford, Jim Gammack, Roger, Duthie, Donald, Buchan, Robertson, Mitchell, Bowie, Mennie, McKenzie.

Aberdeen: Leighton, Dorman, McLelland, Cooper, McLeish, Thomson, Davidson, McMaster, Morrison, A. Oliver, Bell, Angus. Sub: MacGuire.

A Davy Robertson double, against Deveronvale in the League Cup, saw us through to meet Huntly at Bellslea in the quarter-finals. It was that man Robertson again in that game, with another double, that saw us through to the semi-finals, against Buckie at Victoria Park, and what a night it turned out to be as this time the Broch were hit for six. A crowd of well over 1,000 saw Buckie go two up in the first fifteen minutes, with goals from Nicol and Christie. Donald pulled one back for the Broch, but then came disaster. Keeper Clark took a short goal kick to Crawford, but his return went over the keeper and rolled into the net to put Buckie 3-1 in front. Forbes then made it 4-1, two minutes before the interval. Mitchell made it 2-4 in 72 minutes and it was about that time I saw Spicy leave the dugout and head for the dressing room, to return stripped to go on. Who did he take off? Bertie Bowie! (not one of his better decisions.) Scott added a fifth and Adams made it six to add to our misery. The final score was Buckie 6, Fraserburgh 2.

A double header followed v Inverness Caley, both at the Bellslea in the next two weeks. In the first game we were soundly beaten 0-3, but won the Qualifying Cup tie 1-0, with a Dave Robertson goal. An away tie to non-league Fort

William followed and a shock came, when the Fort recorded their first win against the Broch, with a Conlin strike on 55 minutes. Final score Fort William 1, Fraserburgh 0.

The following Wednesday, we were away to Buckie in the league. I missed the bus, but my father gave me a lift to see if we could catch it. I saw it in the distance, so we flashed the lights to get the driver's attention and it finally stopped. I got a shock, when I got on as it was the service bus, so it was back to the car chase. We finally caught our own bus at the, "Broad Mile Stane," but my journey was wasted. The game was adandoned after 57 mins due to a floodlight failure with the score standing at 0-0.

By October 3rd, the Broch were lying 3rd bottom of the league with just three points from six games, but a 7-2 home win over Lossiemouth, with Willie Donald scoring four, lifted our spirits. The club then turned down a bid from Buckie Thistle for Bertie Bowie and by mid November, we had climbed up a couple of places in the league with a 2-0 win v Inverness Thistle and a convincing 4-0 over Ross County, with Davy Robertson getting a double.

The old regime v new regime, about who should be in charge at Bellslea, was still rumbling on. The S.F.A. didn't want to intervene in club business, but to everybody's surprise, after a, "clear the air meeting," Jimmy Brown and Doddie Gray finally agreed to go and a new chapter in the history of Fraserburgh F.C. opened. But let me say this, no matter what happens in the future, without Jimmy Brown and Jimmy McDonald there would have been no Fraserburgh F.C.

By mid December, the Broch were still fourth bottom of the league, having played seventeen games for just thirteen points, while, on the other hand, Fraserburgh United were sitting at the top of the Junior League. The Xmas derby at Bellslea was postponed, due to frost, and a 4-0 thumping at Peterhead didn't help matters. A 4-1 win in the Aberdeenshire Cup at home to Deveronvale, with Davy Robertson netting a hat-trick, gave us an away tie in the semis against Peterhead to look forward to, but a John Sievwright goal was enough to see the home side through. Final score Peterhead 1 Fraserburgh 0. The teams were:

Peterhead: McHattie, Rennie, Morgan, Taylor, Sievwright, Krukowski, Grant, Porter, Brown, Lawson, G. Taylor. Subs: Hunter, West

Fraserburgh: Clark, A. Crawford, J. Crawford, Gammack, Rogers, Duthie, Buchan, McKenzie, Robertson, Donald, Bowie. Subs: Sim, McLeary.

Broch's up and coming right back, Alec Crawford, was getting a few write-ups in the press as the best young defender in the league. Bobby Forsyth said, "He is one of the best signings I've made." Huntly were due at Bellslea on Saturday 22nd March, but never made it as they were stranded on the way in snow drifts four feet high. Sadly for Bobby Forsyth, his time was up. The Broch sacked him, but with no money during his time in charge, he hadn't been able to get many of the players that he wanted. The Broch opted to advertise for a manager, with Scottish league experience, but where would the money come from? Whoever it was, they wouldn't come to the Bellslea for buttons.

More disappointment followed, when we lost five out of our remaining six league games and drew the other. Alec Crawford won the Supporters Player of the Year and Keith were league champions.

	P	W	D	L	F	A	PTS
Keith	30	24	4	2	82	20	52
Broch (4th bottom)	30	7	7	16	39	53	21
Lossie (bottom)	30	2	6	22	21	85	10

FROM BELLSLEA TO BRORA THESE ARE MY HEROES

No time to shower for the players as they posed for a picture, mud and all they are pictured in the Bellslea boardroom in 1958 with the Qualifying Cup.

Almost the entire crowd had gathered for this photograph in 1966, the Broch did not have a large following during this era. The photograph features one of my first heroes Burnett Reid (fourth from left).

Very early on the 1970's the Broch had turned a corner, after some bad times in the 1960's, the team were starting to get some good results and moved ever closer to the top of the table.

A few new faces at the Club with Chairman Doddie Gray (far left) out of uniform, and known throughout the North East as the singing Chairman.

The Black and White Club was where the Supporters celebrated after another famous victory over Peterhead F.C.

The boys at Butlins, from the left back row, B Newlands, G Malley, C.J. Whyte and C Duncan. Front row from the left, M Barbour, B Strachan and B Third.

The Sands Bar was the first stop for the Broch Supporters before the last few steps to Recreation Park, the former home of Peterhead F.C.

Celebrating after the Bells Cup victory in 1977 over Keith at Kynoch Park. The Broch won 2 – 1 with goals from J Crawford and B Fraser.

The Broch side that lost the Qualifying Cup Final in 1969 over two legs, the first leg at the Bellslea saw the Broch go behind 3 - 1 to Nairn County, the second leg was a 1 - 1 draw.

The Broch squad with manager Brian McCann after winning the Aberdeenshire Cup on 27th March 1976, beating Huntly 3 – 1 with goals from D Mckenzie (2) and B Bowie.

Charlie Duncan in his playing days at the Broch is pictured with his fellow team mates and manager George Malley in the early 1980's.

The Broch squad pictured at Kingsmills Park, the home of Inverness Thistle the team who joined Inverness Caledonian to form the current Scottish League as Inverness Caledonian Thistle. I believe the ground is now a housing scheme.

FROM BELLSLEA TO BRORA THESE ARE MY HEROES

On the right of the photograph, Club Chairman at the time Gordon Chegwyn proudly holds the Highland League Cup in 2005, also in the picture Bobby Cowe (Director).

Jimmy (Bomber) Brown, without him there would be no Fraserburgh F.C. today, the work he did for the Club in the 1960's will always be remembered by me.

Club Chairman Jim Adams was very proud when his life's ambition was fulfilled as the Club won the Highland League in 2002.

Celebrations after winning the Qualifying Cup in 1996 at Christie Park,, Huntly. The Broch beat Keith 4 – 3 after extra-time, the goal scorers were P Keith, J Thomson, M McCafferty and J Geddes.

Celebrating the Highland League Cup victory in 2005 at Kynoch Park, Keith after a famous 4 – 1 victory over Cove Rangers, with goals from G Johnston, W West, M Stephen and S Main.

The last time the Qualifying Cup Final was ever played,
4th November 2006. The Broch won the final beating Keith F.C. 2 – 1 with goals from M Dickson and M Stephen

Kitted out for the occasion the management and players pose with the Highland League Trophy in 2002.

Chapter Four

The Eighties
(The Broch go Local Again)

As we headed into the eighties, there came a surprise concerning the post of Broch manager. The new man was to be George Adams, former Aberdeen, Partick Thistle and East Stirling player, then plying his trade at Buckie Thistle. Buckie however, weren't happy at him leaving, so they asked for compensation. Some crazy figures were mentioned, four and five figures to be precise, but we'll never know all of that side of things! George Adams was ready for the Broch, but was the Broch ready for him? The first thing he did was free Willie Donald, Alfie Smith, Gordon Mennie and Jim McLeary, and that was for starters. Kenny Rogers too was calling it a day after 14 years - they don't make them like that any more. Another shock was in store as John Duthie was put up for sale at his own request. A swap deal fell through with Buckie, but Allan Scott and Dave Oxley moved to the Bellslea with John Duthie going to Buckie. Adams wasn't wasting any time. He signed Chris Slavin, freed from Aberdeen, and two eighteen year olds on loan from the Dons, John Boyce and Allan Lyons. Grant Smith also arrived, from Deveronvale.

Pre-season training was no holiday either. Alec Crawford had been, "out," on the Friday night before training. Over the beach on Saturday he was seen with his head between his legs braying like a donkey, never again did he go out on a Friday night, before training. Jim Crawford was back all tanned and looking like a million dollars, till Adams got a hold of him. After an afternoon of sprinting up and down the big hill, most of the players were back at Bellslea. Jim, well he was taking all his time to walk up the stone stairs at the Promenade. That was the first few sessions, but what else had Mr Adams in store?

It was a strange line up for the League Cup tie at Princess Royal which the Broch drew 0-0. The team was: Clark, Slavin, Sim, Gammack, Crawford, Duthie, Boyce, McKenzie, Robertson, Lyons, Bowie. A Davy Robertson goal settled the replay, but Keith then knocked us out, winning 4-0 after a 0-0 draw at the Bellslea. A home tie against old foes Peterhead, in the Qualifying Cup at Bellslea, was up next. Martin Buchan put the Broch in front in the 10th minute, but Copland made it 1-1 in 16 minutes. Just after half time, with tension running high, the Broch were awarded a penalty, but McHattie saved the kick, then Martin Buchan slid in and was sent off for dangerous play. Charlie Barbour scored the winner on 70 minutes for a final score of Fraserburgh 1, Peterhead 2. The teams were:

Broch: Clark, A. Crawford, Sim, Gammack, J. Crawford, Duthie, Buchan, McKenzie, Robertson, Smith, Slavin.

Peterhead: McHattie, Rennie, D'Arcy, Taylor, Sievwright, Krukowski, Porter, Copland, Barbour, Lawson.

After the disappointing cup exit, it was back to league business, with another new arrival, Dave Oxley from Caley, at the Bellslea. By the first week in December, we were lying third in the table next to Buckie and Keith.

	P	W	D	L	F	A	PTS
Buckie	14	11	1	2	42	15	23
Keith	13	10	2	1	30	16	22
Broch	17	9	4	4	30	16	22

With a few games being called off, because of bad weather, the question of summer soccer returned to the fore, e.g. two games a week in August and September. There would be a close down of the season, in December, January, & February, Blah! Blah! Blah! Just get on with it!

Bertie Bowie had been on the bench for a few weeks, he was surely not one of Mr Adams' blue eyed boys just then, but a 3-1 win away to Huntly on January 25th, took the Broch to the top of the league for the first time in many a year. A real old fashioned cup tie then took place at Buckie, with Forbes scoring in 9 minutes and Kennedy in the 16th, to put Buckie 2-0 in front. Oxley made it 1-2 in the 17th minute and squared it at 2-2 in the 42nd minute. A minute later, C. Robertson had Buckie in front at 3-2, but Davy Robertson made it 3-3 in 60 minutes for it to finish 3-3. The replay was at the Bellslea the following week when the Broch took the lead for the first time in this cup tie. Charlie Duncan pulled Brian Sim down in the box in the 11th minute and Slavin converted the penalty. Grant Smith thought he had made it 2-0, but was ruled offside and Gordon Robertson then hit a 35 yard shot to make it 1-1. At full time, the tie was all square at 2-2. Rexy Hunter scored the winner on 114 minutes to make the final score, Fraserburgh 2 Buckie Thistle 3. The attendance had been 1,000 at Buckie, with another big crowd (of 1,050) at the Bellslea.

The pressure of being top of the league had begun to show. Three wins and two draws had the Broch just hanging on in there.

March 14th	P	W	D	L	F	A	PTS
Broch	24	13	6	5	41	24	32
Buckie	21	14	3	4	57	27	31

A Ray McIntosh hat-trick, away to Ross County, put a further spanner in the works with County winning 3-1. That same day Buckie lost 1-3 at home to Brora, but Keith were working away quietly and it all boiled down to the final day of the season. Buckie had to beat Keith and we had to beat Peterhead 5-0 for us to be crowned champions. Buckie drew 0-0 and yes, we beat Peterhead 5-0, through a Davy Robertson hat-trick, with Sim, and Adams the other scorers, but it was not enough. Robbo was like a dog that lost its

bone that Saturday afternoon, and he'd scored the best hat-trick I've seen at Bellslea for a long time. The game was so tense with rumours flying about what was happening at Buckie adding to the atmosphere, but it was not to be.
The league race finished:

	P	W	D	L	F	A	PTS
Keith	30	17	8	5	52	26	42
Broch	30	17	7	6	55	31	41
Forres (wooden spoon)	30	3	4	23	31	98	10

The Player of the Year was that night. As you can imagine, it was held in a sombre atmosphere. John Duthie and Neil Clark shared the award. Fort William failed by 11 votes to 5, in another bid to get Highland League status and Wick Academy lost out by 12 votes to 4.

On the Monday the paper headline read, "Broch Bombshell, Free transfer for Striker Bertie Bowie." A lot of Broch fans, including myself, didn't take too kindly to some of George Adams' decision. Too many of his boys made it a bit of, "us and them," and that was not what Fraserburgh FC was, or is, all about, but time would tell about all of that.

Season 1981-82

Before the season had even started, a row was brewing between the Broch and Buckie. George Adams made a bid for Alan Scott, but Buckie refused to accept the offer. Scott then threatened to hang up his boots if Buckie refused to let him go. Another new face in the squad was Neil Shand, on loan from Aberdeen FC, but there was also some sad news. Alec Crawford had been forced to hang up his boots after being carried off in the Xmas derby at Peterhead following a terrible tackle. Alec was only 23 and had been regarded as one of the most promising left backs in the league.

A 3-0 win at Peterhead was a great start to the season. New signing Ian Grant put Broch 0-1 up in 35 minutes and a double from Oxley sealed the result. The League Cup quarter-final was at Buckie where Robertson put the Broch 0-1 in front in 3 minutes, but, in the second half, Forbes made it 1-1 after 78 minutes and Nicol scored the winner with the last kick of the game for a final score of Buckie 2, Fraserburgh 1. The teams that day were:

Buckie: Wood, Thain, Ellis, Wilson, Forbes, Duncan, Thain, Paterson, L. Duncan, Robertson. Sub: Hunter

Fraserburgh: Clark, Slavin, Sim, Gammack, Slavin, Duthie, Shand, McKenzie, Robertson, Oxley, Grant.

A 2-0 win against Wick Academy in the Qualifying Cup, and an away tie to Fort William, gave us a great chance of making the draw for the Scottish Cup. I travelled on the team bus that day but found it strange. All the local boys went on the bus, but the Aberdeen lads got the train, and we picked them up in Inverness. That's the way things were done in those days. We won the game 2-0, with goals from Oxley and Adams, with Neil Clark saving a penalty when we were 1-0 in front. It was certainly not as easy as the result looked. After the game, I was standing in the Social Club at Fort William having a pint, when Tozy and Jim Crawford came in. They had just got their drinks in their hands when George Adams came in and roared "You and you, bus!" Then he pointed to me. "You as well, the bus leaves in two minutes!" I just laughed at him, as some of my mates had come up in the car so we stayed overnight in Fort William. It's a sad day when a player can't have a drink after a game!!

Mid October arrived and we were not doing well in the League, with just five wins, one draw and five games lost, not very impressive. Another row was brewing when an incident, after the Caley game, in the "Black and White" Social Club came to the knowledge of manager George Adams. He immediately put Tozy up for transfer, telling him he would never kick a ball for the Broch again. Hendry Gracie was the other player involved, so he was freed also and signed for Deveronvale. Tozy then joined Buckie Thistle in a swap deal for Alan Scott, so both parties were happy.

The draw for the Scottish Cup paired us with Clach. That was the last thing that both clubs wanted, but at least we were at home, though it turned out to be a shambles. The tie was due to be played on Saturday, December 12th, but it didn't take place till Wednesday December 30th with a 2 o'clock kick off. Prior to that it had been postponed five times, due to bad weather and, in addition to that, the Broch's goalkeeper couldn't get off work, if the tie took place before the Xmas period. He worked in a Bank and, with no other keeper on the club books, who knows what might have happened.

The tie finally got underway, and the Broch went 1-0 in front with a goal from Gibson in 10 minutes, but Duncan Shearer then hit one of the finest goals I've seen at Bellslea to make it 1-1. Gordon Beagrie then had the miss of a lifetime, lobbing the ball over the bar with the goal at his mercy. I won't repeat what I shouted in frustation at him that day! The game finished Fraserburgh 1 Clachnacudden 1. The teams were:

Fraserburgh: Clark, Scott, Sim, McKenzie, Slavin, Crawford, Adams, Oxley, Gibson, Beagrie, Grant. Sub: Shand

Clach: Arris, Flannigan, Dennison, Dingwall, Shearer, Cowie, Watt, Davidson, Kenny Masson, Stevenson.

Before the replay we had a derby game, at home to Peterhead, to take care of. As Peterhead took the field, they got their usual welcome, especially extended to Joe Harper, from the home support. The Broch took the lead in the first half through Grant, when he hit the top corner with a screamer, but Harper made it 1-1 in the 64th minute. Peterhead then thought they had taken the lead, but Scott raced in and hoofed the goal bound ball to safety. More drama unfolded when Adams was fouled and the referee gave a free kick. After consulting a linesman, changed his mind and gave a penalty only for Slavin's spot kick to trundle past the post. Beagrie then scored the winner in the 72nd minute. Final score Fraserburgh 2, Peterhead 1. It was a pity Beagrie hadn't saved that goal for Clach! The teams that day were:

Fraserburgh: Clark, Shand, Sim, Scott, Slavin, McKenzie, Adams, Beagrie, Grant, Oxley, Gibson. Sub: Robertson.

Peterhead: McHattie, Guyan, Rennie, Taylor, Krukowski, Harper, Paterson, Cormie, Barbour, Bain, Copland

Ref – R. Bissett, Inverness

More drama was to follow. The absence of Jim Crawford at the game was a mystery, till it emerged that he had failed to turn up for a training session. George Adams then dropped him for the Peterhead game and put him on the transfer list. It seemed to some of us that he wouldn't be happy until he got rid of all the local boys.

Grant Street Park, Inverness was unplayable, due to heavy snowfalls, followed by frost. The referee inspected it seven times and each time gave it the thumbs down. That's fourteen times that the cup tie had been postponed since the original fixture at the Bellslea. Four years previously, the same ref' had postponed the Cowdenbeath v Partick Thistle time fourteen times and that was for a 1st round tie! Clach then wanted to play the game on a Sunday, but the Broch said no, as four players refused to play because of religious beliefs, "honestly!"

It was tenth time lucky, when the game finally went ahead on Monday 11th October. Both teams knew what was at stake, an away tie to Albion Rovers and the winners of that tie would play at Ibrox. After a goal-less first half, Robertson put Broch 0-1 in front in 69 minutes and, on 83 minutes, Grant was sent off for kicking the ball away at a free kick, as he had already been booked. Three minutes later, Cowie headed home to make it 1-1. Nine minutes into extra time, Cowie put Clach in front, but the Broch fought back and Oxley made it 2-2. Davidson put Clach 3-2 in front in 110 minutes and that's how it ended. Final score Clach 3, Fraserburgh 2 (after extra time). Clach lost 1-0 to Albion Rovers, so it was Albion Rovers who went to Ibrox. A further game v Clach was played on the 11$^{th\ of}$ January, but the Broch didn't play again until the 30$^{th\ of}$ January when we lost 3-1 at Caley. We don't get many winters like that one now. Elgin City and Peterhead were both interested in signing Jim Crawford, but another young Don to arrive at Bellslea was George Middleton and Doug Davidson from Clach was to follow. It was getting so much like an Aberdeen select that, if you hadn't watched the Broch for a while and turned up at Bellslea, it would be hard to pick out a face that you knew.

An Oxley double was enough to see off Huntly in the 1st round of the Aberdeenshire Cup, which the Broch won 4-2 at home, but we couldn't seem to keep away from Buckie Thistle in those days! A 1-1 draw at the Bellslea followed in the 2nd round, but Davy Robertson scored a hat - trick in the replay for a final score of Buckie 1, Fraserburgh 4. That put us into the final against Aberdeen. I'm dead against Aberdeen being in that tournament, as it just makes a mockery of it. By the way, they won 4-0.

Buckie Thistle wanted George Adams back as manager. It was reported in the papers that the Broch wanted £30,000 in compensation if he went, but rumours were rife that he would have to take a pay cut. Jim Adams finally confirmed that George would still be manager next season. Brian Sim won the Supporters Club Player of the Year, which was presented to him by Mr Jimmy Brown. Dave Oxley was top goal scorer with 23 goals, but we were a disappointing 7th place in the league.
Caley finished the season as Champions.

	P	W	D	L	F	A	PTS
Caley	30	22	5	3	76	28	49
Broch	30	15	3	12	56	48	33
Lossiemouth	30	6	2	22	31	74	14

I'll say a final word about John Duthie (Tozy.) He left Buckie as he had started a new job with an Oil Company. He was one of the most whole-hearted characters to pull on a black and white shirt. One last story about him, before we move on, concerns a night out in Inverness with the team on the way home from Brora. The bus was leaving at midnight but one of the team and a supporter didn't make it, being away on an escapade involving a JCB digger. There was a large sized shovel full of bother about it all.However, some years later later, at Tozy's 40th birthday party, we all chipped in and bought him a model JCB mounted on a plaque. Another night, when we stopped at Forres, Tozy disappeared over a six feet wall and came back with a dozen cans of lager. They don't make characters like him any more. I wonder if George Adams will read these tales? Happy days George!

Then it was off to Spain for the World Cup, for three weeks, to watch Scotland, or put another way, one week of supporting Scotland and the rest of the time supporting whoever England were playing!

Season 1982-83

George Adams was at it again. He released Eddie Gammack and transfer listed Davie McKenzie for breaches of contract. There were then not many more of the local boys left for him get rid of! To fill the gap, he signed Colin Maver and called up Robert Gordon from the Youth set up. Then, on the eve of the new season, he dropped a final bombshell by resigning as Manager of Fraserburgh FC, for personal reasons. All that I can say was that it was, "different," having him in charge. The Broch wasted no time in appointing Allan Scott as player/manager.

An impressive 3-1 win at Huntly in the League Cup, followed by the same score away to Keith, meant a home tie with Elgin in the semi-finals. Blacklaw put Elgin into an early lead 0-1, before Grant (12) brought Broch level at 1-1. Armstrong then put Elgin 1-2 in front and there was no further scoring. Final score Fraserburgh 1 Elgin City 2. Elgin went on to berat Peterhead 4-3 in the final. It was a strange line up for the Broch that day: Clark, Middleton, Sim, Scott, Gordon, Mathers, McKenzie, Davidson, Gibson, Robertson, Grant. Since the departure of George Adams, Dave McKenzie had patched up his differences with the club. Non-leaguers Fort William were our first round opponents in the Qualifying Cup. A 5-0 win in that game set us up for a tricky away tie at Brora, but a double from Dave Jackson was enough to see the home side through to the next round. Final score Brora 2 Fraserburgh 0. The supporters Club donated £500 that season for new boots and socks for the Club. That was a lot of money in those days!

By mid November, we were fifth in the league, having played fourteen, won eight, drawn two and lost four, but then more bad news arrived. After just seventy seven days in the job, Alan Scott quit as Manager. He had been forced to stop playing on medical advice. A couple of George Adams' boys were wanting away as well, Dave Oxley and George Middleton having asked for a transfer.

A devastating 2-6 victory at Nairn lifted the gloom over the past couple of weeks. Joe Harper and John Fitzpatrick had been mentioned for the Manager's vacancy, but, as far as I was concerned, no more Aberdeen based Managers please! My old mate George Malley was keeping the manager's seat warm for the time being, ending the year with a 1-0 win at home in the Buchan Derby that lifted the gloom, with Oxley scoring the winner in the 69th minute. The teams were:

Fraserburgh: Clark, Young, Sim, Middleton, Gordon, Beagrie, McKenzie, Maver, Oxley, Robertson, Grant.

Peterhead: Clark, Rennie, Lawson, A. Smith, Taylor, Porter, McAllan, Morgan, Barbour, Smith, Taylor.

In the Broch line up that day was Jimmy Young, who went on to become a real Broch legend. I can pay him no bigger tribute than to say that, if your son ever played football, he should take a look at Jimmy Young. Well-respected in the Highland League, and what's more a topper of a guy. As I write, Jimmy is still at Bellslea keeping today's young guns in check.

On the 29th of January, the Broch went into second place with another 2-6 thumping of Forres at Mosset Park, transfer listed Dave Oxley hitting a hat-trick. He went on to sign for Nairn County, while Chris Slavin went off to Elgin. The Broch then called up Drewy Whyte from Rosehearty Thistle along with team mate Michael Yule. There followed a stormy Aberdeenshire Cup 1st round at Bellslea against Huntly, which the Broch won 2-1, Huntly finishing the match with nine men. We met Keith in the semi-final with a score of Keith 0, Fraserburgh 2 and the final was arranged to take place at Pittodrie against the Dons, when they could fit us in. When they finally did so, the score was Aberdeen 1, Fraserburgh 0. It's a pity Walt Disney didn't sponsor the Aberdeenshire Cup, because Aberdeen were making it something of a "Mickey Mouse," Trophy.

The new manager of the Broch was confirmed as George Malley, who would start re-building the team for the next season. Caley won the League again, having gone the whole season undefeated. The Broch played them at Telford Street in the last game of the season and were 2-0 up, but Caley fought back to make it 2-2. Late on in the game, Dave Robertson ran on to a through ball into the box and was upended there, Penalty! But what did the ref' give? A free kick outside the box. What a decision! I bet he couldn't sleep that night!

The headline in the paper on Monday was "Fraserburgh Axe Seven Players" and all were free to go. Doug Davidson, George Middleton, Ian Grant, Dave Gibson and Colin Maver (with Chris Slavin and Dave Oxley having already gone.)

Season 1983-84 (A New Era)

A young fan, with a bushy red head, by the name of Finlay Noble, started appearing at the Broch's games, home and away. He was sitting on the team bus the last season when the Broch played Clach in the Scottish Cup, having then taken the afternoon off school. George Adams gave him a stern look and said, "What are you doing here, you've your education to think of?" As everybody knows, Finlay is still with the club and is well known throughout the Highland League. Kenny Rogers came back to the Bellslea, as George Malley's assistant, and there was a return to the club for Rexy Hunter, "again." John and Gavin Fraser were to follow along with Alan West, all three of whom had been at Fraserburgh United. So it was back to basics with an all local policy. I just hoped it would work. Season tickets were £10 adults and £5 for boys and OAPs.

The season got off to a good start with a 2-1 win at home to Deveronvale, with goals from John Fraser and Dave Robertson. A point was then gained in a 1-1 draw at Caley, with new signing, Jimmy Cruise scoring. Jimmy came from the Falkirk area and was a real character. He could have sold ice to the Eskimos and sand to the Arabs anytime. Every time he scored a goal, he would shout "ZICO" (you know, the Brazilian star, not Jimmy).
A seven goal thriller at the Bellslea took place against Ross County, with two penalties missed in the course of the game. Robertson opened the scoring, then Clark saved a penalty from McQueen, but County scored on the stroke of half time to make it 1-1. Hunter put the Broch in front at 2-1, before McQueen made it 2-2 and Jappy put County in front for the first time at 2-3. Robertson was then tripped in the box, and took the spot kick himself, but Ure made a fine save. West made it 3-3 and Robertson redeemed himself by scoring the winner for a final score of Fraserburgh 4, Ross County 3. The teams were:

Fraserburgh: Clark, Watt, Sim, Young, Gordon, Whyte, G. Fraser, Cruise, Hunter, Robertson, West.

Ross County: Ure, McLean, Steven, Urquhart, Lemmon, C. Robertson, McKay, Allan, McQueen, Jappy, Taylor.

It was early days, but we were sitting equal at the top of the league with Keith on 10 points apiece, having drawn

Fort William at home in the Qualifying Cup again. Goals from Hunter, and West (penalty) put us through 2-0. The next game must have provided the shock of the quarter finals! It finished Ross County 0, Fraserburgh 3, with goals from "Robbo" (Davy Robertson) and a double from Cruise. I couldn't believe we were in the Scottish Cup again. Team spirit had carried us through, "WELL DONE LADS."

We lost 1-0 at Elgin in a disappointing league game, then discovered we were drawn away to East Stirling in the Scottish Cup, not a very glamorous tie! Unfortunately, Dave McKenzie was hanging up his boots then, at the tender age of 29. He was off to America through his work, but as one door closed, another opened. In a shock move, Charlie Duncan was on his way to the Bellslea, in what must have been the best signing in years. He was real quality, and, like the saying goes, "the rest is history." Crowds were slipping however, with just over 100 watching the 3-2 victory over Brora. Takings were £65, but expenses, for referee and linesman came to £45. The Herald asked, "Does Fraserburgh Deserve a Team?" Charlie Duncan made his debut in a 4-1 win over Lossiemouth, with goals from Robbo (2), Hunter and Whyte.

Referees had been complaining about matches that were finishing in near darkness in December, so it was decided to bring the winter kick-offs forward, to 1.30. It just showed how far the Highland League has come these days, with everybody having floodlights now. Most fans today just take it for granted.

But, back with the fixture list, just imagine this, the Broch at home to Buckie and 3-1 down, with only twenty minutes to go. Sim, with a penalty in the 71st minute, and West then scored to make it 3-3. Robertson scored twice, for 5-3 before Smith scored for Buckie for a final score of Fraserburgh 5, Buckie 4, real end to end stuff. Another memorable game got a match report of, "Buchan derby halted as hypothermia hits Broch player." Peterhead led 0-2 at half-time, at the Bellslea that day, when Broch player Michael Yule was taken to the Broch hospital for a check up. Other players were complaining as well and referee Charlie McBeath was so cold he couldn't hold his cup of tea, so he had little alternative but to abandon the game, with the score at Fraserburgh 0, Peterhead 2. The scorers for Peterhead were G. Taylor and K. Walker. At Recreation Park the following week, Peterhead collected the points with a 1-0 win, following a Cruickshank goal six minutes before half time.

So to the game we'd been waiting for, East Stirling v Fraserburgh in the second round of the Scottish Cup. There were no Supporters Club buses in those days, so I ran a twenty two seater bus to the game with only the real die-hard Broch supporters there. Shire took the lead in 6 minutes through Meechan and Gibson added a second in the 39th minute. The Broch then came right back into the game, when Robertson slammed the ball past Tulloch to make it 2-1. But, with the Broch pushing forward for the equaliser, Shire broke away and Wilson made it 3-1 in the 84th minute. Final score East Stirling 3, Fraserburgh 1. The teams that day were:

East Stirling: Tulloch, Hamilton, Steen, Meakin, Rennie, Steel, McIntosh, Buchanan, Gibson, Wilson, Wylde. Subs: : Doig, Durrant.

Fraserburgh: Clark, Young, Sim, Yule, Davidson, Duncan, Cruse, Whyte, Hunter, Robertson, Gordon. Subs: J. Fraser, G. Fraser

Referee – C C Sinclair, Forfar   Crowd - 361 Receipts - £202.40.

That was it in the cup for another year, but George Malley went on strengthening the team. He gave a debut to 16 year old Graeme Catto in a 1-1 draw at home to Nairn County and brought in Ian Adams from Fraserburgh United as trialist to have a look at him for next season.

By mid February we were 7th in the league table:

P	W	D	L	F	A	PTS
23	9	4	10	44	49	31

Keith knocked us out of the Aberdeenshire Cup 2-0 at Kynoch Park, my namesake, Charlie Barbour, scoring on his debut. Then a battling 2-2 performance at Bellslea with Caley saw Charlie Duncan scoring twice from the penalty spot. The leading scorers in the league at that point were:

W. Urquhart (Caley)	22
D. Simpson (Nairn)	19
D. Robertson (Fraserburgh)	16
S. Pirie (Deveronvale)	15
H. French (Keith)	13
G. Stephen (Buckie)	13
S. Baird (Huntly)	12
M. McIntosh (Caley)	12
A. Duff (Ross. Co.)	12
J. Bain (Peterhead)	12

The replayed derby, after the abandoned game at the Bellslea, ended 1-1, with Cruise scoring for the Broch. Sievwright equalised for the visitors, who finished the game with nine men when Walker was sent off, and a young John Morgan was stretchered off with a suspected broken leg. This was the second season that 3 points were awarded for a win. Caley were champions and the Broch were eighth in the table.

	P	W	D	L	F	A	PTS
Caley	30	21	5	4	85	28	68
Broch	30	11	7	12	55	55	40
Lossie (wooden spoon)	30	6	4	20	26	82	22

With an all local policy now, though with no money to help rebuild, Georgie Malley had done alright in his first season in charge. So we looked with some confidence to next season.
A wee look at how the amateurs were doing, before we move on to the next session.

	P	W	D	PTS
Sandhaven	15	10	3	23
St. Drostans	16	10	3	23
Rosehearty	13	9	2	20
Redburn	13	9	1	19
Invercairn	15	9	1	19
Easthaven	15	5	4	14
Broch Centre	17	5	3	13
St. Combs	16	5	1	11
Social Club	16	2	1	5
Albion	14	1	1	3

They were changed days, with no Pub names appearing in the League.

Season 1984-85 (New Beginnings)

With all of the Aberdeen based players departed and back to an all local policy, the Broch could move on. There had been just one new signing, Gogs Taylor from Peterhead. Highland League football however, was about to change further, with sponsor's names appearing on the shirts for the first time. The Broch had a new strip, white with a thin black pin stripe and, "Station Hotel," in red letters on the front. Fraser Corbett, the hotel owner, supplied the strip. The Broch used to go back to the Station Hotel after their games then for soup and sandwiches.

A 3 - 1 win at home to Huntly was followed by a 0-2 win at Peterhead. Two goals in the first five minutes by Dave Robertson booked a League Cup semi-final place. Walker of Peterhead was sent off that day, for protesting about a penalty, which Charlie Duncan missed. Forres Mechanics 0 Fraserburgh 0 was the score in the semi-final, so it was back to the Bellslea for the replay on Wednesday August 29th with a six o'clock kick off. A Ronnie Dunbar goal 8 minutes from time was all that separated the teams. The final score was Fraserburgh 0, Forres Mechanics 1. The referee halted the match so they could blow up the matchball after the original matchball had mysteriously disappeared, "SO WHAT'S NEW?" The teams that night were:

Fraserburgh: Clark, Young, Sim, Thomson, Roger, Catto, Cruise, West, Robertson, Duncan, Taylor. Subs: Hunter, Whyte

Forres: Arris, Walker, Winton, McIntosh, Valentine, Lee, Rodgers, Fraser, Dunbar, McCulloch, Cameron.

Kenny Rogers had dug out his boots again and had been outstanding in the last few games. Another new face in the lineup was Brian Thomson (Lugs) who later became a real Highland League legend, scoring goals galore with that famous left peg.

Defeats at the hands of Brora (H) 2-3 Buckie (A) 3-0 Rothes (H) 1-2 in the league didn't make good reading, but it was only September, though we had played Huntly three times. The League Cup tie was won 3-1, the league game 2 - 1 and then we were drawn at home to them in the Qualifying Cup. Two penalties from Brian Sim (39, 58 minutes) and a glorious 20 yard shot from Charlie Duncan were enough to see us into the next round on a final score of Fraserburgh 3, Huntly 1. It was Ross County at Bellslea in the next round. A comfortable 3-0 win meant we were just ninety minutes away from the Scottish Cup. You can't ask for anything more than three home draws. We faced Inverness Caley in the quarter final of the League Cup, but it wasn't the Broch's day, with a final score of Fraserburgh 1, Inverness Caley 6. The Broch's scorer was Sim, with a penalty. After that result, George Malley was sacked, and the Club was back in turmoil again. At that rate, no one would want the appointment. George McRae took the training meantime, but what was that all about?

The Broch turned to Brian McCann as manager again, but, with his work commitments, I didn't think it was the right move, as you can't turn the clock back. We were third bottom of the league by the end of October and, alas, Brian only lasted four weeks and then resigned. His record was three wins and one loss.

The next appointment was no real surprise. It was Charlie Duncan, and, as I said, "the rest, was history!" "Cheekie Charlie," or "Dirty Duncan," was to shake the Bellslea to its foundations and things would never be the same again. It would be Charlie's way or nothing! On Saturday November 24th, Charlie's first game, as manager, was at Mosset Park, Forres, which the Broch lost by two goals to one. A few weeks later, an event occurred which was to change the way I saw Highland League football. I got a phone call from Charlie asking if I would like to join the backroom staff and help with the kit, so I packed away the black and white scarf and accepted the post. What more could I ask for than watching the club heroes at first hand!

My first game with the team was away to Ross County. It was strange being in the dressing room at half past two instead of sitting in the pub having a pint. We beat Ross County 2-3 that day. Taylor put us 0-1 in front, then Jackson hit a double to put the home side in front. The Broch hit back with goals from Brian Thomson (83 & 88 minutes) to win 2-3. After a goalless game at Peterhead, the return was not much better. "Gogsy," Taylor and Brian Sim were relegated to the bench, as they were just back from a sunshine break. Nat Porter scored the only goal, to make it Fraserburgh 0 Peterhead 1. The teams that day were:

Fraserburgh: Clark, Whyte, Catto, Young, Gordon, Beagrie, Cruise, Duncan, Robertson, Thomson, West.

Peterhead: J. Buchan, A. Buchan, Taylor, Bell, Sievwright, Hamilton, Porter, Duncan, Cruickshank, Wilson, Hendry.
On Saturday 29th December, the Broch were fifth bottom of the league.

P	W	D	L	F	A	PTS
20	7	3	10	23	34	24

An exciting 4-4 draw with Buckie at Bellslea seemed just like the old days. Cruise made it 4-3 in the 90th minute, but Buckie hit back through Stephen (91minutes) to square matters. The Broch then won 5-0 away to the University in the Aberdeenshire Cup 1st round. Charlie Duncan scored the winner in a 1-0 win over Deveronvale at the Bellslea, which set us up for a final at Buckie, but, again, it wasn't to be with the final score Buckie Thistle 3, Fraserburgh 0. The season couldn't come to an end quickly enough with three defeats in the last three games. Keith were league champions.

	P	W	D	L	F	A	PTS
Keith	30	19	6	5	70	36	63
Broch	30	10	5	15	39	54	35
(4th bottom)							
Lossie (bottom)	30	5	3	22	33	83	18

Jimmy Young was the Supporters Club Player of the Year.

Season 1985-86

There was joy at last for Fort William as they were finally admitted to the Highland League, which took the number of teams to seventeen. The voting was 9 votes for and 6 against. R.B. Farquhar sponsored the League to the tune of £25,000. It would therefore be known as the R.B. Farquhar Highland League. At the start of the new season, however we were down to the bare minimum of players. Charlie took back Kenny Roger and signed Doug Ellis along with a young lad from Strichen with a big heart, John Thomson (Tossil), who, later on, was to skipper the Broch. Another young lad to join the Bellslea babes at that time was John Chalmers from Rosehearty Thistle.

In the League Cup, Keith were leading 0-1 at Bellslea when Dave Robertson crashed in the equaliser to make the score 1-1, though we lost the replay 3-2 after extra time. A Robertson hat-trick at Brora set us up nicely for the Qualifying Cup against Charlie's old team, Inverness Thistle, at Kingsmills. We drew 1 – 1, but Thistle won the replay 0-1. At the start of November, we were ninth in the league.

FROM BELLSLEA TO BRORA THESE ARE MY HEROES

P	W	D	L	F	A	PTS
13	5	2	6	21	19	17

In the derby at Xmas, Broch had to play for 56 minutes with ten men after player/manager Charlie Duncan was sent off. Guyan was pulled down in the box, but Clark saved Burke's spot kick. Broch went on to have Ellis, Sim, Roger and Robertson booked. Guyan netted the winner, to make the final score Peterhead 1, Fraserburgh 0. The teams were:

Peterhead: Buchan, Walker, Donaldson, A. Buchan, Sievwright, Bell, Porter, Guyan, Luch, Burke, Fraser.

Fraserburgh: Clark, Gordon, Sim, Young, Roger, Chalmers, Ellis, Duncan, Robertson, Cruise, B. Thomson.

Winter weather was setting in, so we didn't have a game for three weeks. Two wins and two draws followed and we thought we had turned the corner, but a 3-6 defeat at Inverness Thistle took us back down to earth. Another young gun to make his debut that day was Richard Cheyne - we almost lost him in the dubs. The Rothes v Caley cup tie was postponed three Saturdays on the trot at snow bound McKessock Park. Keith then ran riot and beat us 5-1 in the Aberdeenshire Cup. Manager Duncan commented that we had played better in this game than we had when we lost 3-2 after extra time, "controversial to say the least," but that's Charlie! The last five league games were lost, with us never scoring a goal and conceding 12, including 5 at Caley. What an end to the season we had, losing 0-1 to Peterhead at the Bellslea, with Robbo heading for an early bath. Robert Gordon won the Player of the Year. Forres were champions while Broch were 4th bottom.

	P	W	D	L	F	A	PTS
Forres	32	22	6	4	77	27	72
Broch	32	8	6	18	38	63	30
Vale (wooden spoon)	32	4	10	18	31	65	22

Season 1986-87

"Highland, "Yes," for Cove."

A new chapter in Highland League arrived as Cove Rangers were admitted to take the league to eighteen teams. Over the next two decades, there would be no love lost between the Broch and Cove, and would you believe it, we were drawn at home to them in the preliminary round of the League Cup at the Bellslea. I've never seen so many players sitting in the stand with blazers on. It was like a row of crows sitting on a telephone wire! Before the season started, we said goodbye to three players, Andrew Whyte, Gordon Taylor and Jimmy, "Zico," Cruise, who were stepping down to the Juniors.. Davy Robertson was suspended for five games and Jimmy Young was getting married, so we called in Alex MacIntyre from the Youth Centre. Another new signing, Ronnie Smith, was to give sterling service for the Broch.

With a depleted squad, we opened the season with an historic League Cup game v Cove Rangers at Bellslea. The game ended all square at 1-1. Cove took the lead through Wallace (38minutes) but Ronnie Smith equalised for Broch (59minutes). The teams were:

Fraserburgh: Clark, A.Thomson, Catto, Gordon, Yule, Chalmers, McIntyre, Duncan, Smith, B.Thomson, West. Subs: Keith, Simpson

Cove: Beckett, McCombie, Watson, Massie, Garner, Selbie, Johnston, Paterson, Wallace, Leiper, Blacklaw. Subs: Smith, Kennedy

Ref – I. Skene, Aberdeen

We had three Thomsons playing for Broch then, John, Brian and Alan, none of them related. The latter was born in the Motherwell area, but his parents were Brochers. He had the nickname, "Dashin." This was based on a story that he was (allegedly) chatting up a young lady one Saturday night and said, "my, you look dashing tonight," so the name stuck!

The replay with Cove at Allan Park was on the Monday night. A crowd of 900 turned up to see an exciting game. The Broch took the lead in 14 minutes with a fine goal by Brian Thomson, but it was all square two minutes later through Leiper. The Broch were still reeling when Gary Clark made it 2-1 for the home side two minutes later, and Johnston secured the tie with a goal in 79 minutes. The final score was Cove Rangers 3 Fraserburgh 1. There was no luck in the Qualifying Cup, as we had the long journey to Wick, though the Broch secured a 1-2 win in a scrappy game there, with Davie Robertson netting the winner. Mosset Park, Forres was up next in the quarter finals of the Qualifying Cup, but it was a disaster. Davidson put the home side one up, in three minutes, from the penalty spot. Sim made it 1-1 in the 15th minute, but a Jimmy Young o.g. and two late strikes put paid to our Scottish Cup hopes with a final score of Forres 4, Fraserburgh 1.

The start of December saw the Broch sixth bottom of the table, with five wins and three draws. Ross County were bottom of the league with only two wins out of eighteen games. Broch 1, Fort William 2 and Broch 0 Rothes 1, didn't make good reading before the Xmas derbies. We lost the first, at Peterhead, 2-0 to end the year on a disappointing note. With a 1.30pm kick off for the return game, we fell behind early on, Loch puting the visitors ahead. B. Thomson then made it 1-1, but Peterhead regained the advantage through Donaldson in the 41st minute to make the half time score Broch 1, Peterhead 2. It stayed that way, despite the Broch being on top for most of the second half. The teams that day were:

Fraserburgh: Clark, Young, Sim, Gordon, A.Thomson, Ellis, J. Thomson, Duncan, West, B. Thomson, Catto. Subs: Robertson, Yule

Peterhead: Buchan, Wilson, Donaldson, Jopp, Sievwright, Bell, Guyan, Walker, Loch, Bain, Burke. Subs: Cameron, Porter

Ref – L. J. Officer

It was with deep regret the death of Jimmy Brown was announced at that time. He would be remembered for how he saved the Broch from disappearing into oblivion and he would be sadly missed.

Elgin City were sniffing around the Broch trying to sign Brian Thomson, but the club's asking price of £3,000 kept them at bay. We got our revenge at Cove with a 1-2 win in the Aberdeenshire Cup, Ellis and Brian Thomson being the scorers, but we lost to Peterhead in the semi-final. Fort William completed the league double over us, with a 2-0 win at Claggan Park, and our final game of the season was a 1-3 defeat at home to Buckie, where a young lad named Paul Keith, came on as a' sub', and made a good impression with his strong running. It was arranged that Neil Clark, Broch's long-serving keeper, would get a benefit match against Dundee (the Broch lost the game 2-3.) Alan Thomson was the Supporters' Player of the Year.

The news item grabbing the headlines at the end of that season was, "Highland Clubs prepare for Split Decision." Thirteen Clubs were in favour and four were for the status quo. The Broch threatened to pull out of the Highland League if there was to be a split, but the 9-7 vote at Elgin against reconstruction threw the idea out of the door. No Broch or Deveronvale representatives turned up at that meeting.

	P	W	D	L	F	A	PTS
Inverness Thistle	34	27	6	1	96	30	87
Fraserburgh	34	9	5	20	48	63	32
(6th bottom)							
Ross County	34	5	3	26	31	92	18
(wooden spoon)							

Season 1987-88

After all the unrest at the end of the season, it was back to seventeen home games and seventeen away games in the

Highland League. Alec Cormack, a former Deveronvale player, was the only new signing who arrived. There were no big names in the pre-season build up games either. Turriff United, Deveronside and Buchanhaven Hearts were the opposition.

Gary Whyte of Buckie Thistle scored four goals in a 0-5 demolition of the Broch, at Bellslea, in the first league game. We then drew 1-1 with Huntly in the 1st round of the League Cup at the Bellslea, but a Brian Thomson hat-trick then saw us through 2-3 to the next round. Thomson also hit the winner from the penalty spot, at home to Lossiemouth, in the 2nd round. We were no match for Buckie Thistle in the semi-final however, losing 1-4, with that man Whyte scoring another two. By that time only five Highland League clubs, Cove, Huntly, Fort William, Lossiemouth and Broch, didn't have a flood lighting system. Our semi-final against Buckie had a 6.15pm kick off. I can't imagine that happening in this day and age.

There was no time for feeling sorry for ourselves though, as we next had Wick Academy away in the Qualifying Cup 1st round. A 1-3 win at Wick brought another tricky tie away to Lossiemouth. The week before, we beat Keith 1-0 in the league at Bellslea. You would have to have been in the dressing room at ten to five, this squad of players were starting to believe in themselves. So it was on to Lossie in the Cup. It was to be the final chapter in Kenny Roger's football career, as the Broch had signed John Duthie, "Butcher," for centre half (he was no a bad singer at the back of the bus as well!) When the game got under way, a Doug Ellis strike and a Dave Robertson double saw us through 0-3 and then the draw was kinder to us, with Forres Mechanics at home in the quarter final. Alec Cormack was the hero, with a chip cum shot in 29 minutes, but after that it was backs to the wall. If you've seen the film, "The Alamo," that's what it was like, but we held on for a final score of Fraserburgh 1, Forres Mechanics 0. The teams for that game were:

Fraserburgh: Clark, A. Thomson, Sim, Young, Duthie, Cormack, J. Thomson, Ellis, Robertson, B. Thomson, Gordon

Forres: Gray, Walker, N. Rodger, Forsyth, McKay, Lee, G.Rodger, Fraser, Dunbar, Winton.

Ref – P. J. Peace, West Calder.

We came back down to earth in the next game with a score of Elgin City 5 Fraserburgh 0, but then it was up against Keith, at the Bellslea in the cup semi–final, and what a marathon it was. John Thomson put us 1-0 in front, but a late strike, in 85 mins through Armstrong, earned Keith a replay. There, Broch took the lead in 13 mins through Smith, only for Keith to make it 1-1 from a Barbour free kick, taking the tie to extra time. Nerves were getting the better of me, so I went into the dressing room for the last 10 mins of extra time to find something to do, but even that extra period couldn't separate the teams. Would it be third time lucky at Princess Royal Park for the replay? Robertson put the Broch in front there, lobbing keeper Thain from 18 yards, but then disaster struck, when Keith were awarded a penalty though Clark guessed right and saved Barbour's spot kick. John Thomson then doubled our lead with a wonder goal and the final score was Fraserburgh 2 Keith 0. What a feeling at that final whistle, the Broch in a Qualifying Cup Final, Wow!! The semi-final teams were:

Fraserburgh: Clark, A. Thomson, Sim, Young, Duthie, Ellis, J. Thomson, Ccormack, Robertson, B. Thomson, Chalmers.

Keith: Thain, McKay, Girling, Masson, Forbes, Strachan, Maver, Armstrong, Barbour, Yeats, Walker

Ref – J. McKinnon, Mid Calder   Att –   580 (mostly Brochers)

In the league, things could only get better. A 1-2 win came at Cove, with Doug Ellis hitting the winner, but we were still lingering in fifth bottom place, having played twelve games for only thirteen points. Forres got their revenge over us, with a 0-3 win at the Bellslea. In the cup final it was to be Caley, at Elgin. The media attention was great, with the players lapping it up and the town buzzing. It was estimated that over 1000 supporters would be making the trip, but, come the big day my stomach was in knots and I wasn't even playing, heaven knows what the players were like. When we went out at five to three, the ground erupted, in a sea of black and white, a reception that made the hairs on the back of your neck stand up!!

Caley struck first through Billy Urquhart in 24minutes, but after that they had to defend really well as the Broch threw everything at them. Our joy, when Dave Robertson headed home, was short-lived, for the flag was up for offside. Polworth secured the Cup for Caley, with a further goal in the 90th minute making the final score Fraserburgh 0, Caley 2, but what a great experience for the Broch players and supporters. The teams contesting that final were:

Fraserburgh: Clark, A. Thomson, Sim, Young, Duthie, Ellis, J. Thomson, Cormack, Robertson, Thomson, Chalmers (Gordon), Duncan

Caley: Morrison, Davidson, Mann, Hercher, Summers, Bellshaw, Doherty, Lisle, Urquhart, Duff, Robertson
Ref – J. Cumming, Carluke

The cup final blues continued through the following games, with the Broch 1, Keith 5 and the Broch 0, Caley 6. What had gone wrong? Then, up at Buckie a week leter, Dave Robertson hit a 30 yard shot into the bottom corner but there was a hole in the net and the ball hit the advertising board and bounced back into play. The referee initially gave the goal, but the Buckie players protested and he gave a goal kick! Justice was done, however, when Doug Ellis hit the winner. Mr G. Gunn was the referee and that was not one of his better decisions! Brian Thomson went on a week's trial with Dundee United, but apparently did not impress Jim McLean enough to sign him. We then drew St Johnstone at home in the Scottish Cup. Peterhead came out on top in the Xmas derbies winning 1-0 and 2-3.

I had a more important fixture than these. My daughter Joanne was born on January 1st at 1.40 in the morning. I always tell her it was the same day we lost 1-0 to Peterhead!

A cloud burst, before the kick-off of the Scottish Cup tie v St Johnstone, nearly put the game in danger, and kept the crowd down. Maskery gave the Saints an early lead in 7 minutes, but J. Thomson made it 1-1 in the 14th minute. Watters made it 1-2 in the 53rd minute, then Brian Thomson hit a free kick from 25 yards. If it was on television it would have been the goal of the season, I don't know why the Saints keeper even bothered trying to save it. A minute later however Alec Cormack tried a pass back only for Johnstone to score easily and make it 2-3. Johnstone in 74 and Powell in 86 minutes made it 2-5 and that was how it finished. The teams were:

Fraserburgh: Clark, Cormack, Sim, Young, A. Thomson, Ellis, J. Thomson, Duncan, Beagrie, B. Thomson, Chalmers. Sub: Catto

St Johnstone: Balavage, Thompson, McVicar, Barrow, McKillop, Johnston, Thompson, Coyle, Maskery, Watters, Heddle

Ref – N. Williamson, Renfrew   Att - 1500.

Other cup scores that day were: Buckie Thistle 2, East Stirling 3 and Stranraer 6, Keith 2.

Speculation surrounded Broch striker Brian Thomson, as a mystery club were at the centre of a transfer rumour. He had been at Dundee Utd for a week, but it was Motherwell who nipped in and signed him. After a 0-0 draw with Huntly at the Bellslea in the Aberdeenshire Cup 1st round, the Broch won away, 0-1, with the headline reading, "Broch Find a New Local Hero." Keith McCredie was the scorer of the winner, and he was just one of a few promising youngsters waiting in the wings.

Peterhead certainly had the Indian sign over us with their third win of the season, 0-1 in the semi-final of the Aberdeenshire Cup, with Jim Guyan scoring. The season was drawing to a close and we were still among the bottom

six in the table. We lost to Forres at Borough Briggs, because their ground was closed for an extension to be made. It was not all bad news however, as the Broch received £1710, for being runners up in the Qualifying Cup. Neil Clark was moving on to become Deveronvale's new manager, and we wished him well. Another name for the future emerged, when Paul Keith scored in his home debut v Fort William. John Thomson won the Player of the Year and the goal of the season trophy.
Caley were champions

	P	W	D	L	F	A	PTS
Caley	34	22	5	6	97	40	74
Broch (7th bottom)	34	9	6	19	37	71	33
Nairn County (bottom)	34	1	6	27	30	110	9

We drew 3-3 in a testimonial for Davy Robertson at the Bellslea, against Dundee, with Davy himself grabbing a double. The journey that season had been exciting, to say the least, and we hoped it would continue. What youngster would be next on the Broch's new assembly line? There was one thing for sure, as an up and coming young player, you'd always get a chance at the Bellslea.

Season 1988-89

With the departure of Neil Clark, the Broch signed Billy Gordon from Longside amateurs. Billy was to become a real hero, another club legend, over many years at the Bellslea. Also signed were Simon Sim from Rosehearty and Mike McCafferty, the latter, born in Dundee, was a class act. Brian Thomson was back at the Bellslea, in Motherwell colours, but the Broch were brushed aside 0-4 by the Scottish League side. A home defeat, 1-3 to Keith, followed in the League Cup and the same opponents were back at the Bellslea the following week, where they won 0-3 in the league game. The Broch team that day was: W. Gordon, R. Gordon, Sim,

Thomson, Duthie, Ellis, McCafferty, S. Sim, Robertson, J. Thomson, McCredie

A 1-1 draw with Deveronvale, at the Bellslea, saw ex-keeper Clark stopping everything the Broch could throw at him, then a 2-0 home win v Ross County in the Qualifying Cup, was a good result, then……., oh no, nae Forres again in the third round, but at least we were at home! Dave Robertson put us 1-0 up in 72 minutes, but alas, it was not to be. Gerry Davidson scored a wonder goal in the 87th minute to square the tie at 1-1. As the Broch trooped back into the dressing room, it felt like a defeat. Davidson finished any interest the Broch had in the Scottish Cup that season with a hat-trick in the replay, Duthie misssing a penalty in a Forres 3, Broch 0 score.

After a run of five defeats, we took a point, at Forres again, with a 1-1 draw and new signing Henry Michie making his debut. I missed the derby game at Peterhead, as I was in hospital to see the birth of my son, Darran. This father and son thing, both going to the game together is alright, but I can never imagine me going to, "Parkhead," if you see what I mean. By the way, we lost 0-2 at Recreation Park. So it was on to another memorable derby at the Bellslea. With the score at 0-0, Peterhead broke forward, and Kevin Walker tucked the ball under Billy Gordon at the Pole's Garage end. Walker then ran by the front of the stand doing his usual wave to the Broch fans. Then, Surprise Surprise, as he looked round, the linesman's flag was up for offside (He-haw! He-haw!) To rub salt into the Peterhead wound, Keith McCredie hit the winner with three mnutes to go. The Bellslea roar was back with that final score of Fraserburgh 1, Peterhead 0. The teams were:

Fraserburgh: Gordon, Young, Gordon, Sim, A. Thomson, Duthie, Ellis, McCafferty, Robertson, Thomson, Smith

Peterhead: Tait, Walker, Massie, Masson, Sievwright, Forman, Porter, Emslie, A. Smith, C. Smith, B. Thomson
Ref – I S Emslie   Att - 800

At the end of January, we were 8th bottom of the league.

P	W	D	L	F	A	PTS
23	7	7	9	31	30	28

John Thomson went on a trial with Dundee Utd and Dunfermline too were keeping tabs on him. A ten man Broch ended Cove's interest in the league with a 1-1 draw at Allan Park, with the player/manager being sent for an early bath. A rare 1-2 win up at Telford Street with two goals in two minutes from J. Thomson and H. Michie, but Caley then knocked us out of the Aberdeenshire Cup 1-3. We managed six wins in the last seven games, with the best being a win against high-flying Inverness Thistle, 3-2 at home, with a Dave Robertson double and John Thomson the other scorer. John Duthie, "Butcher," won the player of the year award, presented by his former P. E. Teacher, John Black. Dave Robertson finished with nineteen goals and won the goal of the season, for a diving header assisted by a Brian Sim cross, against Forres at Bellslea. Peterhead were league champions and the Broch were eighth from bottom. It looked like it wouldn't be long before the Bellslea would have floodlights, thanks to Shell (St. Fergus) who donated four pylons.

Season 1989-90

The nineties were nearly upon us and, as their incredible journey continued, the Broch called up young guns, Marino Keith and Mark Finnie, to the first team squad. A 4-1 win, v Threave Rovers at the Bellslea, set us up, before we played Peterhead at home in the League Cup. What a start the game had, with John Duthie heading the Broch in front in 3 minutes. But Peterhead got an equaliser from the penalty spot, and the game ended Fraserburgh 1, Peterhead 1 The Line ups were:

Fraserburgh: Gordon, Young, Sim, Thomson, Duthie, Ellis, McCafferty, Chalmers, Keith, J. Thomson, Smith

Peterhead: Tait, Walker, Donaldson, Sievwright, Forman, Masson, Stephen, Barclay, Thomson, Porter, Fraser

While the Broch's personnel stayed much the same, the number of players who came and went for Peterhead in a season was unreal. In the cup return match, a Porter double saw them go through to the next round. Our early league form however was good, with three wins and a draw, before we met Caley at the Bellslea in the Qualifying Cup 2nd round. John Thomson turned down the chance of a move to Keith, saying he was happy to stay at the Broch and it was John who put the Broch 1-0 up v Caley in 14 minutes. But goals from Andrew, Christie, and W. Robertson had the visitors in a commanding position. "Robbo," managed to reduce the leeway, but the final score was Fraserburgh 2, Caley 3 and Caley advanced to the next round. A 5-0 demolition of Lossiemouth at home had the Broch at the top of the league, with doubles from Dave Robertson and J. Thomson and a further goal from Mike McCafferty.

Troubled by a recurring calf muscle problem, Doug Ellis was told to take a break from football, but, with Charlie now retired from playing, we would need someone else to look out for the young guns on the park. By Xmas, we had dropped to 8th in the league, though, "Ronnie's Magic Moment" was a Sunday headline after a 2-2 draw with Peterhead at the Bellslea. The derby games have never ceased to amaze me and this one was no different. Ex-Broch man Brian Thomson was just about to pull the trigger when Jimmy Young whipped his legs away for a penalty! Brian took the kick himself, but he hit the post. The Broch then ran up the park, Brian Sim crossed to the back post and big John Sievwright headed past his own keeper, "nice one." "Luggs" wasn't to be denied however, as he scored to make it 1-1. Porter then put the visitors in the lead 1-2, but Billy Gordon kept the Broch in the game with an, "out of this world," save. This was followed by "Rattlin Ron's," mazy run, which ended with a 20 yard chip into the top corner to level the score at Fraserburgh 2, Peterhead 2. Boy, do we miss those derby games! It's not the same playing Cove or Deveronvale. There's just not the same atmosphere.

Not content with being the hero of the hour at the Bellslea, Ronnie Smith was at it again, back at Recreation Park. Peterhead took the lead that day, though Mike McCafferty levelled in 62 minutes for 1-1. Ronnie then took over, and, leaving two defenders in his wake, he ended up lashing the ball past Tait, to the joy of the big travelling support. The game ended Peterhead 1, Fraserburgh 2. That must have been Charlie Duncan's finest hour since he took over the management of the Broch. Had we finally arrived into the big time? It seemed nearly as good as the 10-0 years back! I don't know who started it, but anytime a football is kicked high over the bar at any Broch game, home or away, the roar is, "PETERHEID," from Broch fans!

"Broch Keeper Turns Down Elgin," was the story that then hit the headlines. Billy Gordon turned down the chance of a move to his home town team (Billy was born in Elgin and his father, Jasper, is still an ardent City fan.) It was also good to see Doug Ellis fit and back in the thick of things. We drew 0-0 with Keith in the Aberdeenshire Cup and beat them 1-0 away, with Ellis netting the winner for the Broch. Both teams finished the game with 10 men after Young (Broch) and Wallace (Keith), were ordered off. In the semi-final, we played the Dons at the Bellslea where their keeper, Michael Watt had to make four saves to keep the Dons in the competition, before Robertson put the Broch 1-0 up. Lee Gardiner then made it 1-1. By now you will know my feelings about Aberdeen being in this competition!! Incidentally, we lost the replay 4-1, so no surprise there!

With just one defeat in the last seven league games, our form had lifted us up a few places in the table. Our last home game was against Clach, who were in a real mess and it was rumoured would not be competing in the Highland League the next season. Their problem that Saturday was not in picking a team, it was finding a team. The final score was Fraserburgh 8, Clachnacuddin 0, with Paul Keith scoring four goals. As for Clach', we've all been there and got the T-shirt to prove it, so it was all the best to the boys from Clach' for the next season. Elgin were league champions.

	P	W	D	L	F	A	PTS
Elgin City (1st)	34	26	3	5	103	33	81
Broch (7th)	34	17	6	11	58	51	52
Clach (wooden spoon)	34	0	3	31	26	151	3

Alas, we then lost Hendry Michie, as he was off to Australia to work. Mike McCafferty won the Supporters' Player of the Year.
The Highland league top scorers that season were:

B Thomson (Peterhead)	39
I. Stewart (Lossiemouth)	32
J. Teasdale (Elgin City)	28
McLean (Fort William)	26
Jappy (Elgin City)	25
McDonald (Caley)	22
W. Robertson (Caley)	21
Robertson (Fraserburgh)	20

Chapter Five

The Nineties (Cups, Shields and a League Title to Come)

It was into the nineties, with DVD's and mobile phones, and the Broch with a 3pm kick off at home in the middle of December, what next? On a sadder note, on Friday, May 25th, the front page news read, "Tears as Clach Fall to a Final Defeat." Their problems had persisted and it looked like their hundred year history would soon be just a memory. It was like losing a good friend. There was only one new signing at the Bellslea, Andy Lavelle, from Formartine United. Charlie had resigned himself to final retiral at the age of 42, compared to him Peter Pan hadn't got a look in!

A four team tournament had been planned, to take place in Peterhead, the Broch, Peterhead, Ayr Utd and Airdrie, at the start of the season, and it was billed as the Buchan Cup. In their first game, the Broch, having taken a shock lead in 15 mins with a goal from Ronnie Smith, lost 3-1 to Ayr Utd. On Sunday, we played Peterhead who were defeated by Airdrie on Saturday, so we were playing for pride. Though we were up 2-0, Peterhead fought back to draw 2-2, with the Broch losing out on penalties.

At the 11th hour, a consortium bid rescued Clach, which meant they would be playing Highland League football that season. The Broch Supporters' Club would be active again, under the leadership of Sandy Tasker, and they planned to run buses to most away games. With no Youth League in this area, the Broch entered a youth team in the amateur league, with Brian Newlands and George Malley in charge. It was to prove a worthwhile exercise, with some cracking young talent breaking into the first team squad from the youth set up, e.g. Scott Murray, James Geddes and Marino Keith.

Our interest in the League Cup didn't last long, with a 2-0 defeat up at Huntly, but three wins and two draws in the league set us up nicely for Nairn, at the Bellslea in the Qualifying Cup. A Davy Robertson double saw us through to the next round, with a final score of Fraserburgh 2 Nairn County 0.

The Broch under 18s were defeated 4-3 by Elgin at the Bellslea in the B.P. Youth Cup. Their team read: Innes, Duthie, McCann, Cowe, McGruther, M. Keith, Finnie, Lavelle, Geddes, Murdoch, Murray. A piece of sad news was the death of Rod Clyne. He was only 55, and would be sadly missed in North of Scotland soccer.

A tough away tie to Elgin City stood in our Scottish Cup run and what a cracker of a game it turned out to be. McKay put Elgin 1-0 in front in the 1st minute, but Dave Robertson made it 1-1, before Jappy put the home side back in front. Robbo then made it 2-2, before more drama came in 50 minutes when Duthie was ordered off, but the Broch held on. The final score was Elgin 2 Fraserburgh 2. We were back at Elgin on league business the following Wednesday but lost 1-0.

The cup replay was at the Bellslea on the Saturday. A McArthur own goal was all that separated the teams in the replay, leading to a final score of Broch 1, Elgin City 0, but we'd take that any time. The teams were:

Broch: Gordon, R. Gordon, B. Sim, Young, Duthie, Sutherland, McCafferty, McCredie, Robertson, Lavelle, J. Thomson. Subs: A. Thomson, Smith

Elgin: Watt, McArthur, McLennan, McHardy, Slavin, McKay, Johnston, Teasdale, Jappy, Loch

Ref – J. Kelly, East Kilbride Attendance - 900

Inverness Thistle at Kingsmill was our semi-final fate. The match would be remembered for the chances the Broch had to bury Thistle, before a Robbo strike finally saw us through to win 1 – 0. Cove beat Ross County 3-1 in the second semi-final, so it was Fraserburgh v Cove at Huntly in the final. The Broch were not happy with the venue, saying that it should have been played at Peterhead, but the decision was typical of the S.F.A!!

It was on to the big day, but what a let down when it came! Nerves were getting the better of the Broch when, after a goalless first half, Cove got a dodgy penalty after Billy Gordon took the ball (cleanly) off Baxter's toes, but justice was done when Billy saved Park's spot kick. A goal from Andy Paterson proved enough to take the Cup back to Cove, on that final score of Fraserburgh 0, Cove Rangers 1. There were a few tears shed in the dressing room that day, but me, I just sat in the dugout, trying to take it all in. Football's a cruel game sometimes.

We had little time for feeling sorry for ourselves, as we faced Cove again, on the following Wednesday night, in the final of the Aberdeenshire Shield. We had to admit defeat in that game as well, as Raymond Yule scored the winner ten minutes into extra time for a repeat final score of Cove 1, Fraserburgh 0. We then got a home tie against Borders side Vale of Leithen in the Scottish Cup, with the BBC cameras scheduled to be at the Bellslea to show highlights. A pre-match shock hit Broch fans when Davy Robertson broke his leg at work. Would you believe that, after him being knocked about in the Highland League for years?

We got off to a shaky start with Duthie clearing off the line in 15 minutes, but then, against the run of play, the Broch went 1-0 up, with McCafferty scoring. The visitors drew level in 38 minutes through Hogarth, before Lavelle put Broch back in front (51 minutes). The Bellslea then went delirious as Lavelle put the Broch 3-1 in front and sealed the game. The final score was Fraserburgh 3, Vale of Leithen 1. The teams that day were:

Fraserburgh: Gordon, Sim, Young, Duthie, Thomson, McCafferty, McCredie, Keith, Lavelle, J. Thomson. Subs: Smith, Sutherland

Vale of Leithen: McDermutt, Ross, Graham, Bird, McNauton, Taylor, Thurpe, Mitchell, Spence, Hogarth, Lynch. Subs – Selkirk, Waddell

Ref – M. McLinlay, Clydebank   Att' - 812

After waiting all these years to see the Broch on TV, when the day came there was a power cut due to bad weather, but only in the Broch area, so I'm still waiting to see that game. Peterhead turned down a Broch offer of £1200 to sign Graeme Masson, so that was the end of that matter. I couldn't believe it when the draw for the cup 2nd round paired us with old foes Cove Rangers. Tickets for the stand were £2 and £1.50 for the ground. Before the big match we had Peterhead to take care of and had a comfortable 2-0 win, with goals from John Thomson and Keith McCredie.

There was disappointment again for the big crowd at the Bellslea, as Cove steamrollered the Broch to go into the next round. We had no answer to Mike Meggison, who made two and scored two goals, before Paul Keith netted a consolation goal after eighty minutes. The final score was Fraserburgh 1, Cove Rangers 4. There were two changes in the Broch line-up that day, when J. Duthie and Brian Sim were relegated to the subs bench with Simon Sim and Stevie Sutherland taking their places. Cove Rangers team for the tie was: Beckett, Forbes, Whyte, Brown, Patterson, Cormack, Park, Yule, D. Smith, Baxter, Megginson. Sub: King, G. Smith
Ref – D. Miller, Glasgow   Att – 2500

That Saturday, 29th December, saw the Broch attract the biggest crowd of the round. Another local derby, Montrose and Arbroath, could only attract 650, that's your Scottish League for you. Cove were defeated 1-2 at home by Cowdenbeath in the next round - how different it all might have been! Gray & Adams were the new sponsors of the Aberdeenshire Cup and who do you think we got in the draw? Surprise, surprise, it was Cove Rangers at the Bellslea! The final score was 1-1, with the replay to take place the following week. Then, at last, we got one over on them, with a 1-2 win, following goals from McCredie and Paul Keith. A 6-0 defeat against the Dons at Pittodrie was our reward, with Eion Jess scoring four, but was it really worth playing this fixture?

Dave Robertson's dream of scoring 30 goals that season had been shattered by his injury. It looked as though he wouldn't play again for the rest of the season. Michael McCafferty was leaving also, going on loan to Arbroath Sporting Club. His new job meant he had moved to the town, but he would stay a signed player for the Broch. It was reported that Sheffield Utd were keeping on eye on Billy Gordon after an impressive season in goal. On the way to a game at Nairn, George Watt, Fraserburgh F.C's treasurer, made a surprise debut at, "left back." The bus stopped at Elgin and George went to order the players' evening meal. No one missed him when the bus started off and the next time we saw him was when he came out of a taxi at Nairn. So from now on it won't be, "Taxi, follow that bus."

As another season drew to a close, our form had dipped, with two 3-3 draws at home to Huntly and Fort William. Against Fort William it took an Andy Lavelle strike to get a share of the points to a good "Fort" side. Taking the field in that game were:

Fraserburgh: Gordon, Young, Sim, Thomson, Duthie, McGruther, R.Gordon, McCredie, Lavelle, J. Thomson, Sutherland. Sub: Ellis

Fort William: McLean, Flannigan, Beaton, Jackson, McLean, McKinnon, Drummond, C. McLean, Conlon, Shearer, McBeath. Sub: Rossiter

Ross County only needed to beat us at Dingwall to be crowned champions, but Scott Murray kept the champagne on ice with a late strike and a final score of Ross Co 0, Fraserburgh 1. So it was on to the final game of a sensational season, which finished Cove Rangers 2 Fraserburgh 1, was that five or six times over the season?

Fraserburgh United won promotion as champions of the first division, so it was, CONGRATULATIONS to them. Their league record read:

P	W	D	L	F	A	PTS
22	14	6	2	46	21	48

Ross County finally won the Highland League Championship.

	P	W	D	L	F	A	PTS
Ross County (champions)	34	24	4	6	91	37	76
Broch (6th bottom)	34	11	8	15	54	56	41
Rothes (wooden spoon)	34	2	5	27	36	102	11

John Thomson won the Player of the Year award, presented by Larry Officer. Robbo, well he won the Goal of the Season for the third time, so I nicknamed him, "Roy of the Rovers." Finally, did you know that, from the start of the new season, referees would get £25 per game and linesmen £12? I wondered what it would all have to offer in terms of results on the field, roll on.

Season 1991-92

Hendry Michie was back in Broch colours after a year in Australia and another new face was a young lad from Ellon, Scotty Clark, who went straight into the first team, to perform as though he had played there all his life. The Buchan Cup was again to be played, this time at the Bellslea. With great weather, the crowds were good, especially with it being so early in the holiday season. The Broch lost 1-0 to Ayr Utd and 3-1 on penalties to Peterhead for 3rd place and 4th place. Airdrie defeated Ayr Utd on penalties to lift the trophy which was presented to skipper Ian McPhee by Jim Adams, Fraserburgh's Chairman.

On a sad note Johnnie Strachan, the Broch's goal hero when they knocked Dundee out of the Scottish Cup, died, aged 59. I had got his autograph when he was at Bellslea not so long ago. He was a really humble man, but in the nicest way.

The League Cup had changed to a knock out format. What a nice change that was, instead of the usual Huntly,

Vale, etc and a Ronnie Smith goal saw us through to the next round at Lossiemouth. It was Cove Rangers in the quarter finals at Bellslea and a Keith McCredie header, nine minutes from time, was all that separated the sides. Revenge was sweet for us. As for Dave Watson's comments, they were the usual, "we dominated the game but had nothing to show for it!" The teams that played the tie were:

Fraserburgh: Gordon, Clark, Sim, Young, Thomson, S. Sim, Gordon, McCredie, Lavelle, P. Keith. Subs: Murray, Sutherland.

Cove Rangers: Beckett, Watson, Whyte, Park, Paterson, Cormack, Baxter, Forbes, Stephen, Wallace, Megginson, S. King, Wilson.

A Ronnie Smith penalty earned a draw at Buckie but, with the replay the following Wednesday, the Broch's injury hoodoo struck again. Dave Robertson was nearly fit again, but then Keith McCredie broke his ankle in a bounce game. The Saturday match was a poor preparation for the replay, with the Fort beating us 5-1. Early on in the semi-final replay, things didn't look too promising either as Buckie went into an early lead through McPherson in the sixth minute. The Broch rolled up their sleeves, but had to wait until the fifty eighth minute before the equaliser arrived, a bullet header from Alan Thomson. The score, after ninety minutes, was 1-1, and just five minutes away from penalty kicks, Lavelle headed the winner as the Bellslea erupted. Another Cup Final - I can't get used to this! The teams that night were:

Fraserburgh: Gordon, Clark, Sutherland, Young, Thomson, S. Sim, R. Gordon, Michie, Lavelle, P. Keith, Smith. Sub: M. Keith

Buckie Thistle: Innes, Keith, Bruce, Mathieson, Fettes, Still, Gibson, Smart, Cowie, Ord, McPherson. Subs – Allan, Galbraith

Ref – A. M. Roy   Att' - 1,000

This was the first of some great nights under the new floodlights at the Bellslea, with big crowds making for a great atmosphere. The final was at Elgin against Ross County. They were due at the Bellslea on the previous Saturday and went away with a 1-2 win. With the final looming, Huntly and Keith both beat us 2-0, with Billy Gordon being sent off during the Huntly game.

So it was on to the fnal and, with the Broch's injury situation getting worse, it was anybody's guess what the team would be. On the Saturday, Scott Clark put the Broch 1-0 in front in twenty minutes, but it was only a matter of time before County found the net. The Broch had held on for 59 minutes, when Robertson equalised. The score after ninety minutes was the Broch 1 County 1, but two goals in eight minutes, from Sommerville and Ferries, settled the issue. The final score read Ross County 3, Fraserburgh 1. The teams that contested the final were:

Fraserburgh: Gordon, Clark, Sutherland, Young, Thomson, S. Sim, Keith, R. Gordon, Lavelle, Michie, Smith. Subs: Duthie, B. Sim

Ross County: Ure, Sommerville, Campbell, Williamson, Bellshaw, Allan, Robertson, Grant, Duff, Connely, Wilson, Ferries, McPherson.
Ref – G. Simpson
How differently might it have been if we'd had a full side on the day.

The Qualifying Cup was up next and it was Wick Academy at home for us. In a poor game, the Broch scraped through 1-0 with a Robert Gordon goal deciding things. Up next were Caley at the Bellslea, but that game was a one man demolition job, with Alan Hercher scoring all four goals. Final score Fraserburgh 0, Caley 4. We played Nairn next and, with the score Nairn 1, Fraserburgh 0, the party was not quite finally over over for Charlie Duncan, who came off the bench to play in his last game at the age of 43. There was some good news, however, Robbo was back and he scored one of the goals v Keith to see us through to the final of the Aberdeenshire Shield. The final score that day was Fraserburgh 2, Keith 1.

We finally ended a 15 year drought and won a trophy by defeating Deveronvale 4-3 on penalties at Christie Park, Huntly. Lavelle put the Broch in front in 10 minutes, but Muirhead made it 1-1, and it stayed that way till full time. Muirhead put Vale in front (117). "Not again," we all thought, but Alan Forbes tackled Scott Murray in the box and the referee pointed to the spot before sending Forbes off. Robertson made no mistake, to make it 2-2 and take the game to penalty kicks. Masson missed the first kick, but the penalties finished with Muirhead needing to score to save the Vale, Billy Gordon saved it and the result was Broch 2 Vale 2 (4-3 on penalties.) The Broch were not to be bridesmaids this time. The teams in that final were:

Fraserburgh: W. Gordon, Clark, B. Sim, Young, C. Robertson, S. Sim, Thomson, Lavelle, Robertson, Alexander, Smith. Sub: Murray

Deveronvale: Randall, C. Forbes, Massie, Masson, A. Forbes, Clark, Pirie, Muir, McBeath, Hadden, Muirhead, Montgomary, R. Masson

Ref – A. M. Roy   Att' - 580

Despite all the shield excitement that season, by mid-December we were third bottom of the league, having played eighteen games but gaining only fourteen points. Fraserburgh United weren't doing any better. They were second bottom of the premiership, having played eight games for only three points.

Stevie Doak replaced Billy Gordon in goal for the derby games as Billy had broken one of his fingers. A very tricky, snow covered Recreation Park was the scene for the first Buchan derby. Cheyne put the home side 1-0 in front in 4 minutes but Lavelle squared things at 1-1, in 5 minutes, only for Cheyne to make it 2-1 a minute later. A soft penalty in 85 minutes gave Cheyne the chance for his hat-trick and 3-1, before Smith reduced the leeway in 89 minutes, but the game ended at Peterhead 3, Fraserburgh 2. The return match had everything, with referee Bendal even having a nightmare. After an even first half, the Broch took the lead on 50 minutes through Scott Murray, then enter Mr Bendal. The linesman flagged for offside, but the referee disagreed and gave a penalty for a tackle Jimmy Young had made. Cheyne scored from the spot to make it 1-1 and then McIntosh put the visitors in front in 78 minutes before a superb shot on the run from McGruther hit the bar and denied us a share of the points. The referee blew for time and had a police excort from the park. I hoped he could sleep that night!

The teams that day were:

Fraserburgh: Doak, Clark, Sutherland, Young, Thomson, S. Sim, Murray, McGruther, Robertson, Lavelle, Smith. Subs: M. Keith, C. Robertson.

Peterhead: Tait, Watson, Fraser, Morland, Sievwright, Forman, Bremner, Cheyne, McKenzie, Brown, McIntosh. Subs – Loch, Bain

Ref – B. Bendal Aberdeen

Scottish Cup results involving Highland League teams that season were:

Berwick	7	Ross County	4
Huntly	4	C. S. Strollers	0
Peterhead	1	Cowdenbeath	1
Stenhousemuir	1	Caley	4

We got revenge in the Aberdeenshire Cupo by knocking out Peterhead 0-1, with a Simon Sim strike separating the teams.The Broch had intimated they didn't really want to play Aberdeen in the next round at Pittodrie, but the game went ahead with a final score of Aberdeen 5, Fraserburgh 0. What a waste of time those games were! We never managed to get out of the bottom four in the League, but Jimmy Young won the Player of the Year.

Ross County were champions that season.

	P	W	D	L	F	A	PTS
Ross County (champions)	34	24	3	7	95	43	75
Broch (4th bottom)	34	11	3	20	43	67	36
Nairn County (bottom)	34	3	3	28	23	11	12

There was some disappointing news for Broch fans that summer. Davy Robertson, "Robbo," was leaving the Bellslea to become manager of Fraserburgh United. I didn't think the goalkeepers in the Highland League would be too concerned, more likely they breathed a sigh of relief!

Season 1992-93

Away we went again for another saeson. Nairn County proposed a split in the League for a two year period ("Blah! Blah! Blah!") Seventeen year old Mintlaw lad, Kris Hunter, was to wear the No 9 shirt for the new season, just like his father Rexy had. If he could score half as many goals as Hunter senior, he'd do alright. Away to Keith, in the League Cup, we won 3-5, with new boy Graeme Alexander hitting a hat-trick and two goals for Ronnie Smith. Another couple of new faces training at the Bellslea were Michael Stephen and James Alexander Geddes (Bab a Doo) I remember thinking that we'd hear a lot more of those two in the future!

Cove Rangers knocked us out of the cup quarter finals 3-1 at Allan Park and next came a double header v Buckie Thistle at home. Once in the League which we lost 2-4, then in the Qualifying Cup 1st round. In the latter game, Alan Thomson headed the Broch in front just on the stroke of half time, but Galbraith made it 1-1 (63 minutes) Clark thought he had clinched the tie with a strike on 90 minutes, but Marino Keith scored in stoppage time for a final score of Fraserburgh 2 Buckie Thistle 2. The replay was what Cup football is all about. With the Broch trailing 2-1 and only half an hour to go, John Thomson was brought on and he scored a hat-trick to put us into the next round, with the final score Buckie Thistle 3, Fraserburgh 4. The teams were:

Broch: Gordon, Clark, Sim, Young, Michie, M. Keith, Gordon, McGruther, Alexander, Hunter, Smith, S. Sutherland, J. Thomson.

Buckie: Innes, Smart, Bruce, Mathieson, Fettes, Robertson, Gibson, Still, Galbraith, Clark, Finlay, Keith, Ord.

Striker Andy Lavelle had been unsettled for a while and looked set to join Cove Rangers, but the Broch however wouldn't let him go on the cheap. It was Ross County who came out of the hat with us for the next round of the Qualifying Cup. A Billy Ferries goal was all that separated the teams at the Bellslea for a final score of Fraserburgh 0, Ross County 1. Scott Murray was making a name for himself in the team and continued this with an injury time strike to gain a point v Caley, but Cove knocked us out of the Aberdeenshire Shield 2-1. Fourteen years is a long time in football, but that was how long the Club Captain, Jimmy Young, had been pulling on a black and white shirt and with no apparent intention of hanging up his boots!

A crowd of 1500 turned up at Bellslea for the Xmas derby and they were not disappointed. Hunter and Alan Thomson put the Broch in a sound position though McIntosh scored a consolation goal for the visitors to make the final score Fraserburgh 2, Peterhead 1. The return game was just as exciting. Ronnie Smith gave us an early lead then Peterhead equalised on the stroke of half time through Campbell. Brown put the home side 2-1 in front, but Ronnie Smith denied Peterhead revenge, with an equaliser a minute from the end. The game ended Peterhead 2, Fraserburgh 2.

Fraserburgh: Gordon, Clark, Michie, Young, Thomson, Keith, Murray, McCredie, Hunter, McGruther, Smith. Subs: Sim, Alexander

Peterhead: Tait, Watson, Fraser, King, Coull, Wilson, Campbell, Emslie, McIntosh, Brown, Cheyne. Subs: Keith, McGachie

Stevie Sutherland had decided to return to Fraserburgh United. He left with the best wishes of all at the club and the hope that his experience there had served him well for the future. He had been a really nice lad to have in the squad. James Geddes then went on loan to Buchanhaven Hearts to gain more experience.

On Saturday, January 23rd the Broch v Peterhead tie in the Aberdeenshire Cup was abandoned because of a blizzard, with the players immediately diving into the shower to get a heat. We had to put Scott Murray into the shower with his strip on as his boots were frozen solid to his socks. The score was 0-0, but the following week, we beat our hosts 3-1 with goals from Hunter, McCredie and M. Keith.

It was not often that we beat Huntly around that time, but a 4-2 victory had Charlie Duncan raving about Scott Murray, saying that it was the best performance he had witnessed from an 18 year old. The Broch's youth system was then in full flow, with a succession of its players making an impression in the first team. In arctic conditions, a Graeme Park goal at Bellslea was enough to see Cove through to the final of the Aberdeenshire Cup final on a score of Fraserburgh 0 Cove Rangers 1. Then six wins and a draw came in the final games of the season, with the introduction of some of those promising youngsters, leaving us in good heart for next season.

Scotty Clark won the Player of the Year, which was presented by ex-Broch legend Rexy Hunter. Harry Cheves received a special award, having driven the team bus for the previous fourteen seasons. He was the only man to breach the Lossiemouth defensive wall as he reversed into it and left a ten foot hole in the set up at Grant Street!

Elgin City were champions, but they were later stripped of the title (for unknown reasons.) I hoped that the people who voted for that could sleep after doing so. I think that most people in Highland League circles were against this decision. The best team, over the season, always wins the league.

	P	W	D	L	F	A	PTS
Elgin City	34	24	5	5	110	35	77
Fraserburgh (10th)	34	15	7	12	63	52	52
Nairn County (wooden spoon)	34	1	2	31	26	126	5

Caley striker, Billy Urquhart called it a day and hung up his boots, to the delight of many Highland League defenders.

Sunday July 25th was a very proud day for the club as the youth team beat Elgin City 5-1 to win the Highland Youth Championship play off. The team that day was: Innes, Gauld, Burnett, Farquhar, Keith, Griffin, I. Murray, Hunter, Beaton, Stephen, Milne. Subs: Buchan, Killoh
Ref – B. Christie
There was every reason for Jim Adams, Charlie Duncan and Brucie Buchan to take particular pride in the club's youth policy that they had nurtured. Seven of that youth team went on to wear the famous black and white strips of the Broch. Jim Adams was an excellent Chairman, but he never interfered with Charlie's team decisions. Other Highland League Chairmen, please take note!

Season 1993-94 (The Broch in Europe)

The Broch went off to France to play a couple of pre-season friendlies in Bressuire, which is the Broch's twinned town. I was very disappointed when I couldn't make the trip. The first match was played in thirty degree heat, and the score was Thouars 4, Fraserburgh 0. During the match, twenty four litres of water were consumed by the players (and staff) and after the match fifty litres of beer were consumed - only joking! Bressuire won the second match 3-0 though we the won the final game against a local select 2-1 with goals from Ian Murray and Marino Keith.

What a start to the season back home when we demolished Peterhead 6-1 at the Bellslea in the League Cup with a Paul Keith hat-trick the highlight.

Fraserburgh: Gordon, Clark, Michie, Young, Thomson, J. Thomson, McCredie, P. Keith, S. Murray, Stephen, I. Murray. Subs: McGruther, Sim.

Peterhead: Tait, Watson, Fraser, Knowles, McGachie, Emslie, Campbell, Cheyne, Gray, Brown, Wilson. Subs: Gordon, McIntosh.

Ref – B. Christie, Aberdeen   Attendance - 1,000

A 3-1 win at Deveronvale and 3-0 win v Buckie Thistle at the Bellslea set us up for a home game in the semi finals v Elgin City, and it turned into one of those glory nights under the flood lights. Elgin took the lead in 39 minutes through McGruire, but Ronnie Smith came on in 80 minutes and unleashed a shot that keeper Hinchcliffe couldn't hold. John Thomson was on hand to side foot the rebound into the empty net for 1-1. Then came Rattlin Ron's second touch, when he bulleted a header past the helpless keeper to put the Broch in front. (Brian Sim's theory had been to lob everything over the defenders, into the corners, and make them turn.) Scott Murray then chipped the keeper to make it 3-1. Leslie reduced the deficit in injury time, but the final score was Fraserburgh 3 Elgin City 2. It would be the Broch going on to meet Huntly at Elgin in the final. The teams that night were:

Fraserburgh: Gordon, Clark, Michie, Young, Thomson, Keith, Murray, McCredie, Keith, J. Thomson, Stephen. Subs: Smith, J. McGruther.

Elgin City: Hinchcliffe, Porter, Teasdale, McLennan, Forphy, Dallas, McKay, Cameron, Teasdale, McGuire, Leonce. Sub: Leslie

Ref – A M. Roy   Att' - 850

As the final approached, Charlie Duncan let go a blast, "If I can't keep my best prospects at Bellslea, I'll jack it in." His comments were in response to the report that a Club, not far from home, had been suggesting that they were interested in some of the Broch's young guns. We wondered who it could be?

The build-up to the final was great, with the Press at every training session. We were no match for Huntly in the match however. A goal from Gary Whyte on the stroke of half time made it an uphill struggle. In the second half, further goals came from Whyte and Copland, before Hunter made it 3-1, only for Thomson to score on 90 minutes. The final score to a good Huntly team was Huntly 4, Fraserburgh 1. It's not the first time that I've picked a runners-up medal off the floor and handed it back to the owner at a better time. As for Charlie, he just takes it in his stride, even though he's hurting inside. Scott Murray has been to Anfield, Liverpool, for a trial and has been asked to go back.

It was no rest for the wicked, as we were away to Lossiemouth in the Qualifying Cup with James Geddes back in the team, having recovered from breaking his leg. Scott Murray put us 1-0 in front, but Shaw made it 1-1 to take Lossie to the Bellslea in the replay. Lossie took a shock lead in 15 minutes through Kellas, but Hunter made it 1-1 three minutes later. Then Billy Gordon made yet another crucial save from Stewart to keep the Broch in the game. Two late goals from Michael Stephen and Murray set the Broch on their way to the next round. Next up was Huntly, and another drubbing at the Bellslea. This time it was Fraserburgh 1 Huntly 5, with Gary Whyte scoring four goals. In a B. P. Cup fixture, the Broch defeated Nairn County 12-1, with Michael Stephen scoring six. What goes around, comes around and it came when the Broch finally ended Huntly's thirty two game unbeaten run when we knocked them out of the Aberdeenshire Shield 1-0, Paul Keith scoring with 15 minutes to go.

Huntly: Gardiner, McGinlay, Murphy, Walker, Grant, DeBarros, Stewart, Thomson, Whyte, Selbie. Sub: Copland

Broch: Gordon, Michie, Geddes, Young, Thomson, M.Keith, Gordon (Smith), McCredie, P.Keith, Murray, Stephen

Ref – A. Smith, Ellon   Attendance – 720

The Broch line up was along the same lines as the team that lost to Huntly in the Qualifying Cup. Charlie Duncan had scuppered rumours that Scott Murray had joined Liverpool for a fee of £42,000. Scotty was in his usual place when we defeated Peterhead at Recreation Park 1-3 to march into our second Cup Final this season. McCredie, A. Thomson and Smith were on target for the Broch. The Broch also had a new sponsor, Scot-Net, a local firm owned by Calvin Morrice, who later became a director of Fraserburgh FC and took them to another level in the Highland League.

In the final of the Aberdeenshire Shield, the Broch played Keith at Christie Park and were 1-0 up in 30 seconds from Michael Stephen, who wrote his name all over this match. Robert Gordon, the forgotten man, made it 2-0 before Will made it 2-1. It made a change for us to score on 45 minutes, but John Thomson headed into the roof of the net then to make it 3-1. Stephen made it 4-1 in 60 minutes and Hamilton got a consolation goal for Keith to make it 4-2. Triumphant at last, after lot of hard work, it was not often you saw Charlie smiling! The teams were:

Broch: Gordon, Clark, Geddes, Young, Thomson, R. Gordon, Murray, McCredie, Keith, J. Thomson, Stephen. Subs: Smith, Michie.

Keith: Thain, Thow, Tosh, Watt, Collie, Thomson, Maver, Hamilton, Will, Allan. Subs: Collins, Gibson.

We did play league games, but were included in so many Cup matches, that I wouldn't try to fit them in for this season. In one however, we lost 4-5 at home to Lossiemouth after being 3-0 in front! Winter had set in and both Xmas derbies were postponed. These are the top scorers at that point of the season.

Stewart	Lossie	20
Whyte	Huntly	18
Thomson	Huntly	15
Duff	Ross County	14
Stewart	Huntly	12
Paul Keith	Broch	12
Scott Murray	Broch	10

The Broch lost another stalwart, when Robert Gordon moved to London to work. Robert had been an unsung hero for the Broch, playing anywhere and always giving 100 %. There was some good news however, as Aberdeen pulled out of the Aberdeenshire Cup, but we drew Huntly again, up at Christie Park. Goals from Doug Rougvie and Eddie Copland saw Huntly through 2-0 on a muddy day.

The Broch young guns were going well in the B. P. Cup and were drawn to meet Airdrie in the quarter finals. They wouldn't play us on a Sunday, so the Broch had to play in midweek, a 380 mile round trip. It was ridiculous! Would Airdrie have travelled in mid-week to play at the Bellslea? I don't think so! We lost the tie 4-1, with Airdrie knocking us all over the place and it was no surprise when Ian Murray headed for an early bath, after some of the tackles he received.

Broch: Morris, McLean, Gauld, Milne, McDonald, Norris, Buchan, Murray, Beaton, Killoh, Stephen. Subs: Weymss, McBride

Eight players from this squad graduated to the Broch first team. I don't think any of Airdrie's team ever made it to theirs. It was goodbye then to Scott Murray, who had signed for Aston Villa for £35,000, which was not bad for a Mintlaw loon. At the fifth time of asking that season, we finally defeated Huntly 1-2 at Christie Park. Ronnie Smith scored and Gardiner let one slip through his hands for the Broch's winner. "Charlie Duncan Turns Down Peterhead," was a headline at that time. We hoped that was the end of that situation.

Ross County and Inverness (Caledonian & Thistle) were admitted to the Scottish League. We would miss going to (Victoria Park) Dingwall, (Kingsmills) Inverness Thistle and (Telford Street) Caley, where we have met and made a lot of good friends. I recall one of these especially who was deaf and dumb. I never knew his name nor did he know my name, but a friendly smile and a shake of the hand, when we came across each other, that was Highland League football for you, and that kind of thing happened at every ground. We got a new member Club in the shape of Wick Academy, who, at last, got the good news that they were to be accepted into the Highland League.

It was the middle of March, and with wintry conditions, we still had eleven league games to play. A 1-3 win at Caley and a 1-0 win at Bellslea v Peterhead, gave new Blue Toon manager Dave Watson a few headaches for the future. Another Broch young gun who made his debut, against Peterhead at Recreation Park, was Ian Murray (Molby) We would hear a lot more of him in the future, I thought.

We defeated Caley to keep the Highland League Youth League Cup for the second time. The final score was Fraserburgh 3 Caley 0. Then Peterhead were at it again, with Billy Gordon the subject of a bid. The Broch's reaction was that none of our players were out of contract and we couldn't see ourselves selling anyone to Peterhead!! Paul Keith won the Player of the Year which was presented by John Duthie (Tozy).
Huntly ran away with the league.

	P	W	D	L	F	A	PTS
Huntly (champions)	34	27	4	3	95	21	85
Broch (9th)	34	15	8	11	52	36	53
Rothes (wooden spoon)	34	4	6	24	42	97	18

Season 1994-95 (The Future Looks Bright)

Season tickets that year were £35 for the ground only and £42 for the stand. Admission was £3 and £1.50 for OAPs and kids, which was not bad then for an afternoon at the Bellslea. Peterhead were at it again, sniffing around Keith McCredie. Why didn't they go and produce a few young players of their own instead of always opening a cheque book? What an introduction to Highland League football young fifteen year old Russell McBride made, when he came on for the last ten minutes in a friendly v Albion Rovers.

He scored with a spectacular volley for his first touch of the ball. The final score that day was Fraserburgh 5 Albion Rovers 0, but another Broch legend from the past died about then, Cliff Meldrum, aged only 57.

We lost our first two League Cup games 2-3 at Cove and 0-3 at Deveronvale, so, as we could not win the section, we had a meaningless derby game at home to Peterhead. A McGachie goal for the visitors settled the match at Fraserburgh 0 Peterhead 1. The teams were:

Fraserburgh: Gordon, Milne, Young, Thomson, McDonald, McGruther, Norris, McCredie, Keith, Beaton, Smith

Peterhead: Pirie, Watson, Cheyne, King, Greig, Anderson, McIntosh, Yule, McGachie, Brown, Shepherd.

The next shock news item was that Ronnie Smith had left the Bellslea and joined Buckie Thistle, but that was nothing compared to the shock that was to follow on Saturday September 24th with a score of. Fraserburgh 0 Golspie Sutherland 1 in the Qualifying Cup 2nd round. An own goal from Alan Thomson sent the non-leaguers into the next round and Charlie Duncan's comment was, "I thought I'd seen everything in football in the last 20 years, but this was three years of progress wiped out in ninety minutes". The teams for a really black day in the Broch's history were:

Fraserburgh: Gordon, Milne, Geddes, Young, Thomson, McKeith, J. Thomson, McCredie, Alexander, Hunter, P. Keith, Porter, Stephen.

Golspie: D. Sutherland, Macleod, B. Sutherland, McDonald, Sutherland, McKenzie, Bonnar, Fisher, Cowie, Omen, McKasy.

Ref – A. Gemmill, Linlithgow

The Broch then transfer listed three, "rebels," who were no longer interested in staying at the Bellslea: Keith McCredie, Alan Thomson and Scott Clark. It was no surprise that Peterhead were interested, but Broch Chairman, Jim Adams, told them to, "stump up," or back off. One offer for one of the players was a four figure sum, but Charlie inquired if that was the signing on fee, enough said? With all this turmoil going on, the team's results were affected. We lost 0-1 after extra time in the semi final of the Aberdeenshire Shield and, having played eleven games in the league, we had won six but lost five.

It was about that time, when we were playing Nairn at Station Park, that Charlie was reading out the Nairn team in the dressing room. Not recognising any of the players, his comment was, "just eleven players in red shirts." I looked at Brucie Buchan and we just smiled, as Nairn hadn't played in red shirts since the late sixties! Then, up at Lossie, during another team talk, one of the young guns wasn't very interested, so he put on his earphones and started to listen to a tape, needless to say, he never made it at the Bellslea.

We drew 1-1 with Peterhead on December 3rd, a bit early for a Xmas derby and, the game being so early, there was a poor crowd, but Huntly gave us a real Xmas present with a 5-1 thrashing at Christie Park. This was followed up with a 0-3 win at Bellslea after the New Year. It looked like they would run away with the League again this year.

Our table positions stood like this on Sat 21st Jan'.

	P	W	D	L	F	A	PTS
Huntly (1st)	20	15	1	4	64	23	46
Fraserburgh (4th)	24	11	3	10	40	40	36

At Recreation Park, an Ian Murray goal gave us three much needed points with a 0-1 win. Huntly were due at Bellslea in the Aberdeenshire Cup, the week before they were knocked out of the Scottish Cup (3-1 at home to Dundee Utd.) They started where they left off the previous time they were here, with Eddie Copland scoring in 3 minutes. The Broch earned a replay in 75 minutes through Hendry Michie, but we were no match for them in the second game, losing 3-0 with Copland, and a double from Brian Thompson doing enough to see Huntly through. Our young guns couldn't compete with the experience and strength of that Huntly side. The teams were:

Huntly: Gardiner, Yeats, Dumsire, Mone, Rougvie, Copland, Gray, Stewart, Thompson, Whyte, Lennox, Fettes.

Fraserburgh: Gordon, Clark, Geddes, Thomson, Milne, Keith, Murray, McCredie, Alexander, Beaton, Killoh, Summers, Sim.

"Every doggie has its day, some day we would have ours." We managed four wins and a draw in our last five league games, including a 0-3 at Cove and a 1-3 win at Elgin. We actually won a trophy too, the Aberdeenshire Reserve League, but it was the big one we were after. Marino Keith won the Highland League Young Player of the Year award. James Geddes and Jim Young shared the Player of the Year, which was presented by old friend, and foe, Peterhead legend John Sievwright.

Huntly were runaway champions, 17 points clear of second place Cove Rangers.

	P	W	D	L	F	A	PTS
Huntly (champions)	30	23	4	2	102	30	74
Fraserburgh (7th)	30	16	10	4	56	43	52
Nairn Co (wooden spoon)	30	3	25	2	30	105	11

In the close season, Peterhead finally signed Broch rebels, Alan Thompson and Keith McCredie, but they could have been in trouble, as both players were still under contract at the Bellslea. Supporters wrote into the Herald to voice their disgust at the double transfer. Headlines appeared like:

"No Ambition at the Bellslea."

"The Grass is not Always as Green on the Other Side of the Fence."

Over the years some players were surprised at the criticism they received for signing for Peterhead, but, in this corner, that goes with the territory.

Season 1995-96 (Who's Next on the Broch's Assembly Line?)

Youngsters David Gauld, Clark Killoh and sixteen year old Duncan Summers were all on the verge of the first team. The Buchan Cup would again be played in Peterhead, with hosts Peterhead, St. Johnstone, Dundee United and the Broch competing. The Broch lost 1-0 to St. Johnstone, with Marino Keith missing a penalty. Then an under strength Fraserburgh were 2-0 up against Peterhead, but the Blue Tooners secured two late counters to square the match, though the Broch won 4-3 on penalties.

Kris Hunter had had his usual moan about pre-season training over the beach. After being left behind on one session, he came out with this classic line, "if I wanted to do this I'd have joined the .... Army," - nice one Kris. Another rising star arrived back at the Playing Fields after a session at the big hill, and started hamming in to a tin of cola and a packet of crisps. Two other young guns were caught coming out of the chippie at 1.30 on a Saturday afternoon with a pie supper each, before heading to the Bellslea. "They were Growing Loons".

What a start we had to the season, with a 2-6 win at Elgin. Stuart McDonald opened the scoring, and doubles for the Keith brothers and Mike McCafferty, back in a Broch shirt, finished the rout. The best was still to come however, a 5-1 win v Cove Rangers in the League Cup, but a 1-1 draw at Buckie meant we needed a draw at Banff v Vale. We lost 2-0 and didn't qualify for the semi-finals.
The teams that day were:

Deveronvale: Veitch, Thornton, Simmers, Cormack, Ironside, Dunbar, Ball, M. Stewart, Wolecki, Stewart, Dolan.

Fraserburgh: Gordon, Milne, Michie, Young, McDonald, Geddes, McAfferty, Murray, J. Thomson, Hunter, Stephen.

At a tribunal, Peterhead were ordered to pay the Broch £12,000 for Keith McCredie and Alan Thomson, which was not a bad bit of business. How's this for a score that year?

Huntly 7 Fraserburgh 4. We were 7-1 down with ten men and ten minutes to go, but hit back through Keith (80), Hunter (84) and Clark (90). The following week, the score was Fraserburgh 4 Keith 6. It was like watching the Broch in the 60's. I had thought that these kind of games were long gone. With this rich vein of goal-scoring form, we trounced Forres 4-0 at Bellslea in the 2nd round of the Qualifying Cup, with Marino Keith hitting a double. Then, would you believe it? The Broch drew Huntly away in the next round for a place in the Scottish Cup. With 65 minutes gone and the score at 0-0, Jimmy Young, of all the people to score, put the Broch 0-1 in front. Nerves were getting the better of everybody, as Murray replaced Killoh, but wo minutes later, it was all over for Huntly, when a Murray shot squirmed under Gardiner to put the Broch 0-2 in front and they held on, despite Michael Stephen being sent off. The final score was Huntly 0 Fraserburgh 2. The teams, in a massive result for the Broch were:

Huntly: Gardiner, Grant, Allan, Copland, Rougvie, Morland, Gray, Stewart, Thomson, Selbie, Yeats

Fraserburgh: Gordon, Clark, Michie, Young, Milne, Keith, McCafferty, Killoh, Keith, Hunter, Stephen. Sub: I. Murray
Ref – D. McDonald, Edinburgh

The Broch drew Lossiemouth away in the semi-final, but disappointing news was the Broch selling Marino Keith to Dundee Utd for an undisclosed fee. It was bad timing, considering our chance of cup glory and, with the Broch trailing 1-0 and just half an hour to play, things didn't look bright. Then Gerrard collided with his keeper and Stephen poked the loose ball home via the post for 1-1. It was, "game on," after that but the Broch held on for a replay. The Broch got their noses in front early on in the re-match, with Michael Stephen heading home. We then pounded the Lossie goal for the killer goal, but it never came and Shaw made it 1-1 with ten minutes to go. There was no more scoring, so it went to penalties. With the game evenly balanced, and all square in penalties, Billy Gordon saved from Paul Douglas. So Scotty Clark stepped up for our shot at glory and coolly slotted the ball home to put the Broch through to the final, 5-4. The Bellslea erupted in mass hysteria. What a great experience a cup run like that was for some of those young guns!!

Fraserburgh: Gordon, Clark, Michie, Young, Milne, Thomson, McCafferty, Murray, Killoh, Hunter, Stephen

Lossiemouth: Pirie, Cheyne, Main, Masson, Gerrard, Kew,Still, Paterson, Clark, Douglas, Kellas

The following Wednesday, we knocked Huntly out of the Aberdeenshire Shield at Christie Park, 4-3 on penalties. (I could have got get used to that every week.) We were due meet Keith in the final of the Qualifying Cup at Christie Park, Huntly. The week prior to the game was again pretty exciting. Every day the Press included some kind of write up and at training everybody had a smile on their face. When we left the Bellslea for Huntly, the fans were out on the streets with banners and flags, as the build-up continued.

It was typical cup final weather, rain, that greeted the teams at 3 o'clock, and, after a nervy early spell, Paul Keith opened the scoring in 15 minutes. Taylor squared matters in 32 minutes, to make it 1-1, but then came disaster. In 66 minutes, Milne nudged Will in the box and the referee pointed to the spot for Wilson to hammer his spot kick past Gordon and put Keith in front 1-2. John Thomson then threw the game into the melting pot, scoring to make it 2-2 and with just two minutes of playing time to go, the Broch took the lead again as McCafferty sent an unsaveable shot into the top corner for 3-2. Christie Park was a sea of black and white, but while the Broch were still celebrating, Keith ran up the park and Wilson scored with the last kick of the game for a final score of 3-3. So it was on to extra time, but how would the Broch react to that late, late equaliser and would they manage to get their heads back up?

Geddes replaced the tiring Hunter, but was this a last throw of the dice? Then, with just twelve minutes to go, it happened. Geddes went boring down on the Keith goal. He beat one man and, with everybody shouting, "hit it," he then beat a second man. I was shouting "………" hit it, when his shot sailed into the net. GOAL!!!! What a feeling it was as the bench went wild. It was better than sex, or maybe it just seemed that way at the time. I can't explain my feelings as the final whistle went. I remember hugging Billy Gordon in the centre of the park and then it was Finlay Noble's turn as we just wept with joy. Your mind runs riot at times like that and you think of all the disappointments over the years. It doesn't get any better than that day. The teams were:

Fraserburgh: Gordon, Clark, Michie, Young, Milne, J. Thomson, McCafferty, Killoh, Keith, Hunter, Stephen. Subs: Geddes, Murray, Alexander

Keith: Thain, Taylor, Wilson, Watt, Singer, Gibson, Thomson, Taylor, Lavelle, Will, Allan. Subs: Wolley, McPherson, Nicol

Ref – K. Clark, Paisley   Att' – 1,700

It was back to Christie Park again for the final of the Aberdeenshire Shield against old foes Peterhead. On the half hour, Kris Hunter was upended in the box, "penalty!" and with goalkeeper Pirie the last man, a red card should have been shown, but he got a yellow instead. Clark coolly slammed his penalty home for 1-0 and, just after half time, Hunter headed the Broch into a 2-0 lead. Shepherd pulled one back with 10 minutes to go, but the Broch held on. Two trophies won in one week was, "magic". In a league game at the Bellslea shortly after that, we were 2-0 down to Buckie in ten minutes, but ran out worthy winners 7-2.

Whitehill Welfare, away, were our opponents in the Scottish Cup. I remember leaving the house in pitch darkness to catch the bus, as our opponents didn't have floodlights, and when we arrived at their ground, well, the facilities were nothing to write home about. When the game began, we went behind in 15 minutes with Gowrie scoring from the penalty spot. Two goals, from Clark and Killoh in 28 and 63 minutes, then put us into the lead, before Gowrie made it 2-2 in 80 minutes. A replay at the Bellslea was on the cards and the score stayed that way to finish Whitehill 2 Fraserburgh 2. The draw for the next round was on TV that night and what an incentive it was, Fraserburgh or Whitehill Welfare v Celtic. The whole town was buzzing, but Charlie wasn't getting carried away. We had to do the business with Whitehill first, but sometimes the press don't help. They were running riot with various stories and you can't stop the players from reading those stories.

We started the replay in confident style, but missed chances were to cost us dear. The visitors took the lead in the 37th minute and extended it in 55 minutes. Welfare had done their homework on Michael Stephen and kept him quiet all afternoon, except once, when he managed to escape his marker and score to give us a bit of hope. However, as the clock was ticking down time and our Cup dream was dying. It was a very unreal atmosphere as the referee blew for time. The final score was Fraserburgh 1 Whitehill Welfare 2. Whitehill went on to play Celtic at Easter Road and lost 3-0. It was reported they got £60,000 for a half share of the gate. My biggest wish is to meet them again and reverse the score.

After all the cup excitement, it was back to league business. We still had fourteen league games to play and after one game, Kris Hunter was having a drink with Jim Adams and, so the story goes he started the conversation with, "How's it going Mr Chairman, or do I call you Jim?" His reply was, "You can call me anything you want as long as you score 25 goals this season".

It was March and we had still to play Peterhead at the Bellslea. On a windy day, we beat them 4-0. Dave Watson wasn't too happy about the conditions, but they were the same for both teams. Goals from Jimmy Young (3 minutes), Kris Hunter with two and Paul Keith made the second half a formality. After the match, Dave Watson was having a beer in the boardroom and he was staring at the TV. It wouldn't have been so bad, but it wasn't switched on! Cheer up Dave, though there's more disappointment to come! Scotty Clark won the Supporters Club Player of the Year and Kris Hunter won the Highland League Young Player of the Year award. Huntly ran away with the league again.

	P	W	D	L	F	A	PTS
Huntly	30	27	0	3	103	34	81
Broch (5th)	30	14	9	7	85	46	51
Nairn (wooden spoon)	30	4	5	21	26	85	17

The season's top scorers were:

Yeats	Huntly	32
Hunter	Fraserburgh	29
Whyte	Huntly	29
Stewart	Huntly	28
Bridgeford	Peterhead	25
Clark	Lossiemouth	18
Duff	Wick Academy	18
McGraw	Clach	17
Polworth	Elgin	17

That was it for another season. They don't get much better, or do they?

Season 1996-97

The Broch's penalty kick hero, Scotty Clark, asked for a transfer. I reckoned that, if he wasn't happy, we should let him go, but it would be no surprise who would try to sign him? We were on our travels for pre-season friendlies, over the sea to Ireland that year, where we played Bangor and Ballyclare Comrades. We lost both games, 5-0 to Bangor and 4-3 to Ballyclare. The trip was a bonus for the players for doing so well last season. That season's squad was: Gordon, Young, Summers, Michie, Killoh, Geddes, McGruther, Norris, Murray, McBride, Murdoch, Stephen, Duthie, Herd, Stewart.

What a start to the League Cup, a 6-1 trouncing of Keith with Kris Hunter and Paul Keith running riot. Another double for Paul Keith, in a 4-1 win v Cove Rangers at Allan Park, all but secured a semi-final place against champions Huntly away from home. When that game came, Stewart gave Huntly an early lead. On the hour mark a penalty for the home side was magnificently saved by Billy Gordon to keep the Broch in the game, then Copland was red carded and the Broch sensed that the game was about to change. Murray was tripped in the box, and McCafferty converted the kick to make it 1-1, and all to play for. Hunter then scored the winner in 114 minutes to put the Broch into another final. The teams for that tie were:

Huntly: Gardiner, Grant, Allan, Copland, Paterson, Morland, Brown, Stewart, Selbie, Whyte, Gray.

Fraserburgh: Gordon, Milne, Geddes, Clark, Killoh, Thomson, McCafferty, Murray, Keith, Hunter, Stephen.
Ref – A. M. Roy

What was it about this League Cup? Were the Broch destined never to win it? I think the last time had been 1958. After taking the lead against Lossiemouth in the final, the game just ran away from us. Clark made it 1-1 a minute after half time and a wonder strike from Roy Main settled it for Lossiemouth for a final score of Fraserburgh 1 Lossiemouth 2.

Yet again, there was no time for feeling sorry for ourselves. We had a Qualifying Cup 2nd round game away to Cove Rangers to take care of first. Beattie gave Cove an early lead that day, but McCafferty made it 1-1 from the penalty spot. Beattie then scored his second to put the home side in front again, but a stroke of luck occurred, in our favour, when Megginson deflected a free kick past his own keeper to make it 2-2. Then Michael Stephen put the Broch in front for the first time 2-3 and McCafferty should have wrapped things up when he rounded the keeper and rolled the ball into the net. It was the side net however, making it the miss of a lifetime!! Craigie made it 3-3 as Cove hit back. The final score was Cove Rangers 3 Fraserburgh 3 and this set us up for a mouth-watering replay at Bellslea. That man Beattie put Cove 0-1 in front after 42 minutes, but more drama followed as Park was red-carded for an off the ball incident and there was still time for Paul Keith to bullet home the equaliser before half time. There was no further score in the ninety minutes, so it went into extra time. Six minutes into the extra session McRonald scored, to put Cove into the next round. Charlie Duncan commented, "we didn't want to win this tie."

The teams were:

Fraserburgh: Gordon, Milne, Geddes, Clark, Michie, Norris, McCafferty, Murray, Keith, Hunter, Stephen. Subs: Young, McBride, Murdoch.

Cove Rangers: Christie, Pressley, Whyte, Clark, Smart, Gibson, Park, Wilson, Megginson, Beattie, McRonald.

By mid October we weren't doing so well in the league either, lying 11th in the table, having played 6, we had lost 2, drawn 2 and won 2. If we only played every league game like all the Cup ties, we could walk the league race. The under 18's were drawn away to Dundee Utd in the B.P. Cup but were no match for the Premier club's young guns, losing 8-0. The Broch side was: Stewert, Wheeler, Duguid, McKay, A. Stephen, Summers, Herd, Duthie, Coutts, McBride, Whyte.

The Broch finally ended a four year hoodoo by beating Huntly 2 - 1 at the Bellslea in the Aberdeenshire Shield, with a young gun, who had a big future at the Bellslea, 17 year old Russell McBride, scoring the winner. We went on to play Peterhead at Cove's Allan Park in the final. Peterhead took the lead, in 29 minutes, through Colin Milne who then made it 2-0 after 59 minutes and it looked all over when Killoh deflected a shot past Billy Gordon to put Peterhead 3-0 ahead with just seventeen minutes to go. Hunter then scored a consolation goal, or was it? Then a Stephen free kick on 88 minutes had Peterhead rocking. McBride made it 3-3 in the 91st minute. With extra time looming, you could feel that something special was about to happen. The Peterhead players were standing looking at each other in disbelief, while the Broch players were, "chappin' at the bit," to get extra time started. It took only two minutes for McBride to put the Broch in front for the first time and Murray made it 5-3 four minutes later. Michael Stephen was now running riot, then Hunter made it six. When the referee blew for time, you would have to have been there to experience such a magic moment. "COME AWA THE BURGHY."

Fraserburgh: Gordon, Young, Michie, Clark, A. Stephen, Geddes, McCafferty, Murray, Killoh, Hunter, Milne. Subs: Norris, M. Stephen, McBride

Peterhead: Pirie, McCredie, Cormack, King, Simpson, Bridgeford, McKenzie, Yule, Milne, Brown, Smith, Rattray, Beadie, Robertson

Ref – Alan Freeland

In the Xmas derbies, the honours were even with both games ending in 1-1 draws. Mid-February arrived and it looked like Huntly were away with the league again while we were sitting in 7th place.

P	W	D	L	F	A	PTS
20	8	7	5	35	24	31

Buckie managed a 1-1 draw at the Bellslea in the Aberdeenshire Cup but, in the replay the following week, the Broch were too strong for them, winning 1-3 with goals from Hunter, McCafferty and Milne. We were then to cross swords with champions Huntly at the Bellslea in the semi-final. It turned out to be another classic and it took only 7 minutes for theBroch to take the lead. Former Broch player, Ronnie Smith, tripped Ian Murray, for a penalty which Jimmy Young converted. Gary Whyte made it 1-1 and Copland was then sent for an early bath just before half time. Never mind, "there's hot water for him." Hunter made it 2-1 five minutes after half time and Yeats was also sent packing with fifteen minutes to go. The final score was Fraserburgh 2 Huntly 1. Huntly player/manager, Rougvie, was called into the referee's room after the match over comments he had directed at the referee and linesman.

It was another Buchan Cup final between Peterhead and Fraserburgh at Recreation Park, the teams having tossed a coin for home advantage. We had previously beaten Huntly 2-1 at the Bellslea, with Russell McBride hitting a double. There was a big support at Peterhead for the Cup Final and they were not disappointed. The Broch went 1-0 up in 15 minutes through Geddes, but a double for Peterhead striker, Milne, after 16 and 26 minutes, saw them finish the half in front. Murray squared matters three minutes after the break and the introduction of Paul Keith changed the game. It was a goal from him, which I will remember forever, that won the game,. The ball broke out at the edge of the box and he hit a superb volley into the top corner to take the Cup back to the Broch. Final score Peterhead 2 Fraserburgh 3. This Broch side had a, "never say die approach," and it had been another season for its fans to savour. Huntly won the league.

	P	W	D	L	F	A	PTS
Huntly (champions)	30	23	4	3	86	26	73
Fraserburgh (7th)	30	15	7	8	56	38	52
Fort William (wooden spoon)	30	2	3	25	31	116	9

Jim Geddes won Goal of the Season, which was a surprise to me, as I thought Paul Keith would have walked it. Leading scorers that season were:

Beattie	Cove	36
Stewart	Huntly	35
Nicol	Keith	23
Whyte	Huntly	22
Morris	Brora	21
McRaw	Clach	20
Milne	Peterhead	20
Polworth	Elgin	18

Hunter, McBride and Keith of Fraserburgh were all on 16 goals.

Season 1997-98

It was no surprise when Peterhead signed Scotty Clark. The fee was reported to be £8,500. Scotty had been one of the most consistent players at the Bellslea over the five years he had been here. We returned to Ireland and drew 1-1 with Bangor but lost 2-1 to Ballyclare Comrades, with a BBC, "pundit," guesting for the Broch as a substitute.

We were away to Huntly for the first league game, when they were unfurling the Championship Flag. We spoiled the party, by winning 1-2, with goals from Hunter and Stephen, and carried on the good work with a 5-0 win in the League Cup v Deveronvale. We then beat Peterhead 2-1 and a draw with Rothes was all that we needed for a semi final place, but we won 3-0. The semi-final at Cove was on a knife edge at 1-1 with twelve minutes to go, but Cove then scored 3 goals in 3 minutes, from Coull 80, Nicol 81, and Beattie 82, to scupper any aspirations of a Cup final place. The final score was Cove Rangers 4 Fraserburgh 1. The teams were:

Cove Rangers: Charles, Megginson, Whyte, Smart, Gerrard, Nicol, Park, Wilson, Pillichos, Beattie, Brown.

Fraserburgh: Gordon, Milne, McCafferty, Young, A. Stephen, Murray, Thomson, McBride, Keith, Hunter, Stephen.

Ref – M. Ritchie, Macduff

The draw was kind for us in the Qualifying Cup and a 6-0 win saw off Golspie. A 9-0 win at home to Fort William saw Paul Keith in sparkling form with a hat-trick. That was 15 goals in ten games. Jimmy Young's testimonial was on Sunday and Scott Murray and Aston Villa were the opposition. Charlie described Jimmy as a manager's dream, he never missed training, was rarely injured and what's more he was a topper of a bloke. A crowd of 2,500 saw Aston Villa win 5-3 on a great day for Jimmy and his family.

We drew Deveronvale away in the semi-final of the Qualifying Cup. The week before, we lost 3-1 to them at Banff, but you're never sure with double headers. Stewert put the home side into the lead in 35 minutes from the penalty spot, but a double from top scorer Paul Keith (60 and 85 minutes) saw us through to another final with a final score of Deveronvale 1 Fraserburgh 2.

We would meet old foes Peterhead at Christie Park, Huntly in the final and, in the lead up to the game, our form was good with four straight wins in the league so the players were in a confident mood. Every day in the papers, there were photographs of different ones of them at their work. On the day of the final, as both teams emerged from the tunnel they were greeted by a great atmosphere and torrential rain, but the day was to bring disaster for the Broch. Yule had Peterhead in front in 4 minutes and, before the team knew what had hit them, Milne had added a second goal in 8 minutes. Six minutes later, Milne made it 3-0 and Smith, in 22 and 45 minutes, had Peterhead in easy street. At half time, it was Peterhead 5 Fraserburgh 0 and there was no way back for the Broch. Clark made it six and then Paterson and Cormack made it 8. It was a completely demoralised Broch team that went up for their runners-up medals after a final score of Peterhead 8 Fraserburgh 0. The teams were:

Teams: Peterhead – Pirie, Clark, Cheyne, King, Simpson, Yule, Smith, Paterson, Milne, Brown, Livingstone. Sub: McKenzie, Cormack, Baxter.

Fraserburgh: Gordon, Milne, Michie, Stephen, Geddes, McBride, Norris, Murray, Keith, Hunter, Stephen. Subs: McCafferty, Killoh, Wemyss.
Ref – W. Young, Clarkston

After the game a player from each side was picked to give a urine sample for testing. Mike Stephen was the Broch player. He was unable to comply, so they gave him a couple of cans of lager to help things along. "I can get used to this," he said with a wry smile.

We lost possession of the Aberdeenshire Shield the following week, losing 4-3 to the Vale after extra time. In a frantic game, three players were sent off. Then two new faces arrived at the Bellslea. They were brothers John and Rab Scott from Banff. Their father, Alan, was a former Broch player.

Scottish League side Clyde were our visitors in the 1st round of the Scottish Cup. A week of rain postponed the match and when it finally got the go ahead it should have been welly boots, not football boots as the famous Clinic end was like a sand pit. What a start there was to this match. Ian Murray was sent off for tipping a goalbound shot off the line, with Brian Rice hitting the post from the resulting penalty kick. Two minutes after that the Broch took the lead, Paul Keith finishing off a sweet move. Now I know how John Wayne felt at The Alamo, as we managed to hold on to the end. What a result the final score Fraserburgh 1 Clyde 0 was. The teams who braved those conditions were:

Fraserburgh: Gordon, Milne, R. Scott, Young, A. Stephen, Murray, J. Scott, McBride, Hunter, Keith, Stephen.

Clyde: McLean, McStay, Tortolano, King, Baptie, Rice, McPhee, Campbell, Scott, Gibson, Brownlie.
Ref - D. McDonald, Edinburgh   Att - 1,200

The Daily Record reporter wrote, in Monday's headline, "A Can of Lager and a £10 bonus for Broch Cup Heroes." By the way, we were sitting proudly at the top of the league that Xmas.

P	W	D	L	F	A	PTS
13	11	1	1	36	13	34

The first Buchan derby at Balmoor Stadium on 20th December was a 1-0 win, with Paul Keith's 26th goal of the season. Peterhead then reversed the result with a 1-2 win at the Bellslea, their first win in a Derby there for five years. The Broch took the lead from Paul Keith, but Brown made it 1-1 and Smith put the visitors in front two minutes from the interval. There was no further scoring. Final score – Fraserburgh 1 Peterhead 2. Neil Clark was deputising for keeper Billy Gordon in goal and the attendance at the Bellslea on the Saturday was an incredible 1,400 (the envy of a few Scottish League clubs.)

If there's one team you didn't want to draw in the Cup it's Stranraer, but who did we get in the next round? You've guessed. The Broch party stayed at Ayr on the Friday night, but news was filtering through on the Saturday morning that the game was postponed due to high winds and lashing rain. Jim Adams wasn't a happy chappy, complaining, "it's time the SFA took heed of the weather forecast." An old Skipper told Jim before the Broch left that gales and rain were sweeping through Scotland on the Friday night. Who said you need a Scottish Cup run to make money? Try telling the Broch that with a bus for two days, meals & hotel bills, need I say more?

The following week the Broch again set off at 4 o'clock on Friday afternoon and again stayed overnight at Ayr. On the Saturday morning, the weather wasn't that much better than it had been the week before. A training session was held, though the weather still wasn't great but we kept hoping we would get the go ahead. Neil Clark was standing by to play in goal if Billy Gordon didn't make it, but, after a pitch inspection, the match went ahead. I thought we would never get to Stranraer, although it's only an hour down the road from Ayr, but it reminds you of going to Wick!

The Broch kicked off with Billy Gordon in his usual position. We fell behind after just 17 minutes, following a scorcher of a volley from Paul Kinnaird. Nine minutes later he scored another glorious goal, taking the ball from the halfway line and leaving the Broch defence in his wake, before burying the ball past Gordon. At half time it was 2-0, but, in the second half, the Broch gave it a real go, though Hunter's strike, on 86 minutes, was too little too late. The game finished Stranraer 2 Fraserburgh 1. The teams that day were:

Stranraer: Mathews, Knox, Black, George, Campbell, Watson, McAulay, Landsdowne, Young, Docherty, Kinnaird

Fraserburgh: Gordon, Milne, Michie, Scott, A. Stephen, Young, Norris, McBride, Keith, Hunter, Stephen.

Ref – R. Tait, East Kilbride   Attendance - 676

Charlie's comment after the game was, "if Stranraer and Clyde are typical of their division, I fear for Scottish Football." There were over 100 Broch fans at Stair Park, but, if the game had been played at the Bellslea, I'm sure we would have at least 1,500 of a crowd. Ah well!

Back to league business, a 2-2 draw v Elgin City, with Paul Keith scoring his 100th goal for the Broch at the Bellslea. The following week at Borough Briggs he grabbed another couple in a 4-1 win, that was 30 goals this season. By Wednesday February 14th, theBroch were top of the league with a hard fought win at Lossie.

	P	W	D	L	F	A	PTS
Broch	20	16	2	2	54	23	50
Huntly	22	15	4	3	70	28	49

There's nothing like being brought down to earth with a bump. A 1-0 home defeat to Deveronvale came next, but two nervy 1-0 wins v Clach (h) and Nairn (a) had us back on track and so to another disappointing night at Cove. John Scott missed a penalty to give the Broch the lead and, just after that, Coull put Cove ahead. Beattie then added a second in the 56th minute, before Paul Keith pulled one back to make it 2-1, but Beattie scored again to put the issue beyond doubt with a final score of Cove Rangers 3 Fraserburgh 1.

Another big game came along the following week at the Bellslea, this time a, "must win," game against Huntly. A crowd estimated at 1,800 turned up for this cracker. The Broch threw everything at Huntly but they held on to keep the final score 0-0, though the Broch returned to the top of the league after a 4-0 win away to Fort William. At Forres the following week came one of the worst decisions I've seen in all my years watching the Broch. With the game on a knife edge at 2-2, the Broch scored. The linesman was running to the centre, acknowledging the goal, when, all of a sudden, he stopped, changed his mind and ran back to the corner flag and disallowed the score!! Well, all hell was let loose, but the goal didn't stand and Forres hit a late winner, to make the final score Forres 3, Fraserburgh 2.

The table, with two games left read,

	P	W	D	L	F	A	PTS
Huntly	28	20	5	3	86	31	65
Broch	28	20	3	5	66	30	63

With those two games left, home and away to Wick, what were the chances of a Huntly slip up? With eighty minutes of the home game on the clock and the Broch cruising 2-0, a huge roar went round the Bellslea. What was going on? A rumour spread that Huntly were 2-1 down to Elgin City. At the final whistle, however, the final score was confirmed as Huntly 2 Elgin City 1. Huntly won both of their last two games and were crowned champions. The Broch could only manage a 1-1 draw on the final away game to Wick, bringing acute disappointment at the finish.

	P	W	D	L	F	A	PTS
Huntly (first)	30	22	5	3	92	32	71
Broch (2nd)	30	21	4	5	69	31	67
Nairn Co	30	3	3	24	36	94	12
(wooden spoon)							

The Broch won the Jarlaw Aberdeenshire League for the fourth time in five years, but it was no consolation for the heartbreak of the season. Michael Stephen won the Supporters Club Player of the Year and Paul Keith won the Black and White Player of the Year with a remarkable 39 goals for his season.

It seemed incredible, but some things never change at the end of the season with headlines like, "Breakaway Threat," or, "Reconstruction." (Ach, go away and have a holiday and forget about fitba' for a while.) Last but not least, we said goodbye to referee Sandy Roy, who was hanging up his whistle. He'd be sadly missed as there were a few of the up and coming, short-sighted, arriving to take his place.

Season 1998-99

It had been so close, but yet so far. Now that we'd closed the gap on Huntly, would this finally be the season we would win the league? Former Broch favourite, Brian Thomson (Luggies) returned to the Bellslea, which gave us a real boost for the campaign. It was £48 for a season ticket and £24 for OAP's and children. If a father and two sons were at a Premier game, it would probably cost him £72 for the day out. It might be money better spent watching the Broch for a season.

At Cove, Brian Thomson scored his first goal, with his trusty left foot, from a free kick to square matters at 1-1. Michael Stephen then made it 1-2 and Paul Keith made it 1-3. Beattie reduced the leeway with a penalty to make the final score Cove Rangers 2, Fraserburgh 3.
The teams that day were:

Cove Rangers: Charles, Cowell, Whyte, Johnstone, Rougvie, Megginson, Park, Nicol, Coull, Beattie, Brown.

Fraserburgh: Gordon, Milne, Geddes, Young, A. Stephen, McBride, Norris, Thomson, Keith, Hunter, Stephen.

The following week veteran keeper, Neil Clark was in goal for the Broch against Peterhead when we lost 3-0. We then drew them at Balmoor in the second round of the Qualifying Cup. McBride put Broch 0-1 in front in 72 minutes, but, deep into injury time, Yeats headed an equaliser to take the Blue Tooners back to the Bellslea the following week. It was not to be the Broch's day however. Brown had the visitors in the lead after 16 minutes and Smith made it 0-2 before Brian Thomson hit an 18 yard thunderbolt to put the Broch in the game. Peterhead then wrapped things up when Yule made it 1-3 in 85 minutes for a final score of Fraserburgh 1 Peterhead 3.

On a sad note, the death was announced of former Broch player Eddie Noble (Ebbins.) He had also played for Deveronvale and won a league medal with Elgin City. Eddie was known for his cannon-ball shot, and that was with the old leather ball. He was a good friend and would be sadly missed.

Cove Rangers were setting the pace in the league with the Broch in third place.

P	W	D	L	F	A	PTS
7	5	2	0	22	7	17

Champions Huntly wriggled off the hook at the Bellslea. 3-0 down at half time, and looking dead and buried, they came back to snatch a draw. Goals from Stephen, J. Thomson and Paul Keith had the Broch on easy street, but Moreland, Murphy and Black hit back for the champions. The final score was Fraserburgh 3 Huntly 3.

We made our exit from the Aberdeenshire Shield after a 3-1 defeat at Deveronvale with keeper Billy Gordon and John Thomson being sent off. Brian Thomson took over between the sticks and it was good to see Ian Murray (Molby) back after a knee injury. The Broch's young guns were due to play Hibs at the Bellslea in the B. P. Cup, a great experience, but the Premier side ran out 8-0 winners. The Broch line up was: Stephen, Wheeler, Paul, Scott, Aitkenhead, Fleming, Bruce, McLaren, Duff, Martin, Bissett, May, Stewart. Six of that team went on to play for the first team.

A 9-0 victory over Fort William sent us back to the top of the league at the beginning of December, but bad weather took its toll for the rest of the month. Our next game was at Cove on January 2nd where we won 2-1, Kris Hunter hitting the winner with eight minutes to go. Another four straight wins followed for the team and things were looking good, but, as usual, we came down to earth with a bump. The Broch slithered to a 3-1 defeat at Clach, in a match played in atrocious conditions. At Balmoor the following week a crowd of 2,300 turned up for another top of the table derby. Scott Paterson put the home side in front, but Michael Stephen cancelled it out making it 1-1. Referee Gover then sent off Colin Milne and Andy Stephen in different incidents, but only he knew the reason, very strange. Up at Huntly we dropped another three precious points, in a 2-1 defeat, for them to go top of the league by two points, with a game in hand.

The following week a crowd of 2,300 turned up at the Bellslea for the derby game with Peterhead. Two goals in two minutes knocked the stuffing out of the Broch. Despite Paul Keith's effort in 75 minutes to reduce the leeway, the visitors went straight up the park and scored through Paterson to put the match beyond us. The final score was Fraserburgh 1 Peterhead 3 and the teams for that derby match were:

Fraserburgh: Gordon, Milne, McBride, Scott, Stephen, Murray, McKenzie, Thomson, Anderson, Hunter, Stephen.

Peterhead: Pirie, Clark, Campbell, King, Simpson, Gibson, Paterson, G. Clark, Milne, Brown, Livingstone.
Ref – G. Simpson, Westhill.

With Huntly defeated at Forres, it looked odds on for Peterhead to win the league, but it was on then, to the

League Cup. The four team section set up was baffling. You either had two games at home and one away or vice versa. We drew Peterhead, Keith and Rothes and another defeat came at the hands of our old rivals, despite Keith firing the Broch in front. Two late goals from Yeats had Peterhead in the driving seat for a final score of Fraserburgh 1 Peterhead 2. Keith beat us 2-0 away from home, so the game at Rothes was meaningless, though we hit the goal trail, winning 7-1 through a Kris Hunter hat-trick, a double for P.K. and one for Molby to end the season on a high note.

Peterhead were crowned champions with the Broch finishing in a disappointing fifth place. Russell McBride won Young Player of the Year, but there was disappointing news for Broch fans. After fourteen seasons John Thomson was leaving the Bellslea to play for Longside. They don't make them like, "Tossill," any more, another player who wore his heart on his sleeve.

Season 1999-2000

Departures during the close season included John and Rab Scott and Scotty Anderson, but several new faces from the youth side were set to make their mark: Graeme Bain, Ian Wheeler, Trevor Fleming, Chris Martin, and Scott Mackie.

A young Broch side got a football lesson in a friendly with Ayr United, losing 6-1, then Deveronvale knocked us out of the Aberdeenshire Cup, 2-0 at Banff, with Ian Murray getting a double red card. We bounced back the following week, putting seven past Fort William and, back up at the Vale in the league, we got our revenge, winning 3-5 with Ian Murray getting a hat-trick. The draw was kinder to us in the Qualifying Cup, with a home tie against Fort William. Down 1-0 at half time, the Broch fought back to go through to the next round 4-2, with goals from Hunter, Keith and a double from Derek Milne. We hammered Keith 7-1 at the Bellslea, the following Wednesday night, in the league. A young Gavin Wemyss came on as a substitute at Lossie and scored two cracking goals to put the Broch back to the top of the league on a final score of Lossiemouth 1 Fraserburgh 3.

The Broch breezed into the last four of the Qualifying Cup with a 4-1 win over Forres at the Bellslea, but, would you believe it? We drew Peterhead in the semi-final at home. The Broch were under the cosh for most of the first half, but on 65 minutes, Michael Stephen shot us into the lead. This, however, would not be a Buchan derby without some controversy. Peterhead had the ball in the net and were celebrating, in their usual style in front of the stand, but the linesman's flag had stayed up, for no goal. Brian Thomson then sealed it for the Broch in a memorable match. Final score Fraserburgh 2 Peterhead 0. The teams in that game were:

Fraserburgh: Gordon, Milne, Martin, Young, McBride, Wemyss, Norris, Murray, Keith, Hunter. M. Stephen. Subs: Thomson, Mackie, A. Stephen.

Peterhead: Pirie, Clark, Morrison, King, Simpson, Yule, Gibson, Smith, Milne, Brown, Livingstone.
Ref – S. Conroy.

After going back to the top of the league, with impressive victories, away to Cove, 2-3, and at Elgin City, 1-2, we could only draw 1-1 at home with Rothes. It wasn't the best preparation for the Qualifying Cup final the following week against Huntly up at Borough Briggs, Elgin. A major blow for the Broch was Kris Hunter missing the final, due to suspension, but would the Broch break their duck, not having won a final at Elgin since the 1950's?

Huntly set their stall out from the start and that was to cut the threat of Michael Stephen and Paul Keith. The Broch were therefore forced to play second fiddle for most of the game. It was 0-0 at half time, but Huntly had looked the likelier side to score. Martin Stewart broke the deadlock on 69 minutes and, with the Broch then chasing the game, Gary Whyte struck in 90 minutes. Game, set and match. Final score Fraserburgh 0 Huntly 2. It was a disappointing day for the Club and for the large travelling support. The teams were:

Fraserburgh: Gordon, Milne, Geddes, Young, McBride, Wemyss, Norris, Murray, Keith, Mackie, Stephen. Subs: Thomson (64), A.Stephen(76), Martin (90).

Huntly: Morgan, Black, Allan, Morland, Paterson, Guild, Smith, Wilson, Stewart, Addicoat, McRonald.

Ref – D. Somers

Another final lay ahead, after a 1-4 win at Buckie in the Aberdeenshire Shield. We then defeated Keith 2-1 at Huntly, with Ian Murray turning on a sixpence to hit the winner past a helpless Ian Thain. Nice to win the Shield again, but it didn't compensate for the Qualifying Cup defeat.

Arbroath in the Scottish Cup, down at Gayfield, was our prize. Our form was good, as we were top of the league, after beating Peterhead 3-1 at Xmas. Victory had us ten points ahead of our old foes, setting us up nicely for the Arbroath game. What a great old fashioned Cup tie it turned out to be, with the Broch hanging on for a 0-0 draw, and down to nine men, Kris Hunter and James Geddes having been sent off. With time running out, Billy Gordon had a save, which if it had been shown on TV would have been repeated more times than, "The Longest Day." The final score was Arbroath 0 Fraserburgh 0. This was what the Scottish Cup is all about. Teams:

Arbroath: Wight, Florence, Gallacher, McAuly, Thomson, Crawford, Cooper, Bryce, McGlashan, Arbuckle, Mercer.

Fraserburgh: Gordon, Milne, McBride, Murray, Fleming, Geddes, Norris, Thomson, Wemyss, Hunter, Stephen. Subs: Young, Mackie, Martin Att 1,235

On the way home, one of the young players wasn't too happy at not getting a game, but I told him. "You've played in a Cup Final and been on the bench in the Scottish Cup. This time last year you were playing out on the playing fields, your time will come"

The replay was another story of ifs and buts, as the Broch's dream ended again in disappointment. Arbroath took an early lead, with McGlashan scoring after eight minutes. Mercer added a second three minutes after half time to put the visitors in a comfortable position, till Florence deflected a cross past his own keeper to give the Broch some hope. But a late strike from Devine sealed it for Arbroath. Final score Fraserburgh 1 Arbroath 3. The teams were:

Fraserburgh: Gordon, Milne, McBride, Fleming, A. Stephen, Murray, Norris, Thomson, Stephen, Wemyss, Mackie, Young (30), McLaren (81)
Ref – Ian Frekelton Att' - 2,305

The crowds at the games between Highland League sides, and their Scottish League counterparts, in the Scottish Cup put some of those league teams to shame. I'm sure the likes of East Stirling and Montrose could only dream of getting a gate the size of that at the Bellslea on Saturdays. After nineteen games, we were sitting pretty at the top of the league

P	W	D	L	F	A	PTS
19	14	4	1	59	20	46

Nearest rivals, Peterhead, were ten points behind but three 1-1 draws, twice to Buckie and then with Elgin City, gave our title hopes a shake. The fans were getting restless and it was getting to the players. Another miserable afternoon followed at Mosset Park, Forres when they turned us over 3-1, with Charlie Brown hitting a double. Keith had taken over at the top of the table, so we had to win against Huntly. In a bruising battle we came out on top 2-0, Brian Thomson scoring the second goal a minute from time. So it was on to Balmoor for yet another battle. Ivor Pirie was stopping everything that the Broch could throw at him before Scott Clark opened the scoring and Derek Smith added a second. Michael Stephen converted a penalty to give the Broch a glimmer of hope at 2-1 and we were not finished. Stephen equalised with six minutes to go to give the

Broch a share of the points. The final score was Peterhead 2 Fraserburgh 2. We were then five points behind leaders Keith, but had two games in hand.

The Broch were set for the crunch game at Kynoch Park, minus the suspended Russell McBride, and James Geddes, who was working offshore, but another disappointing night was in store as you can't give Keith two goals of a start and expect to win. A crowd of 1,600, mostly Brochers, witnessed our ultimate chance of the league slip away. The final Score was Keith 2 Fraserburgh 2. The teams, on that disappointing night, were:

Keith: Thain, Brown, Simmers, Craig, Watt, Gibson, Stille, Presslie, Robertson, Nicol, Hendry.

Fraserburgh: Gordon, Milne, Martin, Stephen, Young, Murray, Norris, Thomson, Hunter, Fleming, Stephen. Sub: Keith (57), Wemyss (74).

Headlines in the Press the following day read, "Broch Bid Ends in Bitter Disappointment."

"Keith One Win from Championship." Why did it always happen to us? Those three draws in our final three games earned us only the runners-up spot.

	P	W	D	L	F	A	PTS
Keith (champions)	30	21	3	6	76	38	66
Broch (runner up)	30	17	10	3	75	32	61

We couldn't have asked for a tougher League Cup section, home to Buckie, away to Peterhead and away to Keith. We disposed of Buckie 3-0, but the next tie was to be the final competitive game between Broch and Peterhead, before they took their place in the Scottish League. Never again, when they put the ball over the bar, would be heard the sound of, "PETERHEID!!!" The Broch gave them a good send off, by beating them 3-0, with two from Hunter and one from Derek Milne. A late equaliser up at Keith from Neil McLaren, in a 3-3 draw, saw us qualify for the semi-finals, where we would meet Cove at Allan

Park. It all started so brightly as the Broch were 2-0 up in ten minutes. But disaster then struck and we lost 6-2 after extra time. It was time for a summer break, I thought, after another disappointing season. Ian Murray won the Supporters Club Player of the Year and Elgin City were accepted into the Scottish League, along with Peterhead. It would be hard replacing teams of that status in the league for the future.

Chapter Six

The Noughties (A Dream Fulfilled)

As we entered the new millenium, life had changed and the Highland League with it. The pie shop at Lossiemouth had previously been their changing rooms, and do you remember the tin roofed changing rooms under the trees at Huntly? Having five substitutes would also be strange. As for the Broch, we were to have two dozen new training balls at the start of the pre-season training, and a new strip for nearly every season. What would the players of the fifties and sixties have had to say about that? On match days the, "new generation," players got a T-shirt, for warming up, waterproof tops and towels supplied, plus at least three pairs of new boots, in a season. Some of the younger players have probably had it too easy, take the pre-season, for example, their boots are taken over to the playing fields for them and there's water and juice supplied at the beach. Then, after a gruelling stint on the beach, and on cold nights, there's a cup of tea or coffee waiting for them, courtesy of Brucie Buchan.

On the other hand, I hear the fans having a go at the players sometimes. Well, while they're sitting having a cool pint and playing pool on a warm summer's day, they should think of the players over the beach or sprinting up the, "big hill," (I don't know where they got the, 'tiger hill,' name from.) Dedication, is another priceless word. A guy like Billy Gordon left the house for work at 6am, drove to Dyce and back, arrived home, in time to collect his training gear, drove to the Broch from Cruden Bay, trained, then drove home, arriving there at the back of ten, at bed time. That's what you call dedication, though there are some football, "fans," who couldn't spell the word. The Club now ran like clockwork. Neil Clark, Jimmy Young, Brian Sim, Brucie Buchan and Charlie Duncan saw to that. The players couldn't have been trained by a better coaching staff, who, between them, must have played 2000 Highland League games. (Brucie must have seen 2000 Highland League games.)

Along came another trip to Ireland, where we beat Carrick Rangers 1-0, but then lost 2-1 to Bangor. The Press had the Broch as favourites for the League (now where had I heard this before?) By the way, we won an early trophy that year, by winning at the Maud 5 a sides tournament. The winners cheque was put to good use for some after match refreshments.

A 4-1 win at home to Brora and 2-0 away to Nairn was a good start. Then we drew 2-2 away to Buckie in the Aberdeenshire Cup, but with Paul Keith red-carded. Neil McLaren then netted the winner, at the Bellslea in the replay. Teenager Stuart Finnie hit the winner in the semi-final against Huntly, with Fraserburgh winning 2 - 1. We were then to meet Deveronvale at Balmoor Stadium in the final, but had an early Qualifying Cup exit at the hands of Forres at Mosset Park, losing 3 – 1.

In the final, an injury hit Broch lost 2-1 to Vale. Vale took the lead, with a suspiciously offside goal. The Broch then equalised through Milne, but a dodgy penalty then sealed it for Vale, Cadger scoring with the spot kick. The final score was Fraserburgh 1 Deveronvale 2. It was Vale's first Aberdeenshire Cup win since 1966. The teams that contested the final were:

Fraserburgh: Gordon, Milne, Martin, Young, Stephen, Norris, Murray, McBride, Finnie, Hunter, Stephen.

Deveronvale: Phimister, Dolan, Kinghorn, Chisholm, Henderson, Montgomery, Singer, Nicol, Cadger, Watt, Urquhart.

Brian Thomson was then on his travels again, this time to Buckie Thistle, whom we beat on his debut with a score of 3-1.

It was now mid November and at last we'd got the monkey off our backs, beating Huntly 5-1 at Christie Park, with doubles from Kris Hunter and Gavin Wemyss, but Peterhead were at it again. They had been chasing Ian Murray all summer, but though the Broch put up the, "Not for Sale," sign, Ian wanted to have a go at Scottish League football, and we wished him well. I used to joke with, 'Molby,' that if it hadn't been for Charlie and Brucie, he would either have been in jail or playing junior football, judging from the amount of scrapes they've saved him from.

There were more, "new kids on the block," just waiting for a break into the first team. Guys like Graham Coutts, Graham Bain, Trevor Fleming, Ian Wheeler, Chris Martin, Stuart Finnie and Ian Bissett. Sadly, however, in spite of their promise, a few of them fell by the wayside for one reason or another. It was a strange feeling, not having the Xmas derbies against Peterhead to look forward to, but the rivalry between Cove and ourselves had gathered momentum, so we would just have to enjoy the pleasure of taking six points from them instead.

By mid January however, we were a disappointing 6th in the league table.

P	W	D	L	F	A	PTS
17	8	2	3	31	25	26

Broch manager, Charlie Duncan, was banned from the dugout for three months, following comments aimed at match officials. I don't believe that! One story tells of a referee, who was having a nightmare when, with Charlie passing on a word or two of well intended advice, the linesman intervened. "Calm down Mr Duncan," he says, but Charlie replied, "Do you know anything about football?" "Have you ever refereed, "the linesman returned? Charlie's answer? "Every game." Another incident, was when an opposition player contested every decision, time after time. The referee had had enough and booked him, but he continued arguing so Charlie shouted, "You can't send him off there will be no-one to referee the game." That was just another Saturday, with loads of humour in the dugout. Billy Gordon played his 500th game for the Broch against Deveronvale, that season, but these days some players don't stay minutes with a club.

A comfortable 1-0 and 3-0 win over two legs against Lossiemouth saw us march into the quarter finals of the League Cup where we would meet Nairn County. Trevor Fleming scored the winner in the first leg, while, the following week, Mike Stephen put the Broch 1-0 in front after only 3 minutes, for a 2-0 on aggregate lead. Nairn then hit back and ran out worthy winners 1-4, to make it 4-2 on aggregate. What is it about the League Cup?

Cove Rangers were crowned champions with the Broch in eighth place.

	P	W	D	L	F	A	PTS
Cove Rangers (champions)	26	20	3	3	74	32	63
Broch (8th)	26	12	3	11	47	38	39

Russell McBride won the Supporters Club Player of the Year, with Derek Milne getting the Goal of the Season award. Inverurie Locos were elected into the league How the seasons came and went, I had to be getting old!

Season 2001-02

Fans favourite, Russell McBride bade farewell to the Broch and signed for Elgin City. He would be sorely missed. We drew 1-1 with Cowdenbeath in a friendly at the Bellslea, where Kevin Norris notched his 250th appearance for the Broch. He wouldn't forget it in a hurry. We were then beaten 8 – 0 at home by Vale in the League Cup, but it was too early for a crisis, wasn't it??? The Fraserburgh side was: Gordon, Milne, Geddes, Killoh, Bain, Norris, Mackie, Main, Stephen, Weymss, McLaren, Dewar, Coutts

Forres knocked us out of the Qualifying Cup 1-2 at the Bellslea. With the score at 1-1, and fiveminutes to go, there were two penalty claims. Forres got theirs, but the Broch did not. Main converted, leaving the final score Fraserburgh 1 Forres 2. September had only just arrived and the Broch were out of two Cups, but worse was to follow, when 3-0 up at home to Rothes with 15 minutes to go, defensive jitters saw Rothes come back to snatch a 3 – 3 draw. It was not a happy Bellslea just then! Clark Killoh was on his way, as Formartine Utd signed him. His work commitments meant he couldn't train twice weekly.

Our fortunes however were turning, through beating Forres 2-0 and with an impressive 4-0 win, away to high flying Keith. New boy Ian Bissett played a vital role, up front with Kris Hunter and then Stuart Finnie hit the winner, four minutes into injury time, against Cove in the Aberdeenshire Shield. Deveronvale then beat Buckie 5-1 in the final of the Qualifying Cup, but how about this for a score? Inverurie Locos 8, Cove 2. Now they would know how the Fort Williams of this world felt! Ian Bissett had scored on his debut in a 1-3 win at Buckie Thistle. He went on to play an important part in the season. We then took a point up at Nairn in a 3-3 draw, Nairn finishing the match with only nine men.

A further record worth a mention was that of goalkeeping coach, Neil Clark, who made his Broch debut on the 4th April 1978 at Kingsmills, home of Inverness Thistle. He went on to play in four decades, the 70's, 80's, 90's, even making a few appearances in the 2000-2001 season. Neil was another club legend.

Keith beat us 3-2 at Inverurie in the Aberdeenshire Shield, but, on December 2nd we had a chance to make up lost league ground, but lost 3-1 up at Huntly. The rest of that Highland League card was wiped out due to bad weather. Martin Stewart put the home side 1-0 in front, but Mike Stephen equalised from the penalty spot. Munro then made it 2-1 before Bissett was up ended, resulting in a further penalty kick to the Broch. Stephen blasted it high over the bar, but Martin Stewart then secured the points to make it 3-1. The teams were:

Huntly: Bremner, Campbell, Allan, Guild, Small, Munro, Thomson, Wilson, Stewart, Ogboke, Nicol

Fraserburgh: Gordon, Milne, Wemyss, Geddes, Bissett, Fleming, Norris, Mackie, Main, Hunter, Stephen.

These were the top of the league placings on Saturday December 8th.

	P	W	D	L	F	A	PTS
Deveronvale	13	16	1	2	35	12	31
Huntly	14	8	2	4	29	16	26
Clach	14	7	5	2	28	25	26
Fraserburgh	12	7	2	3	32	19	23

Our New Year's derby this year was with Cove at the Bellslea and what a game it was. The final score was 3-3, with Doug Baxter, a Broch fans, "favourite," taking an early bath that day. Never mind, there was plenty of hot water for him!! The following week saw us play Keith at home. It was not often that Scott Mackie hit the net, but his scorcher kept us in the game at 2-2, before Derek Milne netted the winner for a final score of Fraserburgh 3 Keith 2.

Charlie Duncan refused to be drawn into saying we were in with a shout of the Championship, but the Broch kept winning, 2-0 away to Wick Academy, with late goals from Michael Stephen and Kevin Norris, followed by a 1-0 win away to Rothes with Ian Bissett scoring. "Anything but title contenders," was Charlie's comment. Next up was the big test, Huntly at home and, with Kris Hunter and Michael Stephen both injured, it was up to young guns. Neil McLaren and Ian Bissett to do the business. Bissett made it 1-0 in 7 minutes, McLaren then made it 2-0 and he wrapped up the points in injury time. The final score was Fraserburgh 3 Huntly 1 and the Broch went to the top of the league, for the first time this season.

The February 16th league placings were:

	P	W	D	L	F	A	PTS
Broch	19	13	3	3	51	25	42
Deveronvale	16	13	1	2	47	15	40

The Broch were away to Brora the following week in what was never an easy fixture. With the score at 2-2 and the referee looking at his watch, the Brora bench were howling for time up. The Broch, however, were camped in their box and Michael Stephen finally got his head to a cross to score the winner in the fifth minute of injury time. When you saw Neil Clark jumping about at the final whistle, you knew that this was an important three points!

Up at Forres, a fortnight later, we drew 3-3. This was a fixture which usually ended up in controversy, and this one was no different. Ross had the home side in front in 3 minutes before a rare Steven Main goal had the Broch level. Somerville made it 2-1, but Hunter then squared matters at 2-2. What was it about the stand side linesmen at Forres? Another dodgy decision in that game saw the Broch ship a penalty, from which Roy Main scored to make it 3-2. Fortunately, Hunter squared matters again in 82 minutes for a final score of Forres 3 Fraserburgh 3. Forres pair, McLeod and Reid, were sent off in a torrid final five minutes. The teams for that game were:

Forres: McRitchie, Somerville, Main, Bradshaw, Grigor, Reid, Whyte, Hayden, McLeod, Connely, Ross.

Fraserburgh: Gordon, Milne, Geddes, Fleming, Norris, Mackie, Wemyss, S. Main, Stephen, McLaren, Finnie. Subs: Hunter (60 mins) Bissett (70 mins)
Ref – C. Mckay

Wednesday March 20th and a Gavin Wemyss strike against Buckie Thistle at the Bellslea had the Broch five points in front of Vale at the top of the table, but nerves were getting to the players and it showed. Away to Fort William with the score at 0-0 and half an hour to play, it seemed that the more we tried, the worse it got. Fort William sensed they could maybe steal a point and Charlie had all the subs retrieving the match ball, trying to speed up the game. The breakthrough came when the Fort defence didn't clear their lines and Steven Main thumped the ball into the roof of the net in 64 minutes. With all the subs back in the dugout, the Broch played out a nervous game for another vital three points. The final score was Fort William 0 Fraserburgh 1.

We stayed on course at the top of the league with a 0-4 win at Locos, but Trevor Fleming's season was over as he was stretchered off with a punctured lung. The following week Locos beat us 4-2 at the Bellslea. Another trip to Lossiemouth followed, where the Broch won 2 - 0, while Vale won 1-0 away to Wick Academy. On that Saturday night the table looked like this:

Saturday, April 27th	P	W	D	L	F	A	PTS
Deveronvale	26	18	4	4	63	25	58
Fraserburgh	26	18	4	4	67	34	58

This was getting serious, and we needed a bit of humour. The story was told then of a young Michael Stephen, who had just broken into the first team. Charlie was giving a team talk and he told Michael to take the inswinging corners. A bemused Michael inquired, "is that the curly in eens?" The dressing room erupted in laughter!!

Then came the game we'd been waiting for, against Deveronvale at the Bellslea. It was just like the old days. The kick off was delayed to let the crowd in and the dressing room was tense. Early in the game, Robbie Brown put the Vale in front, but Neil McLaren made it 1-1 three minutes before half time and the Bellslea erupted. The struggle dragged on until, with ten minutes to go, Gavin Wemyss headed the Broch in front. After that, time stood still. Was the referee never going to blow the whistle? When he did it was pure bedlam! Final score Fraserburgh 2 Deveronvale 1. The teams that night were:

Fraserburgh: Gordon, Milne, Geddes, Norris, Mackie, Main, Hunter, Stephen, Dewar, Wemyss (25), Bissett (86), McLaren, Finnie

Deveronvale: Thompson, Dolan, Kinghorn, Chisholm, Henderson, Montgomery, Murray, Brown, Watt, Pressley.
Ref – A. Freeland   Att'- 3,000

Destiny awaited us. We only needed a draw, away to Cove, for the title to be ours. Goal hero, Wemyss, would miss the match with hamstring problems, but the Broch would fly Kris Hunter down from Wick, where he was working at that time. As we crossed the River Dee on the way to Cove, my stomach was in a knot, but I have no idea how the players must have felt. So, on a still May night at Cove, the Broch ran out onto Allan Park to such a tremendous welcome that it seemed just like a home game. Neil McLaren had the Broch in front, with a double in the first half, but a James Geddes own goal then set up a nervous finish. As the referee blew the final whistle for a 1-2 result it was bedlam yet again. Tears were flowing, this was what we had waited to see since I was a youngster. Forget Rangers winning the treble or Scotland winning at Wembley, this was what football was all about, your home town team winning the championship in front of its own fans.

The teams were:

Fraserburgh: Gordon, Milne, Bissett, Geddes, Norris, Mackie, Main, Hunter, Stephen, McLaren, Finnie

Cove: Charles, Summers, Marwick, Murphy, McHattie, Pilicos, Adam, Emslie, Coull, Beattie, Brown
Ref – S. Duff Att - 2,050   COME AWA THE BURGHY!

We all landed back at D.J.'s nightclub and what a night that was!! Jimmy Adams sat in the corner with the Championship Cup, not letting it out of his sight. I was standing with Brucie Buchan and we had a wee toast to, 'Jimmy Brown.' We hoped he was watching, as he would have enjoyed that night. The following week we had an open-deck bus taking the team around the town with the

Cup. I'll remember that for the rest of my life and to be in the photograph with the team was one of my proudest moments in football.
Fraserburgh, at last, were Highland League Champions.

	P	W	D	L	F	A	PTS
Fraserburgh	28	20	4	4	71	36	64
Deveronvale	28	19	4	5	68	27	61
(runners up)							

I said to Neil McLaren at the time, "You won't realise what you've done until about 20 years from now," he just grinned! Michael Stephen won the Player of the Year, but when I think of great players like Bertie Bowie, Kenny Rogers and Brian Newlands, who never won anything important in their careers with the Broch, it brought it all home. I thought once we'd won the league I'd be satisfied, but you always want more. Could it get any better than this?

Season 2002-03

It was a proud day for Fraserburgh F.C, as the Highland League Championship Flag flew over the Bellslea, and certainly a day I thought I'd never see. Johnny Sinclair, a long-serving committee member, had the honour of raising the flag. Arbroath won 2-1 in a friendly at the Bellslea and a Rangers under-21 side had a comfortable 3-0 win on the Sunday. With guys like Hutton, Darl, Duffy and Charlie Adam in their line-up, Rangers were that yard quicker than our young guns.

Buckie Thistle were our first visitors, in the Aberdeenshire Cup, and, with us being champions, everyone was after our scalp. Buckie won comfortably 0-2. A controversial penalty, in a 2-1 win at home to Clach, kicked off our defence of the title campaign. However, what about this for a score, Grill League Cup - Culter 16 Maud 0 with Neil Ritchie hitting a treble hat-trick.

It was going to be a tough season and a 1-5 defeat at home to Keith took us back down to earth. We then met Lossiemouth in a double-header away, from home once in the league, which they won 3-2, and in the Qualifying Cup the following week. Sadly, before that game took place, tragedy struck the club. Young Broch star Mark Dewar drowned in Fraserburgh Harbour after his car skidded off the pier. He was only 18 years old, and known in the dressing room as, "Donald," after the politician. It was one of the biggest funerals I've ever been to, with Broch team mates carrying his casket. We all miss you Mark, thanks for the memories.

It was a strange feeling in the Lossiemouth dressing room. No-one knew if some one present should crack a joke, in order to break the silence? After a minute's silence out on the pitch, the Broch advanced into the next round with a double from Mike Stephen and one from comeback man Paul Keith with a bullet header, sealing a 1-3 victory. Against Keith in the next round, a 90th minute equaliser from Mike Stephen got us out of jail. For a final score of Fraserburgh 2 Keith 2. The teams that day were:

Fraserburgh:Gordon, Milne, Geddes, Finnie, Weymss, Fleming, Norris, Keith, Main, Mackie, Stephen.

Keith: Pirie, Brown, King, Robertson, McKenzie, Murison, Still, Smith, Cadger, Nicol, Reid.

In the replay, Wemyss gave the Broch the lead in 60 minutes from the penalty spot, but late strikes from Still (80) and Nicol (88) made sure there was no way back for us. The final score was Keith 2 Fraserburgh 1. Winger Ian Bissett decided he was not going to continue playing Highland League football and would be allowed to go, if the right offer came in for him. What a waste of a talent it was, as he could have been up there with the best of them, the Bowie's, Newlands and Stephens.

After a 3-3 draw up at Vale, in the Aberdeenshire Shield, we lost 4-3 on penalties and, by mid November, out league title was slipping away fast.

	P	W	D	L	F	A	PTS
Fraserburgh (9th)	10	4	2	4	15	19	14

Trevor Fleming then won the Highland League Player of the Year. He was in good company with the likes of Marino Keith and Scott Murray as past winners. On the park, results varied. A 2-2 draw at home in the first week of December brought a sequence of six home games on the trot. After three weeks lying idle, due to bad weather, impressive wins followed against Locos 4-2, and Huntly 4-1. Down 0-1 at the interval, the Broch hit back with three goals in five minutes to shock Huntly. Our form was erratic, however, and the following week, Buckie cruised to a 0-4 win. By the time the clocks changed in March, Deveronvale were running away with the league, while we were 8th in the table and playing out the season. It was no surprise when Deveronvale lifted the championship.

	P	W	D	L	F	A	PTS
Vale (champions)	28	21	6	1	90	24	69
Broch (6th)	28	14	4	10	61	45	46
Fort William (wooden spoon)	30	2	3	26	19	89	9

Trevor Fleming won the Supporters Club Player of the Year and it was not all doom and gloom. Four Broch players were selected to play for Scotland's semi-professional squad, Derek Milne, Trevor Fleming, Michael Stephen and Steven Main. It was a great honour, for them and for the club, and the kind of thing that every player should be aiming for at the start of the new season. Charlie's comment for the season just ending was, "You've got to take the rough with the smooth."

North Top scorers then were:

Murray	Vale	49
McKenzie	Vale	27
Beattie	Cove	26
Polworth	Clach	26
Nicol	Keith	19
Stewart	Huntly	19
McLaren	Broch	18
Still	Keith	18

Season 2003-04

It had been a busy summer for the Broch in the transfer market. Scotty Clark had rejoined the squad from Peterhead, along with team mate Kevin Bissett. Another summer signing was Neil Main, "junior." The younger brother of Steven Main, Neil had spent a year at Inverness Caledonian Thistle. Fans favourite, Russell McBride also returned from Elgin City, to his spiritual home. Expectations were high at the start of the season, but a Press release reported that the Broch were £48,000 in debt. Were we going back to the bad old days? It took £150,000 to run the Broch for a season. Calvin Morrice confirmed that the situation was serious, but nobody was to push the panic button. With new Directors, Bobby and Peter Cowe, Kenny Rogers, Davie Milne and Gordon, 'Morton,' Chegwyn in charge, the Club was in good hands, and all mucked in when needed. Season tickets were £80 for the ground and £44 for kids and OAP's. Admission was still only £4 (the price of two pints) and McRae was the Broch's new sponsor.

We warmed up with two friendlies, losing 0-4 to Brechin and 2-4 to Dundee juniors Lochee Utd. Old rivals,

Peterhead, had entered the Aberdeenshire Cup and we drew them at Balmoor. It must have been great for them to have a decent gate for a change! They ran out 3-1 winners, but I didn't recognise any of their players. Most had Southern accents, "and must have passed Glasgow in the train." The teams were:

Peterhead: Mathers, McGuiness, Good, Raeside, Perry, Mckay, Tindall, Stewart, D. Stewart, Johnston, Ruddie.

Fraserburgh: Gordon, Milne, Geddes, Fleming, Clark, Bissett, Norris, M. Main, McBride, Stephen, Mackie.
Ref – G. Cheyne   Att' - 847

A 5-1 win, at home to Huntly, was not a bad start. Billy Anderson's comment was, "We handed them four goals," cheers Billy! A late penalty for Keith at Kynoch Park earned them a reprieve in the Qualifying Cup, with a final score of Keith 1 Fraserburgh 1. Kevin Bissett was becoming a real fans' favourite with his strong running and aggression, but Gavin Wemyss stole the show in the replay, scoring the winner in the 87th minute, to put the Broch into the next round. Final score was Fraserburgh 3 Keith 2. Broch utility man, Graeme Bain, was to join Rothes - lack of first team action was given as the reason. We wished him well.

An incredible game at Clach, in the second round of the Qualifying Cup, saw theBroch trailing 1-0. With a minute to go, Clach hit the post, but the Broch regained possession, ran down to the other end and Bissett scored in injury time. Final score, Clach 1 Fraserburgh 1. I missed the replay as I was off to Tenerife for a sunshine break, but I phoned the Bellslea and got Finlay Noble. Finlay said, "are you ready for this, 6-2 to Clach." I nearly fell off my bar stool. Charlie commented, "we were the better side".
Mike Stephen and Gavin Wemyss both secured hat-tricks in an 8-0 rout up at Brora. The following week Deveronvale beat us 4-0 at the Bellslea. We just couldn't get a result against them! By November, Vale were still in front with the Broch and Clach chasing them.

Saturday Nov 8th	P	W	D	L	F	A	PTS
Vale	11	10	0	1	41	13	30
Clach	10	9	1	0	22	4	28
Broch	10	7	1	2	31	14	22

The Broch's under 18's were off to Murray Park to play Rangers in the Youth Cup. They lost 4-0 but what an experience for the youngsters. The Fraserburgh team was: Dickenson, Noble, West, Usher, Fraser, Christie, Noble, Cowie, Willox, Johnston, Mair.

Up at Huntly, we won 2-1 with Billy Gordon's heroics sealing our victory, but we rode our luck, with Gerry O'Driscoll missing a penalty three minutes into injury time. We were on a roll now and winning seven games and drawing one, meant we went from December right through till March undefeated, scoring 34 goals on the way. This looked like real championship form. We still rode our luck sometimes, as in the 2-1 defeat of Keith at Bellslea. In one incident, a shot saw the ball cross the Broch goal line, by a foot, with Keith claiming a goal, but a Broch defender booted the ball off the line and the referee waved play on - oops!! Incidentally, we went top of the league that night.

	P	W	D	L	F	A	PTS
Broch	20	15	2	2	62	23	47
Clach	18	14	3	1	43	13	45

Could we keep this form up? March 13th was unlucky for the Broch, as our run came to a halt with a defeat at Cove and it was their lethal hitman, Michael Beattie, who did the damage in a final score of Cove 3 Fraserburgh 2. But the Broch then pulled off the transfer coup of the season, by signing Ian Murray from Vale. It was nice to see the wee man back in a black and white shirt. Next up was Clach, at the Bellslea with the game being billed as a title decider. Clach struck early on with goals from Polworth (7) and Mitchell (17) to put them in the driving seat. It stayed like that until a Mike Stephen penalty, in 90 minutes, which was too little too late. The final score was Fraserburgh 1 Clach 2. A Mike Stephen hat-trick in a 3-3 draw at home to Inverurie Locos wasn't enough to get back up to the top of the league, as Clach won 1-0 away to Keith.

Sat. April 10th	P	W	D	L	F	A	PTS
Clach	25	19	3	3	57	21	60
Broch	27	18	4	5	80	35	58

Away to Clach in the semi-final of the League Cup, we were well beaten 5-2 after taking an early lead. The pressure in the league was getting to the players and the local natives were getting restless. Leading 1-0 up at Inverurie Locos and with the clock running down, Tommy Wilson hit an equaliser with the last kick of the game, what a disaster! That same day, Huntly beat Clach 3-1, but all Clach needed to do was win at Cove and they could not be caught. Finlay Noble and myself went to that match and saw Clach win 2-0 to become champions. After all of their previous troubles, it was great to see all their celebrations on the park and I was chuffed for guys like Robbie Williamson, Roshie Fraser and Peter Corbett.

So to the final league placings

	P	W	D	L	F	A	PTS	
Clach (champions)	28	21	3	4	60	25	63	
Buckie (2nd)	28	18	7	3	56	32	61	
Broch (3rd)	28	18	5	5	81	36	59	(disappointing)

On a sad note, tributes were paid after the passing of Highland League legend, Dave Johnston. What a player he was and the 72 goals he netted in one season for Nairn in the sixties will surely never be beaten. It was a pleasure watching him play.

Mike Stephen was top goal scorer in the league with 33 goals, a title he had also won last season. Another young man we are going to hear a lot about in the future was Willie West who won the best under 18 player at the club award. He was going to be some player..

It was a great occasion at the Bellslea when Scotland played the Republic of Ireland, in the four nations competition, with three Broch players in the team, Mike Stephen, Derek Milne and Ian Murray. Scotland won 2-0 in front of a crowd of 1,171. The Bellslea erupted when Mike Stephen scored, then Ian Murray made it 2-0 on a proud night for all connected with Fraserburgh F.C.

Season 2004-05

Charlie Duncan's quest went on. I've known him as a friend since 1968, but I still don't know what runs around in his head, a real sly fox, he would make a great politician! Watch your job Councillor (and Broch fan) Brian Topping!!

We went down to Dundee for a four team competition with Raith Rovers, Keith, Lochee United and ourselves. We ran riot against Raith Rovers, beating them 8-0 on the Saturday, but then lost the final, 1-0 to a strong Lochee Utd side on the Sunday. The loss of Kevin Bissett (working in Australia) Scotty Clark (Ellon Utd) and Kris Hunter (Maud Juniors) meant that, with such a young team, it was going to be a tough season.

The Broch got off to a great start, thumping Buckie Thistle 3-0, in the first home game of the season. Inverurie Locos were our next visitors, in the semi-final of the Aberdeenshire Cup. They gave us the run around, but we scraped through 2-1, after extra time, after a rare Kevin Norris strike, with Gavin Wemyss hitting the winner. The teams were:

Fraserburgh: Gordon, McBride, Geddes, Christie, Main, Fleming, Norris, Johnston, S. Main, Stephen, Wemyss (70), Cowie (86), West (111).

Inverurie Locos: Coull, Young, Buchan, Wilson, Simpson, Park, Ross, Taylor, Coull, McKay, McLean.
Referee – A. Freeland

Michael Stephen hit five goals in a 6-2 rout of Nairn at home. The following week, he hit a hat-trick at Nairn in the Qualifying Cup. Aberdeen were our opponents in the final of the Aberdeenshire Cup, at the Bellslea. Four minutes away from glory, we were leading 1-0, when referee Duff gave the Dons a dodgy penalty and they went on to win 4-1 in extra time. Does that mean they will be in Europe next season after winning a trophy? There was no Scottish Cup glory for us that season, as Cove knocked us out 4-2 at Allan Park. Ryan Christie was sent off,, for a handball, early on in the proceedings.

By the start of October, we were top of the league and playing entertaining football, with Michael Stephen scoring goals for fun.

P	W	D	L	F	A	PTS
7	7	0	0	25	6	21

Clach came to Bellslea as champions and won 0-3, then Deveronvale beat us 5-2, at Princess Royal Park, to take more of the wind out of our sails, but we bounced back with four wins and a draw in the following games. A nice Xmas present for the fans was a 6-0 thumping of Cove Rangers at the Bellslea, to stay top of the league. Michael Thomson did an excellent job in goal, covering that day in Billy Gordon's absence. The teams were:

Fraserburgh: Thomson, Milne, McBride, Cowie, Murray, Christie, Norris, Mackie, M. Main, S. Main, Stephen, Wemyss (71), McDonald (88).

Cove: Thain, McHattie, Tindal, Hendry, Flaws, Morrison, Clark, Johnston, Milne, Robertson, Brown.
Referee - S. Duff

Bad weather wrecked the entire fixture list the following week. This gave the summer football guys ammunition once again, but, if you watched Highland League football, you'd know that March can be as bad a month for weather as January. On Monday January 3rd, we came back to earth with a bump, losing 3-1 away to Nairn. There would be a few more twists and turns before the season finished. The league top scorers at that time were:

Stephen	Fraserburgh	22
Shallicker	Lossiemouth	20
Kenny Coull	Locos	16
Johnston	Cove	13
Murray	Fraserburgh	12
Green	Forres	11

Inverurie Locos beat us 3-1 away from home, to knock us off the top spot, but we regained our place with a Mike Stephen hat-trick in a 3-1 win against Huntly at the Bellslea and by Saturday February 22nd, the placings were:

	P	W	D	L	F	A	PTS
Broch	22	16	1	5	63	29	49
Inverurie Locos	20	15	2	3	57	15	47
Huntly	17	13	2	2	48	21	41

Ryan Christie scored the winner at Clach in a crucial league game, before we had a break from league business to get on with the League Cup. We drew Wick Academy away from home, now that's always a journey and a half, with a huge job of arranging to be done beforehand. Before a ball is kicked, you would think, from the amount of kit we take with us, that we were going away for a week. There's a hamper for shin pads and extras, two hampers for boots (moulders and studs) medical kit, orange and water bottles, strips, towels, t-shirts, training tops and all weather suits. We usually leave at 7.30, stop in Forres for a break, stop again, for soup and sandwiches, at Golspie at 12.30, before arriving at Wick around 1.45. The players then stretch their legs, while we get the dressing room organised, by about 2 p.m.This is followed by a team talk, then the players warm up. At 2.50 they get ready for the game. After the game,

Finlay and myself clear out the dressing room, and are usually last out. Many players think that strips jump out of a kit bag and onto a peg, and after the match jump back in and then turn up clean again. The players have the best part, "actually playing." We usually arrive back in the Broch around 12 o'clock, that's seventeen hours on the road and for what? For the love of Fraserburgh F.C, and, by the way, we beat Wick 2-3 that season. We were 2-1 down with four minutes to go when Trevor Fleming scored to make it 2-2. I was just about to get more juice and water for extra time, when Mark Cowie struck, in injury time, to see us through to the next round, but bogey team, Deveronvale, beat us 2-0 at Bellslea in that game.

Our league hopes evaporated the following Wednesday when we lost 0-1 to Vale in the league. The following week Huntly won the league, at our expense, with a 2-2 draw at Christie Park. A Ritchie Taylor goal (which was a mile offside) clinched the league in the 90th minute. It's not much fun hearing all the celebrations in their dressing room, but you just have to grin and get on with it.

	P	W	D	L	F	A	PTS
Huntly (champions)	28	20	5	3	79	32	65
Inverurie Locos	28	20	3	5	81	25	63
Broch	28	19	2	7	75	35	59

Mike Stephen was, once again, the league's top scorer.

Stephen	Broch	25
Coull	Locos	23
Johnstone	Cove	22
Shallicker	Lossiemouth	22

Charlie Duncan won the manager of the year award and Michael Stephen then wrote his name into the history books, by winning the Highland League Player of the Year for the third time in four years. He also won the Supporters

Club Player of the Year award, but is Mike too young to be called a legend? It's been a pleasure watching his career blossom.

Season 2005-06

Star striker, Ian Murray, was getting restless and rejoined Deveronvale during the summer. If they're not happy, then let them go, that's what I think. Some "good," news, was that Aberdeen were not taking part in the Aberdeenshire Cup this season. Broch unveiled their new kit sponsors, North Sea Catering Firm E.S.S. Also on display was a new tartan away strip, which went down well with fans.

It was just like old times, winning 3-0 at Peterhead's Balmoor Stadium. OK it was only a friendly, but we never have friendlies against Peterhead! Goals from Stephen, Cowie and Christie settled the issue. The teams were:

Peterhead: Mathers, Shand, Cameron, Raeside, Good, Stewart, Sharp, Buchan, Bavidge, Linn, Youngson.

Fraserburgh: Thomson, Dickson, Geddes, West, Christie, Cowie, Norris, Mackie, Johnston, Main, Stephen.

A strong Buckie side knocked us out of the Aberdeenshire Cup, at the Bellslea, with a score of 0 - 2, after extra time. Draws at home to Huntly, 1-1, and Inverurie Locos, 2-2, gave us a boost before our trip to Keith, which we had to win to keep up with the top teams. A Mike Stephen double saw us through, with the final score of Keith 1 Fraserburgh 2. We then got our revenge against Buckie beating them 1-0, with Mark Cowie scoring.

What was it about Forres? With the Qualifying Cup game heading for a replay at the Bellslea, they got a free kick in the 90th minute and hit the ball straight at Billy Gordon. He pushed the ball onto the bar, only for it to bounce on the line for Sanderson to blast it into the roof of the net, goodbye to the Scottish Cup! The final score was Forres Mechanics 3 Fraserburgh 2.

A Michael Stephen double saw us through to the semi-final of the Aberdeenshire Shield in a 3-1 win, at the expense of rivals Cove, at the Bellslea. Keith knocked us out 1-3 at the Bellslea in the next round. We wouldn't win the league if we dropped silly points, like the 2-1 defeat at Wick, but we went on to thrash Clach 7 – 0 at the Bellslea. In the Scottish Youth Cup we lost 1-4 to Dundee Utd at the Bellslea in front of a good crowd. The Broch team was: McRobb, Buchan, West, Pirie, Dickson, Walker, Thomson, Elrick, Hale, May, Murray. Subs: Ross, Bruce, Cardno, Watt, Simpson.

In a few seasons time, I wondered, how many of these Broch young guns would be starring in the first team, watch this space!!

Things are different nowadays. In the past, if the matchball went over the dyke, it was returned, but the pastime now is to put it into the boot of a car and drive off with it. Surely these people have better things to do with their Saturday afternoons?

It was a nice surprise to be top of the league at the start of December, after a hard fought 2-2 draw away to Clach.

December 4th	P	W	D	L	F	A	PTS
Broch	15	9	4	2	43	14	32
Vale	14	9	2	3	41	20	29

In the Scottish Cup, Gretna defeated Cove Rangers 6-1 and Stirling Albion won at home by 1-0 against Inverurie Locos. A blizzard halted the match at Inverurie with the score at 0-0. A Lossiemouth side then came to the Bellslea at Xmas, struggling to score goals, and went away with a shock 2-4 win to knock us off the top of the league.

It was sad to hear of the death of another of the team that beat Dundee. Freddy Smith was a real character. There was not much of that team left.

A 1-1 draw at Buckie, that saw them equalising in 90 mins, and an exciting 3-3 draw, at home to Keith, saw us slip a couple of places down the league. Then Gavin Wemyss scored four goals and Graeme Johnston two in a 7-2 rout of Fort William. The following week we saw the other side of the Broch in a 6-0 thumping away to Nairn, shocking!! We dropped from top of the league at Christmas to 9th by mid February.

P	W	D	L	F	A	PTS
22	10	6	6	56	34	36

There was freak weather in March, with blizzards wrecking all of the League Cup ties, but that's typical of the weather in this part of the world. The Highland League then lost another friend, when Huntly Chairman, George Minty, passed away. I knew George quite well, through his handshake and smile, win or lose. Over the years I've met some great people through the Highland League. The likes of Kevin McKay and John Young at Brora, without them there would be no Brora. Roshy Fraser and Peter Corbett at Clach, Willie the sponge man at Forres, Kevin Williams and Fraser Kellas at Lossie, not forgetting old Joe at Buckie and Buckie legend Robbie Nicol. Then on to Keith, and Sandy Stables who, "is Keith." There's, "Dod," McGregor at Huntly, Vale fanatic Stuart McPherson, Duncan Little at Cove and Cove legends, Michael Beattie and Graeme Park and, "cup tie McKay," at Inverurie. I always tell him he wasn't at the Bellslea long enough to get into a team photograph.

Deveronvale looked to have the League won for the season, having moved seven points clear of second placed Buckie, with just three games to play.

We were drawn away to Keith in the League Cup, a tough test at any time, and, after a goal-less first half, Darren Still put the home side in front in the 67th minute. With time running out, my thoughts were, "when are we ever going to win this cup?" Then, up stepped Michael Stephen in 89 minutes, to put the tie into extra time. The final score after extra time was Keith 1 Fraserburgh 1 and so it was on to penalties. With the score standing at 2-2, McKay and Watt of Keith, blazed their efforts over the bar and it was left to Mark Cowie to win the game. He converted easily to take the Broch through 4-2 on penalties.

All that stood between the Broch and a final was Nairn County at the Bellslea. On matchday, conditions weren't good with a howling gale blowing down the park. The Broch chose to kick against it and survived till half time, with the score at 0-0. Nairn then shocked the home side, when they took the lead through Brooks in 56 minutes, but Russell McBride squared matters on 62 minutes. It stayed that way, and extra time didn't produce any more goals, so it was on to penalties again. There always had to be a hero or a villain with this lottery and, this time, it was veteran keeper Billy Gordon who was the hero. With Nairn needing to score to go through, he saved three spot kicks, to put the Broch into the final 5-4 on penalties. We hadn't won a game yet in normal time, but who cared?

Our last league game was away to Rothes, where we got whipped 5-1 with Trevor Fleming getting his marching orders, so he missed the cup final, where we faced old foes Cove Rangers at Kynoch Park. It had been 47 years since the Broch last won the League Cup and this would be the fifth final I'd witnessed. Was our name to be on the Cup at last? The players ran out on a gloriously sunny day, with a large travelling support cheering them on. Me, it's a good job I don't play football as my stomach was in knots, as usual, before the kick off. When Fraser of Cove rattled our crossbar with a header, I thought, "Oh no, nae again," but the game ebbed and flowed right up till half time, when we got a controversial penalty for handball on the line.
"Gizzy," (Graham Johnston) stepped up and slammed the ball into the bottom corner, to put the Broch 1-0 in front on 45 minutes. Then, with less than five minutes of the second half played, the Broch were 3-0 up, with goals from Willie West and Michael Stephen. Steven Main added a fourth to put the Broch on easy street. This was the best time to enjoy a Cup Final, when you were 4-0 in front with quarter of an

hour to go. Colin Milne scored a consolation goal for Cove, but the final score was Fraserburgh 4 Cove Rangers 1. You could get used to days like that one.

The teams who contested that final were:

Fraserburgh: Gordon, Milne, Main, Dickson, McBride, S. Main, Norris, West, Wemyss, Johnston, Stephen. Subs: Cowie (80), Elrick (88), Geddes (89).

Cove: Pirie, Cruickshank, Livingstone, Hendry, Fraser, Tindal, Bain, Cadger, Duncan, Ord, Coutts.

Ref – M Ritchie   Att' – 970

I was fair chuffed for Billy Gordon, as that victory completed his full set of medals, and for supporters like Mike McLean, Gareth Deans and Graham Walker, who had supported the Broch through thick and thin. Deveronvale won the league that season, with the Broch in 7th place.

P	W	D	L	F	A	PTS
28	13	6	9	68	45	45

Season 2006-07

After the euphoria of that famous Cup win, it was back to normal, with a five week break and then back to pre-season training on the beach. We said goodbye to James Geddes (Bab a Doo) then Trevor Fleming went A.W.O.L and Mark Cowie signed for Deveronvale. This again made a mockery of the Broch Youth system, when any player is up for grabs and teams like Vale, Huntly and Locos are first in the queue for their signatures. Charlie Duncan then took a batch of young guns from the under-18s, John Ross, Nicko Marchi, Alan Hale and Michael Rae to bolster the senior squad. If they would do what they were told, and listen to what was said, I could see no reason why these players wouldn't make it in the Highland League.

Fort William were in a crisis and rumour had it that they wouldn't start the season, with Junior side Turriff United set to replace them. However, hard-working committee man,

John Flannigan, and his colleagues turned things around and a, "normal," service was resumed. Peterhead were our opponents at the Bellslea, for the James Geddes Testimonial. Down 0-4 at half time, we pulled back to a 3-4 final score. We still didn't play friendlies against our local rivals! Up at Maud a young Broch side won the 7-a-side tournament, for the sixth time in thirteen years. St Johnstone were our visitors at Bellslea, but the game came too soon for the Broch, and we were hammered 0-7. Then Steven Main hit the winner in a 1-0 win at home to Huntly in the Aberdeenshire Cup. Teams that night were:

Fraserburgh: Gordon, Milne, West, McBride, Christie, Dickson, Norris, Wemyss, Johnston, S. Main. Subs: McLaren, Elrick, McDonald, Marchi, Thomson.

Huntly: Bremner, McGregor, Scott, Anderson, Divgonski, Gary, L. Stephen, Guild, McAllister, Gairns.
Ref – S. McDonald

Cove Rangers were our visitors at theBellslea, on the Saturday, and they went home with all three points, winning 0-2 (they were 0-1 up within 24 seconds.) The next game up was against Deveronvale at the Bellslea, in the semi-final of the Aberdeenshire Cup, we hadn't beaten them since that famous night we went on to win the Championship. It was end to end stuff and an unlikely hero scored the opening goal, when youngster Dean Elrick appeared from nowhere to force the ball over the line and put the Broch 1-0 in front. Graham Johnston made it 2-0 at half time, but, after fifteen minutes of the second half, Vale hit back, with two goals in a minute from McKenzie and Smith. Worse was to follow as the referee showed Steven Main the red card and Broch boss, Duncan, was sent to the stand after having a few words with the linesman. Score after ninety minutes was 2-2, but Vale then got their noses in front, when ex-Broch man Murray scored with his head to make it 2-3. As time was running out, the Bellslea erupted when Dolan scored an own goal to take the game into penalties on a final score of 3-3. Then, with the score at 4-4 in penalties, Ryan Christie missed his vital spot kick and sent the Vale into the final. We'd had our share of luck in penalty shoot-outs in the past, so there could be no complaints. There was more bad news for the Broch however, Russell McBride, who had been stretchered off against the Vale with a knee injury, might not play again till after Christmas. With Michael Stephen's hamstring problems continuing, this left the squad short on experience, but it gave some of the young guns a chance to make a name for themselves.

A 2-0 defeat at Brora and a further 3-0 loss at Clach left the Broch at third bottom of the league, with no points and no goals for, but it was still early days. We got a decent draw in the Qualifying Cup, with Golspie Sutherland at the Bellslea. A Neil McLaren hat-trick and a double from Willie West saw us through to the next round, 6-2 and up next were Clach at the Bellslea for a place in the Scottish Cup. It was nice to see, "Smiler," (Neil Mclaren) back in the fold. His goal, and a Graham Johnston (Gizzy) penalty, saw us through 2-1, to a place in the Scottish Cup for the first time in six years. Saturday September 30th saw the Broch pick up their first league points, winning 1-3 away to Nairn County. A goal down, we fought back with goals from Stephen, Norris and McLaren. The only way was up.

The following Wednesday, we defeated Cove 1-3 at Allan Park in the Aberdeenshire Shield, with youngster Alan Hale scoring his first goal for the Broch. Games don't come much harder than the next tie, against the Vale, away from home, in the semi-final of the Qualifying Cup, considering our record against them over the past few seasons. The Broch kicked off,, with strikers Wemyss and Stephen on the bench, and the first half was quite even, though goal-less. Events were about to take a dramatic turn, when the Broch introduced Wemyss in 55 minutes and Stephen after 64. Stephen swung over a free kick for Wemyss to bullet a header past the helpless Blanchard, then McLaren latched on to a through pass, rounded the keeper and rolled the ball into the empty net to make it 0-2. It was all over in 82 minutes when Dickson scored with a fine solo effort. The final score was Deveronvale 0 Fraserburgh 3. This result had been a long time in coming and it was magic now that it had come. The teams were:

Deveronvale: Blanchard, Dolan, Gilbert, Chisholm, Fraser, Bremner, McWilliam, Urquhart, Cowie, Ewan, Watt.

Fraserburgh: Gordon, Milne, Main, Dickson, Christie, Johnston, Norris, West, McLaren, Main, Hale.

I was looking forward to the Scottish Cup draw, but dreading that we would draw another Highland League side. The draw came and, would you believe it, it was Deveronvale or Montrose away in the 2nd round? I've nothing against the Vale, but I'd have preferred to play Montrose, just for the sake of a change of faces. Our season had really started to take off, with a Qualifying Cup Final against Keith at Princess Royal Park, Banff. Our league form had been improving as well, with a 6-1 win, over Rothes, at the Bellslea. The Broch then went through to another final, beating Huntly 3-1 in the semi-final of the Aberdeenshire Shield. One bit of bad news was that Steven Main would miss the Qualifying Cup final as he was suspended.

Up at Grant Park in Lossiemouth we put in a shocking performance, drawing 1-1 with the home side and equalising, with a penalty, in injury time. I thought the Broch's players minds, must have been somewhere else. Billy Gordon had equalled Jimmy Young's record of 680 appearances in a black and white shirt. Some players don't stay five minutes with their clubs, so what Billy and Jimmy have done will probably never be equalled. They were, and still are, superb achievements! North history would be made at Banff, as this was to be the last Qualifying Cup final. What an honour it would be if the Broch could win the famous old trophy. Next season, every club would automatically go into the 1st round of the Scottish Cup, if a proposal to that effect was passed at the A.G.M. next May at Hampden. The chances were it would go through.

At last, Cup Final Saturday came around. I was up early and went down to the Bellslea to check that everything was packed, though my mind was, once again again, racing. After arriving at Banff at 1.50, the dressing room seemed to be quite chirpy. I remarked on that to Brian Sim, but he just smiled. The bell rang in the dressing room at 2.50, and it was time for the last Qualifying Cup showdown.

Keith started the game brightly and should have been a couple of goals up in the first half hour. The Broch looked to be at sixes and sevens and it seemed only a matter of time before Keith scored, and so it happened, when a simple header in, 39 minutes by Nicol, had Keith 1-0 in front. It was all Keith after that, but could we hang on till half time? More drama was to come however, when Marc Dickson burst through the middle and scored the equaliser, with a low 25 yard shot which Shearer had no chance of stopping. The Broch support went wild (and so did the dug-out.) The second half was a different story from the first. Graham Johnston swung over a corner, for Michael Stephen to flick the ball into the roof of the net and put the Broch in front 2-1. Billy Gordon then had a wonder save to keep us in front and Graham Johnston cleared off the line, though I don't know if he knew anything much about it. Time seemed to stand still. When would the ref eree blow that .... whistle?? In injury time the Broch broke away and sub Dean Elrick missed a chance to settle the matter. He arrived at the back post to meet the ball, only to hit the side netting, but seconds later the referee blew for time. What a feeling it was! It doesn't get any better than winning trophies. When Michael Stephen and Derek Milne went up to lift the Cup together, history had been made. When I look back on some of the players who had lifted that Trophy in the last fifty years, I don't think young players, like Willie West or Marc Dickson, realised what they have achieved. It may sink in when their playing days are over, but never mind that, we had celebrations to get on with! The scenes in the dressing room will live with me forever. This is what makes it all worthwhile and I've had the privilege to be part of it. "COME AWAY THE BURGHY."

Up at Inverurie the following Wednesday, we had to deal with Keith again in the Aberdeenshire Shield final, but that night it was not to be. The Broch left their legs at Banff and were well beaten 3-0. A very young Broch side drew 1-1 up at Vale on the Saturday, with youngster John Ross making an impressive debut. Another youngster hitting the leadlines was Alan Hale who scored a hat-trick in a 5-0 win over Forres at the Bellslea. All ears were on what was happening up at the Vale v Montrose game. With Montrose up 0-2, most of our fans were preparing for an away day down there in the next round, but then Vale hit back with 3 goals in the final three minutes to win 3-2. My dreaded wish had come true and I thought back to Cove and Clach, who had knocked us out of the Scottish Cup in years gone by. Walter Skinner and his mates were sitting in the pub after the Forres game, thinking Montrose had won 2-0. They were looking in Yellow Pages, for bed and breakfast places in Montrose, when the final score came over the teleprinter. You'll never live that down Walter! There was some good news also as Russell McBride played his first comeback match in the Aberdeenshire League and Trevor Fleming was back in the fold. It was, "welcome back," to both of them. The players were signing programmes and autographing a football, though looking a bit fed up, when I said to them "When they don't want your x mark, that's when you start worrying".

The build up for the Vale game went well, with the players again getting a lot of media attention. The Broch had no injury worries, so Charlie Duncan had a full squad to pick from, for a change. We needed to be at our best, if we were to progress, but what a let down the game was. After taking the lead in the 7th minute, when Dolan put through his own goal, we then had a stonewall penalty claim, when Mike Stephen was upended in the box, but the referee waved play on. Vale then made it 1-1, with Smith scoring, and after that there was only going to be one winner. Smith went on to put Vale into the next round, with another header on 75 minutes, to make the final score Deveronvale 2 Fraserburgh 1. The teams that day were:

Vale: Blanchard, Dolan, Gilbert, Chisholm, Fraser, Brown, Urquhart, Smith, McKenzie, Ewan, Watt.

Fraserburgh: Gordon, Milne, Main, (McBride 67), Dickson, Christie, Johnston, Norris, West, Hale, S. Main, Stephen, Wemyss (82).
Attendance was 1500.
Vale drew Elgin City at home in the next round while we were left to dream of what might have been!

This may be the end of my story, but I hope to be around this Club for years to come (or some day I might dig out my old black and white scarf and return to the terraces.) Following the Broch has been a roller coaster experience and we've come a long way since the days of struggling to put eleven players onto the park. I recall such a variety of things, like the day, up at Ross County, when we were getting thumped 6-0 at half time and County striker Lynas then made it seven with a glorious header. Substitute Gordon Mitchell stood there applauding his goal, with a few glares from his team-mates. I think the final score was 9-0 in that game. Then there was the story of Norman (Chippy) Chalmers, whose claim to fame was coming on as sub' up at Caley, for the injured Jimmy Noble.

I intended to finish here, but season 2007-08 saw us lose three outstanding Highland League personalities and I could not end without paying tribute to them. "King," Willie Grant passed away after a long illness. I was privileged to see him play and met him when he was a press reporter. He was a humble man, who was pleased when I reminded him of some of the games I had watched him play in. Campbell Fraser was chairman of Forres Mechanics, and for all the years I've been travelling to Mossett Park, I never knew his proper name. We all called him, "Cherry," and he was a true gentleman. Then our own Gordon Kenneth Chegwyn sadly passed away after a short illness. He was a valued director of Fraserburgh F.C,

FROM BELLSLEA TO BRORA THESE ARE MY HEROES

who led an important process of modernising the routines and administration of the club, and was very well respected in Highland League circles. Gordon ("Kenneth," he kept that one quiet) was a Greenock Morton man originally so it was customary to say something like, "Hi Kenny, how did Morton get on today," when meeting him on match days. His passing was a huge loss at the Bellslea and we all miss, "The Mannie," who took the photos at the fitba on Saturday afternoons.

Above everything else it has been the players, all those players who pulled on a black and white shirt over the years, who carried the club through the bad times and the good. I pay tribute to them all, those whose exploits I've included, and the others whom I've forgotten to mention.

When I dream of bygone days
As I do now and then
I dream about those players
Who were our greatest men.

Johnnie Strachan, Dennis Forsyth, Jimmy Milne, Bobby Forsyth, Bertie Bowie, Brian Newlands, John Thomson, Paul Keith, Mike Stephen, Billy Gordon. We may not see them play again, but their memories keep marching on. They have been my heroes.

Before I bring things to a conclusion, I would like to share a few thoughts on the first one hundred years of the Broch, and on the years to come. The club came near to folding in the Sixties and it was to the great credit of Jimmy Brown and Jimmy McDonald that the Broch survived, yet we were instrumental in the changing of the entry rules for the Scottish Cup, after that memorable day when we defeated Dundee.

So what can we look forward to for the club as it embarks on the next one hundred years? When our own turn comes to move on, is there a Finlay Noble out there, with his kind of enthusiasm to push the club forward, or a management, of the same calibre as those we have now, to take over the leadership of the team because no – one, not even Charlie and Brucie, can go on forever? Will the next generation of our players, like Johnny Chalmers or Jonathan Dunbar, be the stuff of future legend as their predecessors were in their day?

Last, but far from least, are the team's supporters. People like Mike McLean, Davie Henderson, Graham Walker, Gareth Deans, and many more over the years, have travelled up and down the road from the Bellslea to Wick and all points south. They have done it, and still do it, because following the Broch has become almost a way of life for them, as it has been for me. It is my hope that enough Fraserburgh people will emerge, willing to show that kind of loyalty to the club so that the Bellslea, through the next century of it's history, will still resound to the cry of, "Come awa the Burghy!"

Lightning Source UK Ltd.
Milton Keynes UK
16 September 2010
159958UK00002B/75/P